THE
POINTE
BOOK

Revised Edition

THE
POINTE
BOOK

Shoes, Training
& Technique

Revised Edition

Janice Barringer

Sarah Schlesinger

A Dance Horizons Book
Princeton Book Company, Publishers
Hightstown, NJ

To Grace Schlesinger and Ben Sommers
whose love for dance and dancers inspired this book
SMS

To Al Gilbert, my mentor and friend,
and to Edward Stewart who has shared my life in dance,
and to my beautiful daughter, Jennifer Barringer
JRB

Cover photo by Marco Arici and
Paoli Bernardi; copyright © C. Porselli Ltd.
Foot anatomy courtesy Williams & Wilkins.
Pointe shoe anatomy © 1990 John Elfenbein.
Capezio publicity poster courtesy Ballet Masters, Inc.
Copyright © 1998 by Princeton Book Company, Publishers

A Dance Horizons Book
Princeton Book Company, Publishers
P. O. Box 831
Hightstown, NJ 08520-0831

Revised Edition

Printed in Canada

Library of Congress Cataloging-in-Publication Data

Barringer, Janice.
  The pointe book : shoes, training & technique / Janice Barringer, Sarah
Schlesinger. — Rev. ed.
      p.   cm.
  "A Dance Horizons Book"
  Includes bibliographical references and index.
  Summary: Studies the development of pointe shoes and the technique of pointe
dancing, an artistic innovation that allowed female dancers to carry ballet to new
heights of virtuosity.
  ISBN 0-87127-204-0
  1. Ballet dancing — Juvenile literature. 2. Ballet slippers — Juvenile literature.
[1. Ballet dancing. 2. Ballet slippers.] I. Schlesinger, Sarah. II. Title.
GV1788.B37 1996
792.8—dc20
                                                                                96-43844
                                                                                   CIP
                                                                                   AC

Contents

Introduction

David Howard

One of my earliest and fondest memories is a visit to a Christmas magic show. Soon after, when I saw pointe dancing for the first time, I assumed that it was also a feat of magic.

No doubt those audiences that saw pointe dancing at its inception in the early 1800s shared my childlike perspective; seeing Taglioni and her contemporaries ascend to the tips of their toes must have seemed a mythical, magical accomplishment.

Since that first, entrancing glimpse of pointe work, I have spent a large portion of my life becoming intimately acquainted with the reality behind the illusion. Yet in spite of my daily exposure to the mechanics of this process, I am still swept away by the element of magic with which magnificent dancers like Gelsey Kirkland and Natalia Makarova have transformed the art of dancing on pointe.

However, I am also more and more cognizant that the freedom to create such magic is rooted in a command of craft. For many years, pointe dancing and the shoes that make it possible have remained needlessly obscured in a mist of myth and rumor. Often this aura of superstition gets in the way of a sensible approach to pointe as an essential element of the classical ballet technique. In *The Pointe Book,* Janice Barringer and Sarah Schlesinger have created a comprehensive resource of great value for everyone interested in this aspect of ballet, including professional dancers, teachers, students, parents, and audience members.

The authors' goal has been to demystify the mechanics of pointe shoes and pointe dancing. They have been assisted in this mission by hundreds of dancers, teachers, choreographers, school administrators, and medical specialists around the world. In the tradition of the dance profession, these experts have willingly shared their knowledge to help make the next generation of dancers even stronger than their own.

This outpouring of response has afforded the book a special richness that provides the reader with a new level of awareness of an often misunderstood tool of our trade. Revelations abound on every subject from determining pointe readiness to prolonging shoe life. The result is a complete and long overdue examination of the most fascinating component of our art form.

After considering the many facets of pointe shoes and pointe dancing covered in this volume, it becomes evident that the key word in the phrase *pointe work* is *work*. Pointe dancing is not an entity unto itself; introduced at the right time for each individual dancer, it is an extension of training. We are also reminded that pointe dancing is not an inevitability for a ballet student; not everyone is suited to its peculiar demands.

The Pointe Book is an exhaustive guide to many available options, offering intriguing insights into the technical path that we hope leads to artistry. It helps us realize that although pointe dancing has sprung from a classical tradition, it cannot remain in the dark ages. The world of the pointe dancer has been forever changed by expanding technique, technological advances in shoemaking, increased understanding of kinesiology, and medical attention to the special needs of dancers.

The future promises to be equally volatile. The pointe shoe will continue to change to suit the dancer's evolving needs. Perhaps a future edition of this book will have to include tips on pointe dancing in space. Will the trick then be to stay on the ground in a weightless environment? One can only speculate!

In the meantime, secretly armed with the knowledge that we find in *The Pointe Book,* we can continue to mystify the occupants of our planet. For me, the illusion of a ballerina defying gravity in pink satin slippers will forever remain proof positive of the existence of magic!

Preface

Our goal in writing *The Pointe Book* has been to create a resource for students and professional dancers and their teachers that presents a full spectrum of information about this essential tool of their craft.

Following a brief look at the historical evolution of pointe dancing, we consider the structure of the pointe shoe as a foundation for our examination of this unique art form. And since understanding the manner in which pointe shoes are made is a vital first step in understanding how they function, we have detailed the shoemaking process based on our observation in British and U.S. factories.

Next, we consider the fundamentals of buying, preparing, and wearing pointe shoes and provide a concise guide to the complex process of ordering custom shoes. We review the international pointe shoe marketplace by profiling major pointe shoe manufacturers around the world and providing descriptions of their products and services.

In the area of pointe readiness, we present an array of contemporary views on when students should go on pointe. Then we examine the way major ballet schools in the United States and around the world integrate pointe work into their teaching systems. Sample classes for beginning, intermediate, and advanced pointe students are provided.

Pointe-related injuries are a fact of life for most pointe dancers, and we address this issue with a look at minor and major injuries of the foot and ankle. Finally, we present the thoughts and feelings of professional dancers about their pointe shoes.

Since our initial meeting in 1975 as a dancer and pointe shoe fitter contemplating the mysteries of a 2 1/2 A Nicolini, we have been fascinated with the idea of gathering together the available wisdom on pointe shoes. We finally had the opportunity to begin work on this project in 1988, and we quickly realized that very little had been written on the subject. It immediately became obvious that our information had to be gathered from dancers, teachers, students, choreographers, company directors, shoe manufacturers, and medical professionals. Between January 1988 and September 1989, our quest for this information took us from Florida to California and from London to Stockholm. During these journeys, we personally interviewed the exceptional group of individuals whose knowledge and ideas on this subject became the cornerstone of this book. They included:

Dance Shoe Specialists

Michelle Attfield, Freed of London Ltd., London, England

Mary Price Boday, The Dance Works, Distributor for Schachtner, Erie, PA

Glenn Baruch, Leo's Dancewear Inc., Chicago, IL

Edith Bloom, Retired Sales Representative, Capezio-Ballet Makers, Sarasota, FL

Anello and Davide, London, England

Anthony Cosentino, Marketing General Manager, Freed of London Ltd., New York, NY

Craig M. Coussins, Theatrical Sales Executive and Chief Pointe Shoe Fitter, Gamba Timestep Ltd., London, England

Franc Raoul Duvall, Sansha USA, New York, NY

Susan Epstein, Vice-President, Taffy's Manhattan, New York, NY

Graham Fay, Gamba Timestep Ltd., London, England

Gandolfi, London, England

Frank Giacoia, Shoemaker, Capezio Ballet Makers, Totowa, NJ

Scott Harris, Leo's Dancewear Inc., Chicago, IL

Joe Kaplan, La Mendola, Smithtown, NY

Julie Hegge, Shoe Coordinator, English National Ballet, London, England

Bernard D. Kohler, Managing Director, Freed of London Ltd., London, England

Tobias Leibovitz, Owner, Ballet Shop, New York, NY

Dan Leva, Product Development Manager, Capezio Ballet Makers, Totawa, NJ

Scott Lovelady, Cobbler, Taffy's Manhattan, New York, NY

Benedicte Marchois, Product Chief, Repetto, Paris, France

Bob Martin, Gamba Timestep Ltd., London, England

Gayle Miller, Capezio Dance-Theatre Shops, New York, NY

Ushi Nagar, Ushi, London, England

Shinji Saeki, President, Freed of London Ltd., London, England

Alan Schofield, Representative, C. Porselli Ltd., London, England

Estelle Sommers, Capezio Dance-Theatre Shops, New York, NY

Art Stone, La Mendola, Smithtown, NY

Donald Terlizzi, Capezio Ballet Makers, Totawa, NJ

Paul Terlizzi, Capezio Ballet Makers, Totawa, NJ

Judith Weiss, Head, Custom Shoe Department for Professional Customers, Capezio Dance-Theatre Shop, New York, NY

Susan Whildin, Cobbler, Taffy's Manhattan, New York, NY

David Wilkinfeld, Managing Director and Designer, Bloch's Australia, Los Angeles, CA

Dancers, Dance Teachers, and Company Directors

Anneli Alhanko, Principal Dancer, Royal Swedish Ballet, Stockholm, Sweden

Deborah Allton, Dancer, Metropolitan Opera Ballet, New York, NY

Christine Beckley, Teacher, Royal Ballet School, White Lodge, London, England

Michelle Benash, Director, Children's Program, STEPS, New York, NY

Claude Bessy, Director, Paris Opera Ballet School, Paris, France

Nancy Bielski, Director, Children's Program, STEPS, New York, NY

Helene Breazeale, Associate Dean of Fine Arts, Towson State University, Towson, MD

Dawn Caccamo, Principal Dancer, Joffrey Ballet, New York, NY

Nancy Johnson Carter, Manager, San Francisco Ballet School, San Francisco, CA

Nansi Clement, Ballet Teacher, New York, NY

Kerrison Cooke, Director, English National Ballet School, London, England

Clara Cravey, Ballet Teacher, Houston Ballet School, Houston, TX

Alexandra Danilova, School of American Ballet, New York, NY

Daniel Duell, Director, Ballet Chicago, Chicago, IL

Alessandra Ferri, Principal Dancer, American Ballet Theatre, New York, NY

Martin Fredmann, Company Director, Colorado Ballet, Denver, CO

Jennifer Gelfand, Principal Dancer, Boston Ballet, Boston, MA

Natalie Gleboff, Executive Director, School of American Ballet, New York, NY

Lorraine Graves, Dancer and Ballet Mistress, Dance Theatre of Harlem, New York, NY

Nils-Ake Haggborn, Balettchef, Royal Swedish Ballet, Stockholm, Sweden

Cynthia Harvey, Principal Dancer, American Ballet Theatre, New York, NY

David Howard, Director, David Howard Dance Center, New York, NY

Rodney Irwin, Ballet Teacher, Ruth Page Foundation School, Chicago, IL

Margret Kaufmann, Dancer and Choreologist, Geneva, Switzerland

Patricia Klekovic, Ballet Teacher, Ruth Page Foundation School, Chicago, IL

Joanna Kneeland, Ballet Teacher, Las Vegas, NV

Darci Kistler, Principal Dancer, New York City Ballet, New York, NY

Natalia Krassovska, Ballet Teacher, Dallas, TX

Delores Lipinski, Ballet Teacher, Ruth Page Foundation School, Chicago, IL

Larry Long, Director, Ruth Page Foundation School, Chicago, IL

Mikhail Messerer, International Guest Teacher, American Ballet Theatre, New York, and Royal Ballet, London, England

Sulamith Messerer, Ballet Teacher, Royal Ballet, London, England

Rosemary Miles, Principal Ballet Academy, Houston Ballet, Houston, TX

Eugene Mills, Associate Professor and Ballet Director, Western Michigan University, Kalamazoo, MI

Christine Neubert, Director, Neubert Ballet Institute, New York, NY

Sandra Organ, Dancer, Houston Ballet, Houston, TX

Marianne Orlando, Teacher, Royal Swedish Ballet School, Stockholm, Sweden

Janie Parker, Principal Dancer, Houston Ballet, Houston, TX

Patricia Renzetti, Principal Dancer, Colorado Ballet, Denver, CO

Sandra Robinson, Associate Professor, University of South Florida, Tampa, FL

Jo Rowan, Chairman, Department of Dance, Oklahoma City University, Oklahoma City, OK

Edith Royal, Dance Teacher, Winter Park, FL

Richard Sias, Associate Professor, Florida State University, Tallahassee, FL

Larissa Sklyanskaya, Faculty, San Francisco Ballet School, San Francisco, CA

Marina Stavitskaya, Faculty, American Ballet Theatre School, New York, NY

Edward Stewart, Artistic Director, Ballet Theatre of Annapolis, Annapolis, MD

Gosta Svalberg, Director, Royal Swedish Ballet School, Stockholm, Sweden

Allyson Swenson, Ballet Teacher, Houston Ballet School, Houston, TX

Jocelyn Vollmer, Ballet Teacher, San Francisco Ballet School, San Francisco, CA

Katie Wade, Director, Royal Ballet School, London, England

Gretchen Warren, Associate Professor, University of South Florida, Tampa, FL

Martine van Hamel, Principal Dancer, American Ballet Theatre, New York, NY

William Martin Viscount, Director, Southwest Ballet Centre, Dallas, TX

Anton Wilson, Former member, Ballets Trockadero de Monte Carlo, Severna Park, MD

Glenn White, Special Assistant to Artistic Director Gerald Arpino, Joffrey Ballet, and Artistic Director of the Tidewater Ballet Association, Norfolk, VA

Cheryl Yeager, Principal Dancer, American Ballet Theatre, New York, NY

Health Specialists

Dr. Steven Baff, Podiatrist, New York, NY

Dr. Richard T. Braver, D.P.M., Medical Consultant to Capezio Ballet Makers, NJ

Hilary Cartwright, White Cloud Studio, New York, NY

Irene Dowd, Neuro-Muscular Therapist, New York, NY

Margarat Egan, Patient Coordinator, Kathryn and Gilbert Miller Health Care Institute for Performing Artists, New York, NY

Dr. James G. Garrick, M.D., Center for Sports Medicine and Dancemedicine, St. Francis Hospital, San Francisco, CA

John Gossett, Houston Body Conditioning Studio, Houston, TX

Sean Gallagher, Physical Therapist, Westside Dance Physical Therapy, New York, NY

Shirley Hancock, Principal Physiotherapist, Royal Ballet Schools, the Royal Academy of Dancing, and the Remedial Dance Clinic, London, England

Liz Henry, Physical Therapist, Westside Dance Physical Therapy, New York, NY

Katy Keller, Assistant Director, Westside Dance Physical Therapy, New York, NY

Romana Kryzanowska, Director, Pilates Studio, New York, NY

Dr. William G. Hamilton, Official Doctor of the New York City Ballet, New York, NY

Dr. Janiz A. Minshew, Chiropractor, New York, NY

Marika Molnar, Director, Westside Dance Physical Therapy; Physical Therapist, New York City Ballet, New York, NY

Dr. Tom Novella, Podiatrist, New York, NY

Dr. Nathan Novick, Retired Chiropractor, New York, NY

Patrice Whiteside, Movement Analyst, Physical Therapist, Dancemedicine Center, Center for Sports Medicine, St. Francis Hospital, San Francisco, CA

Dr. Alan S. Woodle, D.P.M, Company Podiatrist, Pacific Northwest Ballet Company, Seattle, WA

In addition to these formal interviews, we have gathered extensive information through telephone calls and written correspondence/surveys from dancers, teachers, students, dance store owners, shoe fitters, and shoemakers throughout the United States and Europe.

It would be impossible to thank all of these contributors by name but they are represented on every page because their concerns evolved into the questions that we have chosen to address.

We are especially grateful to David Howard and Robert Cornfield for their encouragement and advice. Special thanks to Jennifer Katz for tape transcription services, Audrey Daniels for her translation services, Mikhail Messerer for his invaluable assistance and generosity, Samantha and Pat from Gamba Timestop Ltd., Miss Pat at Anello and Davide, Marilynn and Jim Dale, Robert and Vivien Altfeld, Gradimir and Margret Pankov, Patricia Renzetti and Martin Fredmann, and Cherry, Mary, Leslie, Heidi, Anne and David of Ballet Theatre of Annapolis.

Today our approach to pointe dancing has been shaped by centuries of experimentation. During our travels to gather material for this book, we have found little agreement about any detail of the process, ranging from how a dancer ties ribbons to when students should begin pointe work. In summarizing what we have learned, we have attempted to reflect this diversity of opinion.

The one truth that united everyone who shared their knowledge and experience with us was a belief in the importance of keeping this unique art form alive as we enter the next century. For that reason, creating this book has been a uniquely rewarding experience for us. We hope readers will find it both useful and provocative.

—Janice Barringer and Sarah Schlesinger, 1991

Chapter 6, "Profiles of Pointe Shoe Makers and Sellers," has been re-written with information on new manufacturers, corrected addresses, and the addition of telephone and fax numbers. The Bibliography has also been expanded to include new books.

We updated information critical to dancers' health and knowledge. Many professionals mentioned have changed affiliations since the first edition, but their expertise remains valuable. Some institutions offer new approaches; others no longer exist. Affiliations listed in the original preface or chapter Notes remain as they appeared in the original edition.

Finally, we would like to thank the following for their help with the revised edition: Victoria Schneider (Harid Conservatory); Betsy Cook (Center for Sports Medicine); Dr. Alan Woodle; James Harren (Houston Ballet's Body Conditioning Studio); Ellen Moran and Christine Neubert (Neubert Ballet Institute); Gretchen Ward Warren and Sandra Robinson Waldrop (Dance Department of the University of South Florida); Chari Nacson, Nancy Bielski, Daniel Catanach, and Kathryn Sullivan (STEPS), and ballerinas Paloma Herrera, Larissa Ponomarenko, and Marisa Soltis.

—Janice Barringer and Sarah Schlesinger, 1998

1

A Brief History of Pointe Dancing

While there is little agreement among dance historians about the precise date and location of the first performance on pointe by a ballerina, there is no doubt that the introduction of dancing *sur les pointes* had a profound effect on ballet technique. The ability to rise to the tips of her toes afforded the ballerina the opportunity for virtuosity on a new plane. With the appearance of pointe shoes, the female dancer's technique expanded, enabling her to create the illusion of incredible lightness and to project an increased sense of daring.

Although dancers may have risen on their toes since ancient times, the first documented performances on pointe appear to have taken place in England and France between 1815 and 1830, 240 years after Catherine de Médicis commissioned the first ballet in 1581. During the intervening years, a number of developments in the evolution of the female dancer's technique paved the way for the appearance of pointe dancing.

When King Louis XIV of France ordered the founding of the Royal Academy of Dance in 1661, the dancers initially performed on ballroom floors. When they were raised up on a stage, the audience had a different view of them and their feet became more important. As the stages grew larger, choreographers became more concerned with sideways movement and created the concept of turned-out legs. The height of the proscenium inspired a new movement vocabulary of elevated steps.

Men dressed as women took the female roles until 1681, when four young ladies danced in a ballet for the first time. These early ballerinas wore shoes with heels, constricted bodices, voluminous skirts, unwieldy headpieces, and enveloping shawls. Their costumes both reflected and dictated the nature of their technique, which was limited to gracefully executed sliding, walking, and running in intricate floor patterns.

During the first half of the eighteenth century, dance technique experienced rapid development and the dancer's dress was adjusted to accommodate these new physical demands. In 1726, Marie Camargo made her debut at the Paris Opéra Ballet and introduced the entrechat. To display these rapid changes of her feet from fifth position front to back and front again, she had to wear a shorter skirt. While initially she danced in the commonly accepted heeled shoes worn by her contemporaries, she soon abandoned them for a flatter shoe that provided an improved springboard for her complicated jumps. Camargo also devised an undergarment to wear beneath her petticoats from which tights later evolved.

In 1734, Marie Sallé, a French dancer and rival of Camargo's, appeared at the Drury Lane Theatre in London, performing a dance called *Pygmalion* for the first time. She replaced her usually cumbersome style of costume with a simple muslin dress that followed the lines of her body and wore her hair flowing loosely down her back instead of binding it up in an ornate headpiece.

The French Revolution swept away the remains of unwieldy costuming, and dancers began to appear in maillots, tights named after a costumer at the Paris Opéra. Flat ballet slippers tied with ribbons became standard footwear. These short-soled slippers with pleats under the toes were developed in response to the need for a more flexible shoe. The new slippers facilitated the fully extended pointing of the foot as well as jumps and turns. They were the foundation upon which the first pointe shoes were built.

During the Revolution, many dancers and choreographers left the Paris Opéra to perform in England and other parts of Europe. One of these emigrants was Charles Didelot, who had introduced the concept of a flying machine in a production at Lyons in 1794. Didelot's contraption enabled dancers to stand briefly on their toes before being whisked upward, creating the illusion of lightness as they portrayed the ethereal, unreal characters in classical ballets.

Didelot's flying machine was enthusiastically received in London in 1796. As theatrical dancing evolved, women had became more athletic, and the audience adored watching them perform such feats as sailing across the stage aided by hidden wires. When the dancers landed on their toes, their fans cheered with delight. This favorable response encouraged choreographers to seek ways for their stars to linger in an elevated position.

During the early 1800s, ballerinas were schooled in an increasingly challenging technical vocabulary including multiple pirouettes, and jumps and leaps. The attempt to dance on pointe without the support of wires was a logical extension of this growing emphasis on technical skill. Dancers discovered that by rising higher and higher on half pointe, they were able to balance on the ends of their fully stretched toes.

A print of ballerina Maria del Caro dated 1804 shows her nearly on the tips of her toes. On the basis of reviews and prints, Geneviève Gosselin, who died at the peak of her career in 1818, is thought to have danced on pointe in a production of Didelot's *Flore et Zephire* in 1815. Prints dated 1821 have been found showing Fanny Bias in the role of Flore, and she appears to be on pointe.

The Russian ballet-master Adam Flushkovksy declared that he had seen Avdotia Istomina dancing on the "very tip of her toe" in St. Petersburg in the years between 1816 and 1820. On the London stage, an unfortunate dancer named Mademoiselle Julia is reported to have lost her balance while standing on pointe in 1827 and fell to a chorus of critical scorn.

These earliest appearances on pointe probably involved little more than briefly held poses on the tips of the toes to give an illusion of weightlessness. They represented isolated tours de force and were not yet part of the fabric of dance technique.

In 1832, Marie Taglioni appeared on pointe in the first performance of *La Sylphide*. Her performance not only ushered in the Romantic Age, but introduced the use of pointe dancing as an essential choreographic element. Romantic ballet as represented by *La Sylphide* did not evolve in isolation, however, but rather as one aspect of a movement that involved every form of art in the early nineteenth century. It was part of a revolt against the eighteenth-century tradition of stressing classic perfection over feeling and meaning.

Ballet was an art form ruled by such traditional conventions when Taglioni demonstrated that pointe shoes could be used as an aesthetic element, to convey a sense of character that was essentially Romantic. She used pointe to bring a new poetic quality to ballet that was consistent with stylistic developments in scene design and dance music.

While there are no films or notations of Taglioni's performance, dance historian Walter Terry suggests that Auguste Bournonville's choreography of *La Sylphide* was probably very similar to the original Taglioni version. There are no extended pointe segments, but relevés on both feet, arabesques, attitudes, and bourées were probably performed on pointe. The elements of technique that could be executed on pointe were obviously limited by the nature of early pointe shoes. However narrow her technique, Taglioni's opening-night performance in *La Sylphide* caused one member of her audience to write, "Hers is a totally new style of dancing, graceful beyond all comparison, wonderful lightness, an absence of all violent effort. She seems to float and bound like a sylph across the stage."[1]

Pointe shoes similar to those worn by Taglioni in the 1800s have been preserved by private collectors. Her cobbler was Janssen of Paris, and several pairs of shoes bearing his stamp can be seen in the Haydn Museum in Eisenstadt, Austria. Upon examination they appear to be nothing more than soft satin slippers, heavily darned at the tip. They had no box to protect the toe and featured a flexible leather sole that supported the foot. Darning along the sides and over the toe kept the slippers in shape. They were essentially a one-sized tube of satin and leather that bound and squeezed the toes into a uniformly narrow pointe that had little relevance to the shape of the wearer's foot.

In order to work in such soft shoes, early pointe dancers probably stuffed the toes for added protection. Stitched ribbons and starch were the only other primitive attempts at reinforcement, leaving the dancers to rely on the strength of their feet and ankles. Wearing these slippers, a cloudlike costume, and wings, Taglioni created the image of the ballerina as a vision of perfection. Her performance pulled together the elements of a style that had been evolving for decades and quickly spread to England, Italy, Denmark, Germany, Russia, and the United States.

In 1832, Amalia Brugnoli danced on pointe in London, causing a critic to observe that her staccato work on the tops of her toes was unequaled by anything except Paganini's bow. Pauline Montessu performed a slow turn on pointe in 1833, and Angelica Saint-Romain astonished the public by performing "capriccios" on the tips of her toes.

Three other great Romantic ballerinas made their debuts following Taglioni's triumph—Fanny Elssler in 1833, Carlotta Grisi in 1836, and Fanny Cerrito in 1840. Fanny Elssler was particularly skilled in pointe technique. When she visited the United States, it was said that her admirers drank champagne from her slippers. A similar myth claims that some of Taglioni's Russian fans bought a pair of her shoes for three hundred rubles, cooked them, and had them for supper.

Ballerinas influenced by the theories of Italian dance master Carlo Blasis again expanded the technique with exuberant new physical pyrotechnics in the late 1800s. For example, Pierina Legnani introduced thirty-two fouettés in a performance of *Swan Lake* in 1892. Dancing on pointe became a means of expressing fire and strength as well as fantasy. This expanded technical vocabulary gave the ballerina a supremacy over the male dancer, which lasted until Nijinsky took Paris by storm in 1909.

Inspired by the feats of dancers like Legnani, the Russians invited Enrico Cecchetti to teach them the Italian technique, which they subsequently combined with elements of their own technique and French technique into what we now know as the Russian style. In addition to Italian technique, the Russians also embraced Italian pointe shoes. The shoes worn by Legnani were less pointed than the shoes worn by Taglioni and had a flatter, sturdier base. They also had stronger soles and a box that was molded with more substantial layers of fabric.

Pointe shoes created by the Italian shoemaker Nicolini were imported to Russia for use by the Russian Imperial Ballet until shipments were suspended during the Russian Revolution. These shoes had no nails and were lined with white kid leather. Since only their tips were stiffened or blocked, they were soundless on stage. Russian dancers used various techniques to stiffen the toes such as cutting up old pasteboard suitcases for support.

By the time of the great neoclassical ballets of Petipa and Ivanov, pointe work in the Russian ballet had become a series of intricate steps performed entirely on the toes. When *Sleeping Beauty* premiered in 1890, the dancers performing the fairy variations wore pointe shoes with a blocked toe made of newspaper and floured paste, which was reinforced by a light cardboard insole stretching between the tips of the toes and the instep.

As pointe dancing spread, variations in technique began to emerge. For instance, while the Italians tended to rise to pointe with a sprightly spring, the Russians rolled smoothly. The French rise was a cross between a spring and a roll.

In spite of the fact that her shoes weighed only one-half ounce more than the unblocked shoes of Taglioni's day, Anna Pavlova added a new dimension to pointe dancing in her portrayal of *The Dying Swan*. She was constantly on pointe in bourrée, a feat which had previously been thought impossible. Pavlova was rumored to have a secret process for preparing her slippers; after having a student break them in, she ripped out the cardboard and the fabric and leather liners and replaced them with a mysterious inner sole of her own design. She was reported to wear shoes with very wide platforms which afforded her superior balance. However, she supposedly took special care to have the platforms touched up in photographs to look narrower and more delicate, creating the illusion that she balance on "nothing."

The ballets created by Michael Fokine, Léonide Massine, and George Balanchine for the Ballet Russes under the direction of Sergei Diaghilev between 1909 and 1929 brought pointe dancing into the twentieth century. For the first time, the ballet audience saw ballerinas performing backward bourrées, slow balances, and traveling relevés in arabesque on pointe.

These advances were followed by further feats of skill performed on pointe by the "baby ballerinas" of the New Ballet Russe in 1931. Teenage ballerinas Irina Baronova and Tamara Toumanova performed sixty-four fouettés on pointe, six unsupported pirouettes, and extended balances to the delight of cheering audiences. The company rechoreographed the classics to incorporate these new "tricks" on pointe.

In the 1920s, one of the most popular stars on Broadway was Marilyn Miller, a toe dancer. Harriet Hoctor, another Broadway favorite in the 1920s and 1930s, stunned audiences at the Hippodrome in London by tapping up and down an escalator on her toes in shoes supported by steel shanks. Other Hoctor tricks included executing a backbend while doing bourrées on pointe, zooming through a circle of piqué turns at breakneck speed, and tapping out the meter of Edgar Allan Poe's poem *The Raven* with the tips of her shoes. Other revue dancers wore steel reinforcements to allow them to perform the Charleston on pointe.

In this "trick" pointe dancing tradition, Gloria Gilbert used ball bearings in the platforms of her shoes to allow her to turn at a dizzying rate while performing backbends. Toe-tap became a national craze as entrants in local amateur nights performed such feats as tapping on toe and playing the trumpet at the same time. A "shoe-biz" approach to pointe continued to spill over into the classical realm during the 1950s, when audiences expected ballerinas to do such tricks as sustaining attitude on pointe for an extended time period while the conductor had the orchestra play the same phrase over and over, waiting for the choreography to resume.

During the Second World War, shoes were often in short supply due to the upheaval throughout Europe. Alexandra Danilova recalled trying to extend the life of her shoes by darning them and coating them with a kind of shellac used to make straw hats stiff. Other dancers speak of strengthening their feet to be able to stand on pointe without shoes in order to dance in footwear that had been reduced to shreds.

By mid-century, pointe shoe boxes had become considerably harder in order to accommodate the technical demands on the dancer's foot. In the process of creating harder shoes, however, shoemakers produced pointe shoes with little flexibility, making it difficult for the dancer to have a sense of contact with the floor.

The continuing evolution of contemporary ballet technique led pointe shoe manufacturers to nonstop experimentation in succeeding decades. The result has been a wide range of pointe shoe designs from extremely strong to ultralight, in a variety of styles and shapes that enable dancers to jump higher, move more quickly, and accomplish increasingly difficult pointe technique utilized by choreographers such as George Balanchine. A typical pair of contemporary pointe shoes weighs about four ounces more than those worn in 1932.

Custom-constructed shoes ordered by various companies reflect the demands of their dominant choreographic styles. New York City Ballet dancers tend to "pounce" on their pointes, jumping rather that rolling up. Therefore they may be more dependent on their shoes for support than dancers whose main concern is creating the illusion that a pointe shoe is an extension of the foot.

Balanchine once said that if no pointe existed, he would not be a choreographer. Walter Terry quotes Balanchine as explaining,

Ballet is artificial. It is like poetry, it is invented. Where words fail, poetry can succeed and the same is true of ballet: something you cannot explain can be expressed on pointe. You can't tell a story on pointe but it can, when imaginatively used, give you an extra feeling similar to modulations in music or color intensities in light. In this sense, the pointe, even if it cannot tell a story, communicates drama. A ballerina on pointe is the maximum in dance.[2]

But what about the future of pointe dancing post-Balanchine and in the twenty-first century? While pointe dancing is sure to live on in the "museum" works of the past such as *Swan Lake* and *Giselle,* questions have been raised about its relevance to newly created works, since both choreography and the tools of the dance tend to change as the culture does.

Writing in 1986, dance critic Clive Barnes observed that the influence of modern choreography on classical ballet companies was tending to diminish the significance of the pointe shoe in new repertory. He suggested that toe dancing may be perceived as an unnatural movement, and "there is actually an aesthetic against the pointe work now, just as the cultural climate favored pointe work in the age of Romanticism."[3] Barnes wondered if pointe was an organic part of ballet technique or only a technical aid. However, works by such choreographers as Peter Martins, Clark Tippet, and Twyla Tharp for the New York City Ballet and American Ballet Theatre have clearly demonstrated that the dimension of pointe is still very much alive at the end of the twentieth century and that contemporary ballet artists are indeed integrating pointe into their creative visions.

NOTES

1. Trucco, Terry. "To the Pointe," *Ballet News,* vol. 3 (March 1982), p. 21.

2. Terry, Walter. *On Pointe.* (New York: Dodd Mead, 1962), p. 100.

3. Barnes, Clive. "Barnes On...," *Ballet News,* vol. 7 (February 1986), p. 39.

   For more information on the Romantic period see Guest, Ivor. *The Romantic Ballet in England* (Middletown, CT: Wesleyan Press, 1966) and Guest, Ivor. *The Romantic Ballet in Paris* (Middletown, CT: Wesleyan Press, 1972) and refer to the Bibliography.

2

The Foot and the Pointe Shoe Making Process

ANATOMY OF THE FOOT

The "real" pointe is the foot itself and not the shoe, which is only a covering. To meet the unique demands of pointe dancing, the foot has to be strong, supple, and as sensitive as the hand. Rather than serving as a passive weight-bearer, it must assume positions and execute movements beyond its normal limits. The original nature of her foot can be either a plus or minus for a pointe dancer.

The foot is a complex structure containing twenty-six bones, with a maze of ligaments connecting them. Ligaments are bands of tissue that bind bones together. The foot is animated by muscles and tendons, the tough fibrous tissue that connects muscle to bone and originates either in the foot itself or in the lower leg. Some muscles and tendons are large and visible through the skin, while others are quite small and impossible to see.

Nerves control the foot and give it feeling. Bones, ligaments, muscles, tendons, and nerves work together to operate a structure that is extremely resilient and has a broad range of motion.

The skeleton of the foot is composed of three major parts—the tarsus, consisting of three tarsal bones; the five metatarsals; and the fourteen phalanges (see fig. 1). The bony point that appears in the middle of the foot is part of the fifth metatarsal. Each of the toes has three phalanges, with the exception of the big toe which has only two. The metatarsal joints at the ball of the foot connect the phalanges or toe bones and the metatarsals or foot bones.

The solid back part of the foot is made up of seven tarsal bones. They are divided by cartilage, a tough elastic substance, and bound by ligaments which permit movement. The largest of the seven tarsal bones is called the calcaneus or heel bone.

Above the calcaneus is the talus or ankle bone, which fits into a concave receptacle formed by the lower leg bones, the tibia and the fibula. The talus receives the weight of the body through the tibia and then transfers it to the calcaneus.

The connection between the talus and the lower leg bones is cushioned

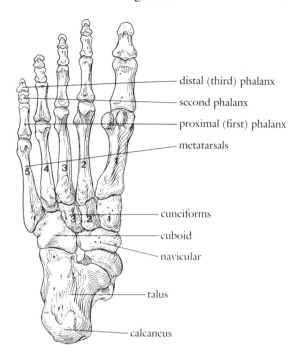

Figure 1
Bones of the left foot

distal (third) phalanx

second phalanx

proximal (first) phalanx

metatarsals

cuneiforms

cuboid

navicular

talus

calcaneus

by dense cartilage and held together by ligaments that run along the outside of the bones. There is no muscle around the ankle joint.

The part of the heel we can see and feel is an extension of the calcaneus. There is a protective bursa, or small, moist, friction-reducing envelope, between the calcaneus and the Achilles tendon. The sustentaculum tali offers support on the inside of the calcaneus; its edge can be felt about an inch below the ankle bone. On the outside, there is a similar projection called the peroneal tubercle.

The cuboid, found in front of the calcaneus, is situated between the calcaneus and the two outer metatarsal bones. On the inside it forms a joint with the outer cuneiform and navicular. The navicular is on the inside of the foot; it forms a joint to the rear with the talus and to the front with the three cuneiforms. These three cuneiforms form a joint with each other and the three metacarpals in front, and with the navicular behind. The outer cuneiform also forms a joint with the cuboid.

The bones of the foot form two arches—the longitudinal arch along the inner side that is made up the calcaneus, talus, navicular, the three cuneiforms, and the first three metatarsals; and the transverse arch which is formed by the convex arrangement of the tarsal and metatarsal bones and crosses the forefoot. When dancers speak of their arch, they are generally referring to part of the sole between the ball and the heel, while the term *instep* describes the surface of the arch.

The arches are held together by long ligaments and maintained by muscles. The spring ligament is the most important long ligament in the foot and is attached to the sustentaculum tali and the plantar or sole surface of the navicular, supporting the talus.

Long and short plantar ligaments run under the foot between the bottom of the calcaneus and the three middle metatarsals. The short plantar ligament is situated under the long plantar ligament; it begins at the calcaneus and is then passed forward and slightly beyond the cuboid. The medial or deltoid ligament begins at the end of the tibia and spreads into three bands attached to the navicular, the sustentaculum tali, and the body of the talus. The lateral ligament is on the outside of the foot and attached to the end of the fibula. It divides into three bands which connect with the front of the talus, the calcaneus, and the body of the talus.

MOVEMENTS OF THE FOOT AND ANKLE JOINT

The foot both bears weight and executes movements such as propulsion. Four layers of short muscles along the sole of the foot, called the intrinsic muscles, adjust the bones of the foot to the shape required for weight-bearing and hold this position. The long muscles attached to these bones and traveling up the leg are used when performing various movements.

There are eight possible movement patterns of the foot. The first two, plantar flexion or pointing the foot downward and dorsi flexion or pointing the foot upward, take place in the ankle joint. They are limited by the shape of the bones and tightness of surrounding ligaments and tendons. Inversion or the raising of the inner border of the foot and exversion or the raising of the outer border happen in the back part of the foot between the talus and calcaneus. Adduction, the turning in of the forefoot, and abduction, the turning out the forefoot, take place in the midtarsal region between the talus, navicular, calcaneus, and cuboid bones. Finally, supination is the combination of adduction and inversion, while pronation is the combined action of abduction and eversion.

The toes stabilize the foot when it is bearing weight. Toes can move by curling downward or flexing and by extending.

MUSCULAR ACTION

Weight-bearing, propulsion, shock absorption, lifting (e.g., relevé), and free movement without weight-bearing (e.g., battement frappé) are performed by a series of muscles extending between the bottom of the knee and the bones of the foot as well as by the previously mentioned four layers of short intrinsic muscles on the soles of the foot. The only deviation from this pattern is the gastrocnemius, the large muscle at the back of the calf that originates at the lower end of the femur above the back of the knee. It acts as a knee flexor assisting the hamstrings. As it passes through the leg it joins with the soleus; these two muscles form the Achilles tendon which is inserted into the back of the calcaneus. The flexibility of this tendon determines the depth of demi-plié possible.

Four muscles turn the foot up and raise the inner or outer border; they are the tibialis anterior, the extensor hallucis longus, the extensor digitorum longum and the peroneus tertius. The tibialis anterior helps maintain the arch of the foot.

Five other muscles point or plantar flex the foot; they are the peroneus longus, peroneus brevis, tibialis posterior, flexor digitorum longus, and flexor hallucis longus. Tibialis posterior is an important supporter of the arch, and flexor hallucis longus fixes the big toe to the ground and assists in takeoffs during propulsive movement. Tibialis anterior and tibialis posterior as well as flexor hallucis maintain a normal relation between the front and back of the foot.

To achieve a position on pointe, the anatomical progression is through a rise to half pointe and then to three-quarter pointe or full pointe. To achieve a rise, the trunk and pelvis move as one and come slightly forward with the line of gravity, to lie over the toes when the rise is completed. Anatomically, the calf muscles contract, lifting the heel and hindfoot against gravity. Tone must be maintained in the muscles of the leg and hip, including the gluteals, the adductors, the hamstrings, and the quadriceps. Complete control requires full strength in the intrinsic muscles of the foot as well as the calf and other leg muscles.

When dancing on pointe, the weight of the body is supported by the intrinsic muscles of the foot and the longitudinal arches, but it rests on the metatarsals. The pointe shoe is designed to protect the toes and force them to stretch out in a gentle curve instead of buckling under the weight of the body.

ANATOMY OF THE TRADITIONAL POINTE SHOE

Since the foot of a pointe dancer changes shape every few seconds when she is in motion, she needs a shoe that can adjust to provide comfort and support whether she is on pointe or in a flat position. The contemporary pointe shoe does just that.

Inside the end of most contemporary pointe shoes is the box or block made from densely packed layers of fabric and paper, which are shaped and dipped in glue. It is this hardened glue that makes the shoe stiff. This "box" of fabric and glue extends over the phalanges, encasing, protecting, and supporting the toes and giving them a small round platform on which to perch. The blocking is thickest at the tip but extends as far as halfway down the shoe in a thinner form, providing a sturdy structure under a skin or "upper" of satin, canvas, or leather. Shoe blocks come in varying degrees of hardness, and varying widths and vamp lengths.

A short outer sole made of thin leather allows for flexibility and contact with the floor, while a sturdy but pliable insole made of various combinations of leather and fiber reinforces the dancer's instep. A narrow supportive spine called the shank is usually placed between the outer sole and the inner sole. This centerpiece is the core of the shoe, extending from the middle of the heel to just under the ball of the foot and usually shaped like a flattened spoon. The shank must be supple, but not brittle, to conform to the arch of the dancer's foot as it lifts off the floor. It can be made from leather or fabric. In the United States we sometimes refer to the entire unit formed by the insole and its attached reinforcement as the shank. To prevent confusion, we use the term *shank* to refer only to the inner reinforcing tongue. An additional protective sock lining is usually glued over the insole.

The side and top of the shoe are covered with a cotton lining and an outer layer of satin, canvas, or leather. The "upper" extends over the toes, across the box or block, and under the foot to connect with the sole in carefully crafted pleats.

The descriptive terms given in figure 2 are commonly used by American and European manufacturers to describe the parts of the pointe shoe.

THE POINTE SHOE MAKING PROCESS

To more fully comprehend the unique nature of point shoes, we begin with a basic understanding of how they are made. While pointe dancers and their makers are usually strangers to one another, they depend on each other for their livelihood.

Sulamith Messerer, the renowned former Bolshoi star who taught company class for the Royal Ballet at the time of our research, recalled that very young ballet students at major company schools in Russia learned how pointe shoes were made. Since their pointe shoes were made by the company's own shoemakers, they were able to observe the process directly. As a result, they had a much clearer understanding of their shoes and were better able to communicate about them.

Since few American dancers have such an opportunity to observe the process for themselves, we have synthesized the steps of pointe shoe construction as we observed them in four factories in the United States

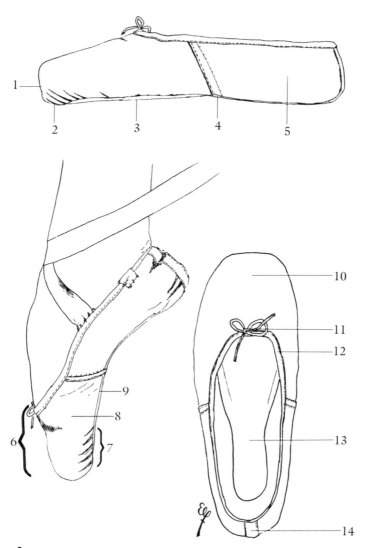

Figure 2

Anatomy of the pointe shoe: (1) platform or tip; (2) edge of the pleats or feathers; (3) outer sole; (4) waist seam; (5) quarter or heel section; (6) vamp—the top of the box that covers the toes (vamp length is the distance between the drawstring knot and the top edge of the box. Some European manufacturers refer to vamp length as the distance between the drawstring knot and the edge of the pleats or feathers); (7) pleats or feather—area underneath the box where the satin is pleated to fit under the sole; (8) wings or supports; (9) shank or narrow supporting spine, which is attached to the back of the insole; (10) stiffened box or block made of layers of glue and fabric and surrounding the toes and ball of the foot; (11) drawstring knot; (12) drawstring casing—piece of bias tape stitched around the edge of the shoe to contain the drawstring; (13) insole; (14) back seam, which divides the quarters.

and England. Pointe shoe construction varies from manufacturer to manufacturer, yet the basic process, while quite complex, is much the same. One manufacturer estimates that it takes 137 operations performed over three days by seven people to make one pair of pointe shoes. Thus it is not surprising that no two pairs are ever alike, even when crafted by the same maker.

Traditionally, pointe shoes are made by the "turnshoe process," which means they are lasted and sewn inside out, slipped off the last, and then turned right side out for shaping, drying, and finishing. Until the 1870s, all shoes were made in this fashion, but now only pointe shoe makers and some running shoe manufacturers use the method. Pointe shoes are made on a straight last and have no right or left since this kind of "no-footed" construction gives better balance and a truer, straighter point. A straight last allows the foot to tell the shoe what to do, rather than having the shoe establish the form of the foot.

While some of the cutting and sewing phases of the process have been automated, the majority of the work on pointe shoes around the world is still done by hand. Since efforts to bring pointe shoe making into the twenty-first century by creating a machine capable of pleating and shaping them have yet to succeed, the process remains a nineteenth-century craft. Shoemakers in British factories still often stand at their work stations, although those at Capezio sit at low benches.

The Process

STEP 1. CUTTING OR CLICKING
The vamp section, quarter sections, and linings that form the upper of the toe shoe are cut from special patterns. After inspecting the fabric for imperfections, cutting-room employees do multicuts of yards of satin and lining material for stock shoes using a hydraulic press to cut many layers at one time. Special orders are hand-cut from individual patterns, and alterations related to the height of the vamp, sides, and back are done at this stage. Uppers are stamped with a date and lot number.

STEP 2. SEWING OR CLOSING
Seamstresses at sewing machines join the front and backs (vamp and quarters) of the upper and sew satin and cotton lining sections of the upper together. The back strap is sewn on and opened flat. At some factories, the binding and drawstring that adjust the snugness of the shoe are attached at this time. At others they are added when the shoe is near completion. When working on stock shoes, seamstresses usually work on a batch of ten of a size. Excess threads are removed at a trimming table.

STEP 3. PREPARING THE INSOLE, SHANK AND OUTER SOLE
The insole, shank, and outer sole are cut to the shape needed out of large

YOU'RE A STAR IN CAPEZIO® TOE SHOES

SALVATORE CAPEZIO   NICHOLAS TERLIZZI, SR.

From the time Salvatore Capezio made his first pair of toe shoes, three generations have honored that unique tradition. Shown here are Salvatore Capezio, the founder, and Nicholas Terlizzi, Sr., the present Chairman of the Board and a nephew of Mr. Capezio, who represent the first two generations. The third generation is represented by Mr. Terlizzi's sons Nicholas, Jr., Alfred and Donald.

Many of the craftsmen in the Capezio factory are also third generation. Making toe shoes is a labor of love for them—from the cutting of the fabric to the final pleating by hand. Second only to her technical skill is a dancer's toe shoes. These craftsmen not only recognize that, but find it a challenge. That's why they continue to refine their craft by watching dancers perform, talking to dancers and choreographers and experimenting so the Capezio shoes they make can continue to earn the reputation as the finest and most prestigious in the world.

So, to the people who create Capezio's Nicolini, Assoluta, Pavlowa, Contempora and Ultimo toe shoes—bravissimo!

Capezio's
been dancing
since 1887

1 The uppers of the toe shoe are carefully cut by hand from special patterns.

2 The front and backs are sewn together. Then the entire uppers are stitched.

3 The many layers of satin and fabric that will form the toe box are glued with Capezio's own special formula glue.

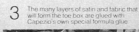

4 The upper is put on a last (or form) inside out, pulled taut, and then the pleats are formed entirely by hand. This is a crucial step because the fit and flexibility of the toe shoe depend on the pleating.

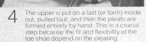

5 Pleats are stitched down tight with linen thread, and excess cloth is trimmed. Upper is then stitched to sole in a pre-cut channel.

6 The shoe is turned right side out.

7 After the inside of the toe is tamped and shaped and the inner sole is glued in, the craftsman relasts the shoe with an enormous shoe horn.

8 Now the shoe is shaped from the outside and pounded with a satin-smooth hammer.

9 The pleats are deepened and checked. Then deep, criss-cross cuts are scored on the sole, and the finished shoe is placed on a rack to dry naturally for 2-4 days, depending on humidity.
Bravissimo.

pieces of leather by heavy mechanical presses or by hand, with knives that look like cookie cutters. Shoulder leather is frequently used. A number of makers commented on the difficulty of finding a steady supply of leather in an age of synthetics. The leather soles and insoles are then shaved to perfect the surface and establish uniform thickness. Then, on a machine that looks like a sewing machine, a channel or groove is cut around the perimeter of the sole. Later, when the shoe is assembled, this groove becomes the stitching line. After the channel is cut, the soles may be buffed in a wringerlike device.

STEP 4. PULLING OVER
The upper is stretched inside out over the last, which is a foot-shaped form. At some factories the last is covered with tissue paper to make it easier to remove the shoe. Once made of wood, most lasts today are constructed of heavy plastic. As many as eight thousand lasts may be required to make a full line of pointe shoes. The shape of each last—designed to mold the shoe into a curve somewhere between the flat and arched foot—is a compromise. While a professional dancer may have her own last molded to her foot, most student dancers wear stock shoes formed on standard factory lasts in the size, shape, and style of their choice. Lasts may be wrapped with leather and tape to change their shape temporarily for a special order.

STEP 5. BLOCKING
The shoemaker assembles the blocking over the lining of the upper in layers. Fabric (often burlap), paper, and special formula glue are used to build up the inside of the box. In some processes, a burlap triangle is added to form the platform. The specifics of this part of the process differ greatly from manufacturer to manufacturer. Many place special emphasis on using materials and a method that ensure the shoe will be "noiseless." Glue formulas are usually kept top secret. The combination of fabric and glue must stay malleable enough to be worked on through the day.

STEP 6. THE LASTING STEP
The lasting step begins as the shoemaker pulls the uppers taut and uses his hands as well as various pushing and pulling instruments to mold the still-soft block into its finished pointe shape—square, long, flat, oval, or curved. He inserts the pleats by hand and pushes them into position with an awl-like instrument called the bone. This step is critical because the fit and flexibility of the shoes depend on the pleating. Many shoemakers feel that pleating is the most difficult part of the process. At Capezio, pointe shoes are made with ten pleats. One disappears from view when the shoe is turned, leaving a broad central pleat with four smaller pleats on either

side. After the pleats are formed, the shoemaker holds them with his thumb and ties them in place.

STEP 7. STITCHING AND TURNING
The pleats are stitched down with linen thread, and excess cloth is trimmed. The upper is stitched to the sole in the precut channel. Then the shoe is turned right side out.

STEP 8. INSOLE INSERTION
The insole and attached reinforcing shank are placed inside the shoe with glue and nails. Next the shoemaker tamps and shapes the inside of the shoe and glues on an inner sole or sock lining.

STEP 9. HAMMERING OUT
Using an enormous shoehorn, the shoemaker reinserts the last. Then he shapes the shoe from the outside, using a smooth-edge hammer to mold the block or box over the shape of the last, particularly at the toe to get rid of any bumps or uneven edges. He deepens the pleats, scores cuts on the soles for traction, and stamps shoemaker, size, and last information on the soles.

STEP 10. DRYING
Finished shoes are placed on a rack to dry for two to four days. At some factories, the shoes are baked in a hot-air oven. Some manufacturers sponge finished shoes with a nonabrasive soap solution to remove excess glue and other residue.

STEP 11. INSPECTION
Dried shoes are inspected for quality and either stored until needed or prepared for shipment.

About the Shoemakers

Pointe shoe makers are usually trained on the job and many remain in the profession for a lifetime. They are almost always men, although women are often involved in the preparation and finishing stages of the process. Most of the makers are highly skilled craftsmen who do not necessarily have any interest in ballet or knowledge of the dancers for whom they create shoes.

In the early days of American pointe shoe manufacturing, shoemakers were recruited as they got off the boat from Italy. Many apprenticed at factories as young men and remained a lifetime. According to legend, one

Capezio shoemaker was so dedicated to the company that he asked to be buried in the factory; his ashes are rumored to be there today.

While the older shoemakers used to bring their entire families into the business, fewer members of the younger generation are joining the profession. There is apprehension in the industry about the eventual loss of a willing and capable work force in an area that requires long practice, devotion to craft, and exceptional skill.

3

The Pointe Shoe
Fitting Process

No other event in a dance student's life is anticipated with as much excitement as being fitted for a first pair of pointe shoes. Often this initial enthusiasm is replaced with disillusion at the fitting session. Not only do pointe shoes feel extremely uncomfortable on the novice's feet, but the first fitting can be a confusing, frustrating experience for everyone involved. With careful forethought, a teacher can greatly simplify this experience for the student, the parent, the dance shop, and the school.

TEACHER INVOLVEMENT

If possible, the teacher should accompany the student to the first fitting or arrange for representatives from a dance shop to visit the studio for a group fitting. If this is impossible to arrange, the teacher should be sure to provide students and their parents with a complete orientation to the fitting process. This orientation should include a discussion of how pointe shoes should fit, their cost, and the importance of not wearing them at home without the teacher's supervision. The school's preferences in ribbons, shoe padding, and use of elastic should also be explained.

In view of the rising cost of shoes, it is essential that teachers inform parents about the economic commitment involved in placing a child on pointe and clarify the importance of an exact fit. Inevitably, parents seek to have their children fitted in shoes "to grow into." The teacher must help them understand why this concept cannot be applied to the process of buying pointe shoes.

Since the bones of the feet do not complete their final ossification—hardening and joining—until the dancer's twentieth to twenty-third year, incorrect fitting can damage the future growth pattern of a young dancer. The shoe must fit snugly; otherwise it could cause calluses and bruises to joints or accidents to ankles and toes. Shoes that are too large make it impossible to achieve proper support and balance.

Pressure from parents because of the cost of pointe shoes to have their children fitted in shoes that are too large has led some teachers to compromise their standards. Allowing students to pad their shoes for longer wear is an unsafe and irresponsible solution to the problem.

If parents are not able or willing to make the necessary investment to keep their child in correctly fitting pointe shoes, it would be far more advisable and healthier for the child to remain in soft slippers. Making parents aware that advanced pointe students go through a pair of shoes in one to three weeks and that a ballerina at the height of her profession might wear out sixty-five pairs a month can help put the realities of starting a student on pointe in an accurate perspective.

The teacher's knowledge of the student's foot structure, overall strength, and potential for advancement should prompt a suggestion for a specific brand, style, and possible size of pointe shoe to try. The more information imparted in advance, the higher the probability the student will be fitted correctly and not have to return to the dance shop to exchange her shoes.

Finding a shop with skilled fitters is the most important step in the pointe shoe buying process. This is one purchase that should not be made on the basis of discount shopping. Most pointe shoes are identically priced from store to store in a given state. However, prices may vary slightly from region to region because of shipping costs.

A store dedicated to selling dance shoes offers the best prospect of finding experienced fitters. While children's shoe stores, general shoe stores, and department stores stock dance shoes, they frequently cannot offer the same specialized fitting services.

Ordering pointe shoes by mail is always risky, but is absolutely out of the question when buying a first pair. If there is no local source where shoes can be tried on, a trip should be planned to the nearest location where this is possible.

PREPARING FOR A FITTING

A number of preparatory steps a dancer can take before a pointe shoe fitting will greatly simplify the process. She should be sure her toenails are properly cut. The nails should not be allowed to hang over the toes; they should reach only to the tips of the toes. The corners of the nails should be slightly rounded.

Dance tights that are the same weight as those that will be worn in class should be brought to fittings. If nylon socks or stockings are worn, an improper fit may result.

It is important to know the exact size and width of current ballet slippers and street shoes. Although American pointe shoes are marked from two to two and a half sizes smaller than a street shoe and foreign shoes are sized on a variety of different standards, current shoe sizes can be helpful to the shoe fitter. While some shops measure the feet to determine a first pointe shoe size to try, trained fitters can quickly identify this size on the basis of ballet slipper and street shoe sizes.

AT THE FITTING

Pointe shoe fitting is not an exact science. It involves a great deal of trial and error. All fittings take time, but first fittings can be especially lengthy. Ample time needs to be allowed for the fitter to find the best shoe for a particular foot within the limits set by the teacher's requirements. The handmade nature of the shoes means that no two pairs are ever identical, and this further complicates the process.

Some stores make advance appointments for pointe shoe fittings. Otherwise, it is a good idea to call and ask for a suggestion about the best hour to come in for a fitting. Hectic times such as Saturdays at the beginning of dance semesters should be avoided.

The best time for a fitting in terms of a dancer's feet is after class in the late afternoon. Feet are generally smaller in the morning; as circulation increases during the day, they tend to swell.

The dancer should be sure to show the shoe fitter her bare feet before the fitting begins. Although tights are worn for the fitting itself, they can obscure important information about toe and foot shape and alignment that the fitter needs to observe. The foot should then be covered with tights and whatever padding is going to be used in class.

FINDING THE RIGHT SHOE

Pointe shoes have to feel right in addition to looking right. Although this is very hard to discern when trying on a first pair of pointe shoes, it will become much easier as time goes on.

The goal of the fitter is to find a pair of shoes that will fit the customer's foot like a glove, providing support and helping to prevent the foot from buckling. The more information a fitter is given about the way the shoe feels, the more chance the wearer has of getting a perfectly fit shoe. Since pointe shoes are initially quite hard and conform snugly to the foot, a great deal of important information about their fit is hidden inside a barrier that the fitter cannot penetrate. Consequently, it is extremely important for the wearer to describe what is happening inside the shoe as accurately as possible.

While a measuring stick reading or ballet shoe size may give the fitter a place to start in terms of pointe shoe size, most of the work must be done on the dancer's feet in a lengthy trial and error process. The dancer needs to have control of her feet for balance and the ability to move freely and with ease. The need to feel the floor and be able to work on demi-pointe is as important in pointe shoes as in soft shoes. Normally, pointe shoes are fitted anywhere from one to three sizes shorter than street shoes and one width wider.

STOCK SHOES

Ideally, each pair of pointe shoes should be custom designed and specifically molded to a dancer's feet. This is obviously not possible in a world where the demand for pointe shoes has created the need for mass production. Since the skilled labor force required to create special shoes is limited, priority is given to professional dancers.

While many professionals have their own last and a particular shoemaker who creates their shoes, students are usually limited to shoes purchased "off the shelf." Although these shoes are created in a factory environment and produced in standard sizes and widths, each pair is worked on by hand by experienced cobblers.

Some professional dancers actually prefer to wear stock shoes, believing that shoes that have been "freshly made" for a custom order may not last as long as shoes that have been on a warehouse or store shelf for several months "hardening up."

Manufacturers are constantly involved in research and development efforts to improve their stock shoe lines. For example, during the past several years, Gamba has spent hundreds of thousands of dollars researching standard shoe design and shoe sizing with the aid of computers.

The dancer who wears stock shoes is well advised to find a dance shop that carries a large selection of sizes and widths in a variety of styles and brands of pointe shoes. The more latitude of choice, the more chance for a perfect fit. Stock shoes are designed to provide different degrees of support for various kinds of feet. Many manufacturers now produce stock shoes varying in strength of the shank and box, width and shape of the box, and length of the vamp.

THE HARD SHOE – SOFT SHOE DEBATE

While most teachers want the shape of a pointe shoe to be determined by the student's foot, they may set a uniform policy about whether first shoes should be very hard, hard, medium, or soft. These terms relate to the strength of the box, which corresponds to the arch strength.

Some teachers recommend a classic, harder shoe for beginners and gradually work toward having students wear lighter shoes as their bodies develop. They believe that a strong shoe will strengthen the foot as the dancer works in it. This is a popular choice with parents because harder, heavier boxes mean longer wear.

Other teachers suggest a softer shoe, feeling that the dancer must depend on the strength of her foot and not her shoe. They believe that a lighter shoe forces the foot to build its own strength on the theory that once dependence on hard, stiff shoes has been established, it is often impossible to make the change to lighter slippers because it involves learning a new way of dancing on pointe.

In some cases hard shoes or soft shoes are dictated by the nature of the dancer's foot. Many professional dancers have worn hard shoes throughout their careers. Once a dancer reaches performance level, soft shoes or hard shoes may be required due to the nature of the choreography.

Over the years, a variety of techniques have been explored in the effort to develop a longer-lasting, heavier student shoe to satisfy those who endorse a hard shoe for beginners. The earliest of these, the suede-tipped durable toe shoe, remains a popular beginner's choice in many parts of the country.

In recent years, some teachers and orthopedists have expressed concern that the design of these shoes is not ideal for young, growing feet because of the concentration of weight at the toe. The value of the suede tip feature, which has been a major selling point, has also been questioned. While it is designed to prevent the bottom of the point from wearing out, it may actually limit the dancer's mobility.

The appearance of the bottom of the pointe shoe is actually of little importance. Sturdy beginner pointe shoes with satin toes and a more classic shape are rapidly replacing the suede-tipped shoe and should be given serious consideration by teachers who have not yet adopted them.

Another early experiment for "hardening" shoes was use of the steel shank. These have almost disappeared from the market and should be avoided completely. The steel shank has no flexibility and can cause severe injury to a dancer who falls off pointe with her foot caught in this rigid vise.

In recent years, an inevitable development in the quest for a hard, durable student pointe shoe has been the introduction of plastic boxes. Lacking in flexibility, such shoes have already been responsible for a variety of injuries. Writer Joan Lawson[1] found that in Australia, dancers who wore shoes with plastic boxes suffered an increased occurrence of stress fractures to the second and third metatarsal bones of the toes. Many of them had inflammation of their Achilles tendons and ankles as well as bursas on their heels. When wearing shoes with plastic blocks, dancers cannot rise slowly through the quarter, half, and three-quarter pointe positions. They must simply go up or down because the rigidity of the shoes do not allow the muscles of the feet to work properly. Dancers tend to sink into the blocks of these shoes with their insteps clenched and their toes drawn under. They do not feel a stretch of their feet and legs as their bodies lift away from their hips.

In other words, the hard shoe–soft shoe choices must be made within the range of boxes hardened with standard cloth-and-glue construction. If a dancer is not given any guidelines on shoe weight from a teacher, a good choice for a beginner might be a medium-weight shoe in a shape appropriate for her individual foot.

PROTECTIVE PADDING

Whether protective padding is necessary or advisable is widely debated among dancers. Ideally, if the shoe has been fitted properly, toe pads and lamb's wool should not have to be stuffed in the shoe's platform. Without additional padding, a dancer's toes should just touch the edge of the inside of the platform, allowing her to feel the floor.

If a dancer decides that protective padding is needed, conventional foam rubber or fur toe pads are the worst choice. These pads prevent the toes from moving freely, keep the foot from having contact with the floor, and cause shoes to be fitted too large. In addition, pads made from man-made materials tend to heat up and make the feet perspire, which can encourage the formation of soft corns. A toe pad made by some European manufacturers provides a small layer of foam under the toes in the shape of the pointe shoe platform and covers the sides and front of the foot with thin suede. This pad is less bulky than conventional foam pads and does not greatly alter the fit of the shoe.

A small amount of lamb's wool can be used to keep shoes from rubbing blisters. This wool can be wrapped around individual sensitive toes or placed over all five toes in a thin layer before the shoe is put on. To keep the lamb's wool from slipping, some dancers place a thin padding of it over the joints of the toes before putting their feet inside their tights. The theory behind the use of lamb's wool is that it allows the toe to slip slightly against the soft fibers to avoid contact with an abrasive canvas lining. If a dancer uses lamb's wool, it should be purchased at the dance shop, since drugstore lamb's wool is of the wrong texture. In some parts of the world where wool is not available, soft cotton is used as a substitute.

Many teachers believe students are better off if they develop calluses on their toes early in their pointe training. Some suggest that wrapping the knuckle of each toe in a Band-Aid or masking tape and avoiding any padding inside the shoe prevents blisters and help develop calluses. Others feel that taping the toes prevents them from toughening and suggest other techniques. For instance, Claude Bessy, director of the Paris Opéra Ballet School, encourages her students to clean their feet in alcohol and to avoid soaking them in water since water tends to soften the skin.

Another suggestion for avoiding blisters is to use a lot of talcum powder in shoes since the powder absorbs the moisture which is largely responsible for causing blisters. Sprinkling talcum powder between the toes is a good way to prevent abrasion. However, powder should be applied over a trash can and kept far away from the studio or stage floor since it is very slippery.

Some dancers wear small quantities of various kinds of paper products in their shoes as padding. In fact, finding the specific type of paper can become an obsession, as it did with one dancer who had to have paper toweling from the rest rooms of the Pentagon in Washington, D.C., wrapped around her toes to be able to function properly on pointe. Kleenex, brown paper, and newspaper are also popular choices. However, paper can crinkle inside the shoe and cause blisters.

In England, a product called surgical spirit is used to deaden the top layers of the epidermis, which helps the dancer with tender feet get used to wearing pointe shoes. This product cannot be used if the dancer has developed blisters. Some dancers use antiseptic liquid bandages such as New Skin, which are found in pharmacies. Other possible toe coverings are the top of a cotton sock or old pair of tights, or a nylon stocking.[2]

TOO BIG OR TOO SMALL SHOES

Many of the problems dancers experience with their feet are due to incorrectly fitting pointe shoes. The most common culprit is shoes that are too big. Remember that pointe shoes stretch out as the dancer works in them, and she may end up sinking into a shoe that seems snug in the store. When the foot sinks into the shoe, the big toe twists. Big shoes are a frequent cause of bunions, corns on toe joints, blisters, and bruised nails.

The fitter should check to be sure there is no excess room between the drawstring and the foot, or at the heel. If the heel is too baggy, the dancer may pull the drawstring too tight and the shoe will dig into the Achilles tendon. If a big shoe gives inadequate support to the arch, the shoe may collapse, causing the dancer to go over on her pointe. The platform in a big shoe may also collapse when a dancer has softened the edge of the toe by continuously sliding down into it.

On the other hand, a shoe that is too short can bring great discomfort to the Achilles tendon when the dancer is standing flat. Short shoes can cause the ends of the toes to become pressed and inflamed. Shoes that are too narrow squeeze the toes and joints and do not allow them to work properly. When the toes press against each other, soft corns can form and toenails can become ingrown.

The shoe should hold the toes snugly, but not so snugly that they are bunched together. They should be able to spread slightly sideways, and the tips of the toes should just feel the end of the shoes when the weight is evenly distributed. The right and left edges of her feet and her large and small toe joints should be slightly tight against the edge of the shoe. The shoe must support the foot, and any room for movement inside the shoe may leave the foot unsupported.

The toes must not be bent, pressed against the tip, or feel sore inside the shoe. The dancer should demi-plié in the shoe to see if her arch has room for expansion. An arch that does not have room to expand can gradually lose its elasticity.

Dancers with longer second or third toes should be careful not to cram them into a shoe that is too short. This can cause the longer toe to bend, resulting in corns and callous formations, or possibly disjoint from its normal structure, which can lead to an arthritic condition.

ADDITIONAL SIZING PROBLEMS

Vamp Length

The length of the vamp, the part of the box that covers the top of the foot, must be determined by the length of the dancer's toes. A long-toed foot requires a longer vamp than a short-toed foot. The vamp should be long enough to cover the joint at the base of the big toe, otherwise the joints of the toes may pop out of the shoe. The inside edge of the binding at the center front of the foot should reach as far as or just beyond the third phalange of the first and second toes.

If the vamp is too short, it will cause the foot to break over the toe, making it look extremely ugly. If, on the other hand, the vamp is too long, it will throw the dancer back and prevent her from attaining a full-pointe position. It can also cause the front tendons to strain.

Box Shape

Usually students with long toes and narrow feet need a more pointed box, and those with short toes and squat feet require a squarer box. In some cases the location of the instep forces a different choice. Those with shallow feet often do well in shoes with flatter boxes.

The Outer Sole and the Width of the Box

The end of the outer leather sole does not come to the outer edge of the heel as it does in a street shoe. This is to accommodate the drawing inward of the muscles and the stretching downward of the toes, which both narrows and shortens the foot. Therefore, the shoe must be wide enough to hold the metatarsal arch with the toes slightly spread when flat, but still narrow enough to hold the foot securely when the dancer is on pointe.

The outer edge of the binding at the heel should cover the rounded portion of the heel so that the back of the shoe stays in place when the dancer is on pointe and the outer sole slips upward. When the dancer is on pointe, with the foot and leg fully stretched and the toes uncramped, the leather outer sole should reach the end of the heel.

One Foot Larger Than the Other

It is imperative to have both feet fitted for pointe shoes. Most people have at least a slight variation of size or width in their feet, and a shoe that is perfect on one foot may be a disaster on the other. If the dancer has a significant difference in size and/or width between her feet, she can circumvent this problem by buying two pairs of shoes in different sizes at the same time. Since pointe shoes are made on straight lasts and there are no rights or lefts, she can create two mixed pairs and alternate between them. Another possible approach is to experiment with inserting a thin insole in one shoe.

TESTING FOR PROPER FIT

After pointe shoes have been placed on both feet, the student should first stand up with her feet flat on the floor. The ends of the toes should be stretched out, straight, and just touching the front wall of the shoe. If the toes are pushed back, the shoes are too small. If wrinkles appear in the box area, either the box or the entire shoe is too narrow. If a finger can be slipped between the edge of the box and the top of the foot when the foot is flat or on pointe, the shoe is probably too wide. The metatarsal arch should be held firmly and comfortably within the toe piece of the shoe.

Next the dancer should stand in second position and demi-plié. This stretches the heel and toe. Assess the way the foot feels in this position. Is it touching the front? Is it bent? Since the foot naturally contracts when it goes on pointe, the shoe should be slightly tight when the foot is flat on the ground and in an expanded state. The big toe should just touch the edge of the platform, and the sides should be supported with a sensation of slight pressure but not pain.

Next the dancer should stand in first position. While keeping her right foot flat, she should cross her left foot in front of her right leg, placing the platform of the left shoe gently on the fitting surface and pressing down on the large toe. When the foot is in this position, is it touching the front and back of the shoe? The heel of the shoe should lie smoothly over the heel of the foot. If too much material can be pinched together at the heel, the shoe is too long. Is there any extreme pressure? Can the toes move? Then repeat this movement, crossing the right foot over the left. The end of the leather sole should come to the end of the heel in this position.

There should be adequate room through the width of the shoe. The dancer should not feel as through her feet are in a vise, but there should not be a gap on the side of the slipper. If there is a gap, it may be coming from either excessive width or excessive length and width combined.

Next the student should rise carefully to demi-pointe. If the shoe pops off the heel in this position, it may be too wide.

Finally, the student rises to full pointe. For the first-time pointe shoe customer these procedures should be followed: (1) Have the student face an adult and hold both that person's hands. (Some dance shops have barres for this purpose.) (2) The student should step directly onto pointe with her right foot and then step directly onto pointe with her left foot. She should not relevé. (3) The fitter should then examine the fit in pointe position, while the student remains supported by another adult or the barre. Dancers must remember that their shoes are not secured with ribbons when they try this maneuver. Also, they should be careful not to break a pair of shoes they may not buy.

THE PROBLEM OF RETURNS

Dancers should be sure before buying shoes that the store has a return policy that allows them to return or exchange the shoes if the teacher finds them unsatisfactory. The teacher should check the shoes at the first possible opportunity, and the student should be careful not to wear them, attach ribbons or elastic, or soil them in any way until the shoes have been approved.

The student should stand on a sheet of clean paper when trying on shoes for a size check. If the fit is not satisfactory, the teacher should be very clear about the nature of the problem. If possible, a suggested alternative should be put in writing since many beginner pointe students are unfamiliar with the terminology involved and may not be able to communicate their teacher's wishes correctly to the fitter.

The issue of returning worn shoes that appear to have "factory flaws" is a problem for both dancers and shop owners. Since the shoes are handmade, such flaws are well within the realm of possibility. However, they are often difficult to prove once a dancer has worn her shoes since the breaking-in process may actually create the problem. To further complicate the matter, sometimes a legitimate flaw does not appear until a shoe has been worked in for the first time.

Each shop has its own policy on handling returns. If a customer sincerely believes that a shoe has a factory flaw, she should bring it in to the dealer for examination. Usually when a customer comes in with a reasonable complaint, a dealer is anxious to solve the problem amicably. The dealer may offer to exchange the shoe at once or ask the customer to wait until it has been returned to the factory for evaluation.

If the factory feels the complaint is justified, it gives the dealer a refund on the shoe, which will be passed along to the customer. However, if the factory rejects the request, the dealer must absorb the cost of replacing the shoe. Factory allowances might be made on shoes that have limited wear and have been incorrectly sized or shaped, made with faulty materials, or exhibit poor workmanship.

When dealers refuse to accept a pair of worn shoes as flawed, they believe the damage was done by the dancer. The fact that some dancers abuse return policies and constantly seek to return worn shoes can make dealers especially wary. At best, returns are a no-win situation for everyone involved. If a dancer feels her dealer is responding unfairly to a return request, she can either contact the manufacturer directly or seek another dealer. The best protection is to examine shoes carefully in the store and again before sewing ribbons on them or altering them in any way.

TIME FOR A NEW PAIR

Beginners frequently outgrow their shoes before they wear them out. Teachers have to watch beginners carefully and question them when they suspect a shoe may have grown too tight. Some children will complain loudly, and others will suffer in silence.

Shoes that wear out may become soft and mushy in the box and shank; sometimes the block or shank may crack or be severely bent out of shape. In any case, the shoe no longer provides the needed level of support. The condition of the satin upper is rarely a factor in shoe replacement.

Many dancers remove the ribbons from their old shoes, launder them, and put them on new shoes. Others strip the shanks and insoles and use old pointe shoes in place of soft slippers in class. While this process is endorsed by some teachers, others feel that it is an unwise practice. Patricia Klekovic, who teaches at the Ruth Page Foundation School, explains that the argument for wearing de-shanked pointe shoes is that they allow the dancer to feel as if pointe shoes are always part of her foot. On the other hand, if a dancer always wears pointe shoes, she may find it difficult to perform without them, lacking the sense of freedom gained from working in soft slippers.

Students at the Royal Ballet School in London wear soft slippers for the first years of their training and then switch to de-shanked pointe shoes. Students at the Paris Opéra Ballet School also wear de-shanked pointe shoes for technique class.

Proponents like de-shanked shoes because they provide added support as well as resistance, so a dancer has to work harder to point her toe. De-shanked pointe shoes accustom the dancer to dancing with the added bulk of pointe shoes. Some dancers find that the ribbons on de-shanked pointe shoes offer added ankle support and caution against wearing the shoes with only elastic across the instep since severe ankle injury can result.

Dancers and teachers who look with disfavor on the idea of wearing de-shanked pointe shoes are concerned that the foot does not have enough contact with the floor when it is always encased in such a hard shoe. They feel that the muscles supporting the metatarsals are not worked adequately since the stiffness of the de-shanked shoe inhibits the full use of the foot. Opponents believe that no foot can work well and be supple if it is restricted in heavy and unworkable de-shanked pointe shoes with blocked toes.

If a dancer lives in an area where shoe "trade-ins" such as those annually sponsored by Taffy's are held, she should hold on to her old shoes. They can be traded in for discounts on new shoes during a limited sale period. Otherwise, there are few functional uses for old shoes until a dancer reaches star status. The New York City Ballet, which has a $500,000 yearly shoe budget, sells autographed shoes used by company ballerinas in the lobby during intermission.

When a dancer returns to the dance shop for new pointe shoes, it's a good idea to bring her current pair with her. The wear patterns provide the fitter with useful information in making needed adjustments in style and size. For instance, a lot of dirt on the satin at the heel of the shoe or a split on the heel seam may indicate a shoe that is too short.

Dancers are constantly experimenting with slight adjustments in width or length or changes in style or brands. As progress is made on pointe and total body strength develops, lighter and less restrictive shoes may be appropriate. Many dancers also find that their feet grow wider as they continue to dance on pointe.

Since the shoes are crafted by hand, a dancer cannot expect a shoe to be exactly the same each time she purchases a new pair. No two pairs ever feel identical, and tiny flaws can alter the fit of a shoe. One imperfect pleat can throw the balance of a shoe off center. Performers can become quite disoriented by the slightest variation in a shoe. For this reason, many professional dancers keep dozens of pairs of shoes in their dressing rooms to select and test before performances.

Even if a dancer has been wearing the same style and size for months or years, it is essential to try each new pair on in the dance shop. Often a factory flaw cannot be detected by the shop's staff until the shoe is seen on a dancer's foot.

It is a good idea to keep a journal and identify each pair of pointe shoes purchased by date first used, brand, size, width, and date last used. As shoes are worn, make notations about their positive and negative aspects. This information can save a lot of money and time shopping for pointe shoes. It can also provide information about a possible back-up choice if a customary size is not available. At times, shops are unable to stock specific sizes for weeks at a time if the factory is out of a particular length and width. If shoes are needed immediately, it is very useful to be prepared with an alternative.

Dancers wearing custom shoes or foreign shoes should keep journal notations on stock American shoes they can wear in a pinch. The possibility of not being able to get delivery on a custom shoe order, particularly from a foreign factory, is always present.

NOTES

1. Lawson, Joan. "Shoes and Injuries," *The Dancing Times* (September 1983). Production changes since 1983 might change the significance of these early findings.

2. Another protective possibility is ToeFlo Pointe Shoe Pads, gel-filled toe pads, which are available from Dansant Boutique, 1020 S. Wabash Ave. – #50, Chicago, IL 60605. ToeFlo Pointe Shoe Pads are sold in S/M (which fits up to size 3B) and M/L (which fits 3C and over). Dansant Boutique also carries Bunheads Ouch Pads and Jelly Toes. These products are more widely available than at the time of this book's first edition. Check with your favorite dance product distributor.

Perhaps no aspect of point shoes has been less written about than the fitting process. Information for this chapter was gathered from dance shop owners, managers, and fitters as well as dancers and teachers throughout America, England, Sweden, France, and Norway. Craig Coussins, senior pointe shoe fitter for Gamba, has published a helpful guide for pointe shoe fitters called *A Fitting Manual for Ballet and Pointe Shoes* (London, England: Gamba Timestep Ltd., 1988). Fitting clinics and information sessions at national or regional sales meetings are frequently held by manufacturers for dealers and fitters who in turn sponsor fitting clinics for their customers. Representatives of pointe shoe manufacturers are also present at major dance conventions around the country. Edith Bloom, a sales representative for Capezio Ballet Makers for many years, who has now retired to Sarasota, Florida, and the late Ben Sommers, who was known as "Mr. Capezio," were both walking encyclopedias of pointe shoe fitting lore, much of which is reflected in this chapter.

4

Preparing and Caring for Pointe Shoes

The preparation of dance shoes is a process that is highly personal to each dancer and shrouded in the mystique of several hundred years of dance history. Each dancer develops a system of preparing her shoes that grows out of vanity, personal taste, and the demands of her anatomy. The following guide to preparing pointe shoes is a basic orientation to the process that incorporates traditional techniques and practical concerns. It has been written with the dancer who is still paying for her own shoes in mind.

DARNING SHOES

Although darning has gone out of style in our mechanized society, it remains a special tradition that is actually quite practical. Darned shoes offer improved traction and can also extend the wear obtainable from a pair of pointe shoes because it prevents the satin from fraying.

Darning shoes requires a large, curved darning or embroidery needle and cotton embroidery thread the same color as the pointe shoes. A thimble and a pair of pliers are helpful for pulling the needle through the boxing in the toe. Gamba sells a special mercerized cotton darning thread for pointe shoes.

The darning covers the entire toe of the slipper underneath the shoe and the tip of the end. Some experienced darners suggest sewing over the ridge of the toe block to avoid having the satin rip away from the block. Before starting to darn a pair of shoes, the dancer should put them on and slightly soil the satin by putting one pointe at a time on the floor and turning them from one side to another. This soil spot indicates the area to be darned.

The darner starts as close to the leather sole as possible and stitches a series of bars of thread back and forth across the pleats adjacent to the sole until they reach as far as indicated by the soil. The needle should be stuck into the satin deeply, and the fabric should be picked up with each stitch. Beginning at the sole again, the dancer blanket-stitches over each bar of thread. Then she connects the rows by pushing the needle through the loops of the row below, continuing until all the bars are covered.

After the darning is finished, it can be covered with a thin layer of colorless shellac and the slippers hung up to dry for several days. As the shoes are worn, wear patterns in the satin on the sides of the toe and under the big and little toe joints may appear. As this happens, these areas can also be darned. Some dancers also use darning as a technique for changing the shape of their shoes. A quick alternative to conventional darning involves cutting the satin away from the toe platform and stitching around the edge of the cut.

In England and Sweden, dancers also crochet toe caps, which they sew onto the tips of their shoes. Some English pointe shoe manufacturers include crocheted toe caps in their product lines. When the caps are attached, they must be completely stitched onto the shoe or the cap will stretch and come loose, possibly causing the foot to slip.

SEWING ON RIBBONS

After the teacher has approved the fit of a new pair of a pointe shoes, ribbons can be sewn on. Pointe shoes require about two to two and a half yards of ribbon either $5/8''$ or $7/8''$ wide. The actual length varies according to the size of the dancer's ankle. A variety of ribbons are on the market, including those that are satin on one side and grosgrain on the other. The rougher, grosgrain side is placed toward the leg and helps grip the tights and hold the shoe in place.

The entire length of ribbon is folded in half, and the two ends are placed together. It is then cut into two equal pieces. If the dancer is going to sew her ribbons on in four pieces, she should fold each piece of ribbon in half and cut again. There will now be four pieces of ribbon that are each approximately twenty-two inches long. Some dancers prefer to sew one piece of ribbon forty-four inches long to each shoe, attaching the center of the ribbon to the inside of the sole under the heel.

Some dancers like to sew about five inches of cloth tape to their ribbons to give them added strength and keep them from slipping. This tape needs to be a little narrower than the ribbons and is attached from the point where the ribbon is sewn to the shoe to the point where the ribbons first cross. The easiest way to attach the tape is to baste it to the ribbons before sewing them onto the shoes.

To attach ribbons, the dancer folds the back seam of the shoe against the sole and toward the front. The ribbons are then placed inside the shoe in the angles made by folding the heel forward. Their raw edges should be facing the lining of the shoe. A light pencil mark is drawn on the shoe lining on either side of the ribbon to use as a sewing guide.

Ribbons are usually sewn tilting slightly forward so they will lie flat on the instep. The location of the instep may dictate sewing them more forward or backward. Some dancers do not sew the ribbons at an angle but prefer to sew them on straight.

In the case of a sickled foot, a dancer can experiment with sewing one ribbon slightly forward and the other stitched slightly backward of the pencil mark.

About one inch of the ribbon should be folded under before sewing it to the shoes in order to make the attachment strong and avoid raveling. Some dancers make one five-eighth inch fold and then fold the ribbon over again. Place the folded end between the pencil marks. The fold should be even with the bias tape edging of the shoe. The ribbons should be pinned to the shoes and tested before sewing.

If the placement seems correct, sew small whip stitches around the two sides and bottom of the ribbon using a double strand of thread or heavy dental floss. Advocates of dental floss find it stronger and easier to thread through a needle. Go through all thicknesses of the ribbon, but only through the white canvas shoe lining. Ideally, stitches should not show through the exterior satin.

When sewing across the top of the ribbons, use a running stitch. Avoid sewing ribbons to the upper binding and drawstring around the top of the shoe or it will be difficult to adjust the drawstring as the shoe takes the shape of the foot. Avoid finishing the stitches with a large knot since this could bruise the skin. The ends of the ribbons should be clipped on the bias to prevent fraying. If nylon ribbon is used, raveling can be prevented by running the ends very quickly through a match flame, which will melt the fibers.

If a dancer has extra fabric at her heel because of a broad front foot, a high instep, and a narrow heel, she may be able to help the problem by sewing her ribbons on at a slightly more acute angle than usual toward the front of the shoe. Those dealing only with narrow heels may want to try sewing their ribbons slightly farther back than normal.

For performance, some dancers sew their ribbons with the shiny side of the satin in to reflect less light. This is also said to tie a tighter knot. If the dancer has an option of which width ribbon to use, the narrower ribbon is a good visual choice for someone with thick ankles or a shorter, heavier build. Some teachers have their students wear ribbons on ballet slippers during their pre-pointe years to get used to working with them.

ELASTIC

Elastic can be used on pointe shoes as a ribbon insert, across the vamps, or on the backs of the heels to keep the shoes on the feet.

Dancers often sew elastic into their ribbons so the ribbons adjust to the changing size of the ankle. This allows a dancer to have a more normal demi-plié while wearing pointe shoes.

To insert elastic in ribbons, sew the ribbons on the shoe as described above. Then mark each ribbon where it touches the back of the ankle bone. Cut the ribbons straight across, melt the ends in a match flame, and sew a two- to three-inch length of three-quarter-inch elastic to the ribbon. This can be done by hand or machine. Then sew the remaining ribbon to the other end of the elastic. After this has been done on all four ribbons, tie them as you normally would and cut off any extra ribbon.

Elastic can also be attached to the base of the ribbons at the spot where they are sewn to the shoes. This is helpful because it gives when the dancer jumps. When using this technique the ribbons must be sewn on sloping forward.

A wide piece of elastic can be sewn across the vamp of a shoe for added support if a dancer has weak ankles and highly developed arches. It must not be too tight, however, or it can stop circulation. In England, dancers are able to buy an elastic cloth through Frederick Freed Ltd. that is similar in texture to the elasticized fabric that girdles are made of in the United States. Dancers then cut the cloth to any desired width and configuration. Although it is difficult to find elastic or elastic cloth in the United States which approximates the weight and taut elasticity of this fabric, it is worth searching for as a means of added support. The average width for vamp elastic is one and a half inches, but it needs to be "custom" cut to suit the individual foot size. Check with Freed dealers to see if they have this helpful product in stock. If a dancer wants to extend the shoe vamp, she can also sew a piece of heavy ribbon across the top of the vamp at the inside.

Whether to wear elastic on the heels of pointe shoes remains controversial. Although it is a common practice to wear an elastic loop around the ankle or to run ribbons through an elastic loop on the back of the heel, many teachers with British training believe that a shoe requiring elastic is a badly fitting shoe. They feel that elastic in any form is dangerous for the soft tissue at the ankle, restricting the bend of the Achilles tendon and inhibiting the blood flow through the important veins of the foot and leg. As a result the Achilles tendon and bones of the heel can become inflamed. Teachers who oppose elastic contend that if ribbons are correctly attached, the slight pull forward should hold the shoe on firmly at the heel after the ribbons have been wrapped across the instep and around the ankle.

If elastic is used at the heel, it should be between $3/8''$ to $5/8''$ wide and sewn to the outside of the shoe so it cannot rub the heel. A length that will fit snugly from the back of the heel, around the ankle, and back to the heel again should be measured. The elastic should fit snugly, but not be too tight. It can be attached to the shoes with a whipstitch, starting at the top edge of the shoe, down the right side, across the bottom and up the left side of the elastic. The elastic should be sewn at a slight angle at the back of the shoe and not secured to the casing. When the shoes are worn, the foot is slipped through the elastic and into the shoe before the ribbons are tied.

TYING ON THE SHOES

Shoes should be pulled on the feet with both hands. Using only one hand tends to twist the shoe around the foot. Ribbons should be tied carefully to allow the shoe to remain correctly positioned on the foot.

There are a variety of techniques for tying ribbons. In the first, the shoes should be tied while the dancer is kneeling on one knee and leaning back slightly. The knee of the free leg is bent, with the foot placed flat on the floor. If the shoes are tied with the toe on pointe or the leg straight, the ankle may not be allowed enough room for flexibility, and it will be difficult to move the foot fully on pointe and demi-pointe. Some dancers find that flexing the foot while tying their ribbons keeps them from tying the shoes too tightly.

One ribbon should be extended forward of the foot, crossed over it, and allowed to lie flat in the center of the foot in line with the ankle bones. Then the same ribbon is brought around to the back of the ankle and to the front again so it lies flat on the center front of the leg at a point slightly above the first cross. Then the ribbon is taken to the side of the leg and held firmly.

The second ribbon is brought forward and crossed over the first ribbon so that it lies flat in the center front of the leg. It is taken around the ankle and knotted with the first ribbon in the hollow between the anklebone and Achilles tendon. The ribbons are tied in a small, tight double knot that is tucked under or between the ribbons so no ends are visible. If the ends of the ribbons are visible on the shoes of students at the Royal Ballet School, the offending ends are disparagingly called "pigs ears." The knot should not be tied over the Achilles tendon or the shinbone, to avoid pressure which can lead to inflammation.

In another technique, both ribbons are crossed over the instep. They are wrapped around the foot, crossing the Achilles tendon, and brought back across the instep. The ribbon which is on the outside of the foot is brought across the Achilles tendon to meet the ribbon on the inside of the foot. A knot is tied between the inside ankle bone and the Achilles tendon. It should fit into the small hollow on the side of the foot.

Excess ribbon is folded and tucked from the top under the ribbons which are wrapped around the ankle. The ribbons which cross the ankle should lay on top of each other rather than wind up the lower leg.

Ribbons that are tied too tightly can keep the calf muscles from working properly and inhibit the foot from contacting the floor. They can also impair circulation and cause damage to muscles, tendons, and ligaments in the feet and ankles.

DRAWSTRING

The drawstring in the front of the shoe should be tightened until the shoe feels snug and secure on the foot. It should only be tightened when the foot is in the pointe position. Never pull it by one end. Some teachers suggest tying the drawstring in a small bow and tucking the ends in. Others feel that this can induce scar tissue and bruising when the knot presses in the fine blood vessels and causes constriction. They prefer to gently pull the drawstring to the tightness required, knot it, and cut the excess off. In either case, the drawstring should not be cut until the shoes have been worked in several times. Then any needed adjustments can be made, and the drawstring can be tied in a double knot.

Some shoes are manufactured with elastic drawstrings, which can press on the Achilles tendon if pulled too tight. Even conventional drawstrings can dig into the heel and stop the stretch of the Achilles tendon. Tight drawstrings can dig into the tendon sheath, causing inflammation, or press on either of the two bursas at the heel area, causing bursitis. To avoid this, the drawstring can be stitched in place one-half inch on either side of the heel. This will hold the drawstring in place over the heel without pressure, while allowing it to be tightened as needed over the front of the foot. It will also prevent the development of Achilles tendonitis, bursitis, or heel lumps, which can result when the up-and-down motion of relevé causes the tendon to stretch in a constricted shoe.

OTHER TECHNIQUES FOR KEEPING SHOES ON

In addition to traditional ways of attaching and adjusting ribbons, elastic, and drawstrings, dancers have developed a number of other methods to fasten the shoe securely to the foot. A customary practice, which is also reputed to bring luck, is to spit on the knot as it is made when the ribbons are tied. Some dancers take a stitch through the knot as well.

At the Houston Ballet, dancers use clear Johnson & Johnson surgical tape packaged in a red dispenser and wrap it around their knotted ribbons. This secures the ribbons but still allows a quick change of shoes since it can be slipped off.

Slipping heels are remedied by dabbing a few drops of water-soluble glue between the heel of the tights and the heel of the slipper. Alicia Markova is reported to have glued her whole foot into her shoes.

Another technique is to rub the heels of tights in crushed rock rosin before putting shoes on.

Some dancers dunk the heel of the shoe, foot and all, into a bucket of water before class or performance. Others wet their tights before putting on the shoe and then wet the shoe after pulling it on. In either method, as the water dries, the wet shoe clings to the foot, shrinking in the process. Those who argue in favor of water point out that rosin can be abrasive to the foot, while water is not. However, water can destroy the resiliency of the shank and dissolve some glues, possibly causing the shoe to lose its shape.

MAKING SHOES SLIP-PROOF

Darning shoes or cutting the satin off the tips helps cut down on traction problems. Some dancers rub the satin off the tops of their new shoes by scraping them on gravelly pavements or driveways. A carpenter's knife or Exacto knife is useful for roughing up the bottom of a pointe shoe to gain traction, or the sole can be scored with a scissor point or sandpaper.

A box of rock rosin is kept in many studios to provide protection from slipping. Rosin is a sticky, rocklike substance made from pine tree sap. Dancers apply it to their shoes to increase friction with the floor. A rosin box is placed in a studio corner or in the dressing room, and dancers simply grind their toes into the rosin as needed. A rasp is often kept with the rosin box for students to use to score the toes and soles of their shoes for added traction. Excess rosin can be removed from shoes with a wire nail brush.

In emergencies, dancers have sprinkled detergent and cleansers on a stage or studio floor. While they do retard slippage, these substances often create problems for dancers, orchestra members, and audience patrons who subsequently inhale them. Coca-Cola and Sweet and Low are also used to de-gloss a slippery floor when nothing else is available.

In extreme circumstances, dancers who must dance on very slippery surfaces can have one-eighth inch thick rubber soles put on their pointe shoes by a shoemaker. The rubber may cover the platforms, the pleats (which are particularly slippery), and the entire sole or it may be in two pieces, leaving the middle of the sole uncovered. Freed of London sells these rubber soles through its catalog.

Other nonslip measures include spraying shoe tips and soles with glue products. While a number of dancers recommend Scotch 77 spray adhesive, David Howard advocates rubber cement. He has developed a method of preparing pointe shoes for dancers who must perform on slippery surfaces. He scrapes down the edges of pointe shoe soles to "get rid of the ridges." Then he paints the soles and tips with five or six coats of Contact rubber cement. After the cement has dried, rosin is then applied to the soles. This treatment lasts long enough to see a dancer safely through one performance.

BREAKING IN THE SHOES

Dancers generally feel the need to "break in" new pointe shoes, which means to mold them to their feet and make them more comfortable. Dancers are seeking a workable compromise between the original rigidity of the shoe, needed for support, and the right amount of "give" needed for fluid motion. Since heat and perspiration from the feet further soften the shoe, breaking in is a tricky business. Students should not attempt to break in their first shoes on their own.

Once a dancer is sure she is going to keep a pair of shoes, she can take several preliminary steps to ease the discomfort of wearing them for the first time. She can soften the shoes slightly by molding them in her hand. The insole can be eased by lightly pressing it back and forth at the instep level between the palms. The box can be pressed gently with the heel of the hand or it can be flattened by placing the shoes flat on the floor and carefully stepping on the box with the heel of the foot.

Some dancers like to wear a pair of new pointe shoes around the house the night before working in them for the first time, walking around in them and rising from quarter- to demi- and three-quarter pointe to mold them to their feet. If a dancer is experienced on pointe, she can rise to full pointe several times on each shoe and turn the toes back and forth.

Many dancers indulge in more extreme tactics to break in their shoes, including banging them in doors, whamming them with hammers, and having large men jump up and down on them. Manufacturers are not creating pointe shoes to withstand this kind of abuse and estimate that these tactics can reduce shoe life by 50 percent. Any abusive technique that breaks the shoe down over the edge of the sole can also cause stress to the metatarsals and the arch.

Another popular box-softening technique involves the use of rubbing alcohol or water. A cotton ball is lightly soaked and rubbed across the box of the shoe at the place it should bend on demi-pointe. Pouring these liquids directly on the shoe could weaken it and make it unwearable. Shoes which are softened with water or alcohol must be allowed to dry completely before wearing or storing. Those dancers who prefer alcohol to water for breaking in shoes feel that water takes too long to dry and can cause the shoes to shrink. In addition, alcohol on the box is thought to offer protection against blisters.

Alcohol is sometimes used to make a "noisy" shoe quieter. Noise can be reduced by hammering the shoes or banging them against a wall. A piece of suede is sometimes glued to the tip of the shoe for the same reason.

Some dancers, because of inflexible ankles and insteps, find it very difficult to break in the shanks of their shoes. They may resort to cutting off the inside shank near the heel where the sole of the foot bends. This is usually done with a utility knife. The process involves cutting the shank carefully layer by layer until the small section at the back of the heel can be removed along with the nail which has held it to the shoe. The edge of the remaining shank has to be beveled with the knife and tapered toward the heel for comfort. If the bottom sole of the shoe is difficult to balance on, the edges can also be cut with a utility knife and tapered toward the satin.

OTHER ALTERATIONS

Shoes that are being used in performance may need to be altered in a variety of other ways. If the satin is too shiny, it can be dulled by applying a light shade of pancake makeup such as Max Factor Natural #1 to both the shoes and ribbons with a sponge and a small amount of water. The shoes must be dried thoroughly before wearing. Pancaking shoes can tighten them up and hide smudges. However, George Balanchine did not want his dancers to use pancake on their shoes because he liked their feet to be "obvious."

While pointe shoes can be ordered in black, white, and sometimes red as a special order and can be special ordered dyed to match a costume color, dancers can dye their own satin pointe shoes without too much difficulty. A brand of dye called Evangeline that is used by the bridal industry does an excellent job and can be painted on with a brush. Evangeline can be found at a shoemaker's or through a company that sells shoemaking supplies. A bridal shop might be a good source of information on where to buy Evangeline dye in your area.

Powdered Rit or Tintex dye can also be used to change pointe shoe color. While using liquid Rit or Tintex might seem an easier approach, it tends to streak and does not do an acceptable job. Instead, mix powdered dye with rubbing alcohol, starting with a small amount of dye and adding granules until you get the color you want. You can test colors on old pointe shoe ribbons. Paint the dye on with a brush. Since you are not using heat, the dye granules do not dissolve and you will have to brush them off after the shoes are dry.

A bump on the top of a pair of new shoes can be gotten out by wetting it and beating it flat with a hammer or a rolling pin or beating it on the floor. Shoes with vamps that are too long can be modified to make them more flexible by carefully ripping the stitches around the vamp with a seam ripper, trimming the satin to the proper length, and sewing the drawstring back on by hand or machine.

Shoes may also be altered to accommodate a temporary foot problem. For instance, Sandra Organ of the Houston Ballet cuts a hole out of the satin of her shoe over a bad blister to give it air. Dancers may slit the shoe over a bunion and stitch around the slit to keep it from raveling. This slit looks like a big buttonhole and provides enough give to take the pressure off the bunion.

THE COST OF POINTE SHOES: EXTENDING THEIR LIFE

While major ballet companies order hundreds of pairs of shoes for their principal dancers each year, most student and professional pointe dancers find themselves laboring under much more limited footwear budgets. Deborah Allton reports that members of the Metropolitan Opera Ballet are only provided with two pairs of shoes a month by the company and must fill in with shoes they buy themselves. Martin Fredmann, artistic director of the Colorado Ballet, can only afford to buy his dancers one pair of shoes a week.

Pointe shoe prices have risen dramatically during the past ten years, and steadily increasing costs of production do not indicate a change in this pattern in the immediate future. Although the costs of the pointe shoes seem exorbitant to the dancer, manufacturers actually make limited profits on them because they are labor-intensive. To put the matter in a broader perspective, it is very difficult to find hand-made street shoes of any kind on the market today and those that are available often cost hundreds of dollars a pair.

Pointe shoe dancers and manufacturers are locked into a seemingly impossible set of circumstances. In order to perform correctly, dancers need handcrafted shoes made of natural, flexible materials. In the process of doing their work, they destroy their shoes rapidly. Due to the poorly subsidized state of the arts in this country, neither dancers nor the companies they work for can afford the cost of shoes. On the other hand, manufacturers cannot turn to automation or plastics as a means of controlling prices.

Various changes in ownership have taken place in the pointe shoe industry in recent years. When Selva decided to close, no buyer was found to continue manufacturing their pointe shoes largely because of the economic infeasibility of the process. Capezio bought the Selva name and retired the line with the exception of some specialized products like taps. In 1987, Frederick Freed Ltd. was purchased by Chacott, a Japanese pointe shoe manufacturer. The fact that only other pointe shoe makers exhibit any interest in these companies when they go "on the block" is evidence of their limited profit potential. For many companies, pointe shoes are a labor of love, largely subsidized by sales in more profitable types of dancewear and footwear. Since price cuts are not in sight, there are a variety of techniques used by dancers to extend the life of their shoes.

Alternating Shoes

Pointe shoes have no right or left. While some dancers like to have each shoe take the shape of one foot of the other, others prefer to alternate their shoes. If a pair of shoes starts out identically shaped, they can be changed from one foot to another on a daily basis to keep them in balance. Quite a few dancers have found that alternating shoes can actually double the life of a pair of shoes by avoiding consistent wear on the same spot by the big toe. Alternating also helps dancers identify foot-use problems such as a tendency to "roll" in their shoes.

However, dancers whose feet are not similar to one another will have difficulty alternating shoes. For instance, those with toes of uneven lengths may find that their shoes take the shape of their feet with just one wearing and make alternating impossible.

Caring for Shoes

Since as much as a half pint of sweat can be produced by a dancer's feet during an hour class, pointe shoes become damp during each wearing. In response to this condition, the dancer needs to smooth any wrinkles that may have formed and stretch and arch shoes carefully.

After taking shoes off and before putting them away in a dance bag, stuff a plastic bag into the box of the shoe and fill it tightly with paper. Plastic lasts, which are available at dance shops, can be inserted in the shoes as they dry and used as pointe shoe "shoe trees" to prevent them from becoming misshapen. After smoothing out the wrinkles, allow them to dry in an airy, nonhumid environment. Hang shoes over a heater, place them in the oven with the heat turned off but with the pilot light on. When trying this, leave the ribbons hanging out the oven door to avoid forgetting that pointe shoes are inside. In humid climates, shoes can also be placed in a refrigerator since the air is dry.

Drying out usually takes three days. After they have dried, arch them gently, collapse the heel, fold one side over the other, wind the ribbon flat around them, and put them away.

Buying two pairs of shoes at a time and allowing each pair to rest and dry between wearings seems to make them more durable. Alternate shoes for each class and change after an hour of wear at a long rehearsal. Wearing the same pair of shoes for each class and rehearsal and stuffing them into a dance bag sopping wet destroys them rapidly. Alternating shoes can extend total life by up to 50 percent.

If a dancer takes three classes a week, she needs three pairs of shoes to allow each pair the required three days to dry. In the long run, this approach prevents the shoes from going soft prematurely and results in extended wear from each pair. Wearing dry shoes is also much healthier for the feet.

Shoes worn for class and rehearsal may begin to show signs of wear that are only cosmetic and do not require discarding that particular pair. For instance, if the satin on the toe tears, cut it off. If the canvas insole that covers the shank comes loose and bunches up, pull it out. A dancer can often continue dancing on shoes with loosened shank nails and frayed side seams.

Solid shoes can be cleaned with commercial pointe shoe cleaners or cleaners designed to be used on silk and satin shoes. Mild, nonabrasive soap and water can also be used unless the shoes are made with water-soluble glue.

Rehardening

Even with careful treatment, the box and tip of the shoe will become softer and softer until they can no longer provide adequate support. Once this disintegration takes place, many dancers try to revitalize the blocks of their shoes to make them last longer. Before reblocking, pointe shoes should be stuffed with paper or a plastic last as soon as they are taken off and allowed to dry out in a warm place.

One reblocking technique involves pouring several applications of a liquid shellac into the toe of the dry shoe and letting it soak into the block between applications. Allow the shoes to dry thoroughly before wearing.

Another technique involves applying commercial liquid floor wax to the outside of the tip, pleats, and box of the shoe with an old toothbrush. The wax is only applied where hardness is desired. The boxes are then stuffed with paper, and the ribbons are folded inside the shoes. The shoes are put on a baking sheet in a cold oven and baked for three minutes at 250 degrees. It is important not to preheat the oven. Turn off the heat after three minutes and leave the shoes inside the oven overnight.

The Houston Ballet uses a hot box, which is a wooden box about four feet tall and two and a half feet wide. A door extends the entire length of the box. Inside are drawers with wire bottoms to allow heat to circulate. Light bulbs are used as the heating elements and surround the drawers. A dancer pours Future floor wax in a pair of shoes, allows it to soak in, and then dabs out the excess before placing the shoes in the hot box. Houston dancers report getting as many as seven additional wearings from a pair of shoes by using this method. You can duplicate the hot box by turning a regular oven to 200 degrees, placing your shoes in the oven, and leaving the temperature set to 200 for ten minutes, then turning off the oven and leaving the shoes in until the oven cools. When trying any of the methods involving an oven, be sure to heed the warning of Sandy Organ of Houston Ballet who noticed that her shoes smelled like garlic bagels the day after she dried them in an oven she had recently used for making croutons.

Dancers have tried block strengthening with a variety of shellaclike substances and floor waxes, but the one most frequently mentioned around the country is Pratt and Lambert's Fabulon, a clear floor finish. There has been some experimentation with Super Glue and various cements. However, any substance composed of chemicals should be used with caution and not allowed to get into cuts or abrasions of the feet. Students in Chicago also reported using Future Floor Wax on the shanks, boxes, and sides of their Freeds before wearing them the first time to prevent box disintegration.

Jackson Competition gold medalist Jennifer Gelfand dips Crazy Glue inside the tips of her shoes. She says, "they stay hard for three and a half weeks, even when I use them every day." She also uses the spray shellac Zinsser to stiffen the arches. It can be bought in a hardware store and takes about twenty minutes to dry.

Gamba has created a hardener which is a specially blended combination of high-quality shellacs. Unlike the substances described above, it is water-soluble and also flammable; consequently, it must be handled quite differently.

The best way to use this hardener is to pour a small puddle of it into the pointe shoe box, let it penetrate the platform, and paint it around the areas to be strengthened with a long-handled half-inch paintbrush. If the hardener gets on drawstrings or ribbons, they become quite rigid. Contact with the outside of the shoe results in an orange stain. Often the hardener seeps through the shoes and makes them look unattractive, so this is a method for prolonging the life of rehearsal shoes and not performance shoes. Allow the shoes to sit out in the open air to dry for three days, avoiding contact with heat.

Most of these hardening techniques only last for one wearing and have to be repeated. When the process is repeated too often, the hardener builds up inside the shoe, making it smaller and sometimes uncomfortable to wear. Hardeners provide perfect quick-fixes in emergency situations when new shoes are impossible to obtain and can be helpful in squeezing a few more hours of class or rehearsal out of a used pair of shoes.

Gamba Turning Pointe Reshaping Feature

Gamba has formulated its Turning Pointe shoe with a special water-soluble glue that can be steamed and remolded to a dancer's specifications.

This can be useful when breaking in shoes and for remolding them after each use.

Gamba advises holding the shoes over the steam from a boiling tea kettle for five to six seconds. Remove the shoe from the steam, reshape, and let dry. When the shoe is removed from the heat, the glue hardens again. The shanks in the shoes also become malleable when steamed and harden as they dry. Be careful not to steam the shoes longer than six seconds or the glue totally dissolves. Other brands of shoes not made with water-soluble glue will not respond to steaming.

Recycling Shanks

Some dancers remove the shanks of an old pair of pointe shoes they are discarding or converting into flat shoes and place them under the inner soles of a pair of softening pointe shoes as a reinforcement.

NOTE

Virtually every dancer and teacher interviewed for this book is a contributor to this chapter. We like to think of it as a wonderful dressing room jam session with all of them sitting around after a class sharing this wisdom with the rest of us.

5

Custom Ordering Pointe Shoes

Most pointe shoe manufacturers offer custom construction services for an added fee, which may vary from maker to maker. Custom shoe orders for American shoes generally take four to six weeks, while the waiting time for foreign shoes can be as long as ten months. Be sure to check the current delivery period when placing an order. While custom ordering involves increased expenditures and a longer delivery period, many dancers find the advantage of a shoe with special features that meets the needs of their individual foot structure well worth the added investment of money and time.

The key to successfully ordering custom shoes is to develop a technically specific "prescription" for the feet in question. Finding the right combination of changes is a speculative effort which often takes several attempts to produce the desired result. Ideally, a dancer should visit a store with fitters experienced in designing custom orders in the brand of her choice. In New York, these include the Capezio Dance Theatre Shop, at 1650 Broadway, for Capezio custom orders; and Frederick Freed Ltd., at 922 Seventh Avenue and 200 Central Park South, for Freed custom orders. Shops around the country that service large numbers of professional dancers in regional companies may also have expertise in this area.

If a visit to the New York stores is not possible, orders for custom shoes can be placed through the mail-order departments of these shops. (See mail-order information on pp. 67–70.) When ordering a first pair of custom shoes by mail, send tracings of both feet and a detailed description of the reasons for the special order. Describe the problems experienced with stock shoes and unusual features of the foot such as long toes, a high arch, bunions, and so forth. It is also possible to call these shops to discuss your custom-order specifications. After a first custom order, the shop keeps the shoe "prescription" on file for future reference.

While local dance shops may be able to process special orders, it is often difficult to find fitters with broad experience in evaluating custom needs. After a custom prescription has been formulated, placing an order locally may be more feasible.

We worked with Judith Weiss, in charge of special orders for professional customers at the Capezio Dance Theatre Shop in New York, to develop the following list of changes that are possible in Capezio pointe shoes. Although other brands may offer a slightly different range of custom features, this list will serve as an overall guide to the process of ordering a custom shoe.

When ordering a pointe shoe with custom changes, described by Capezio as an SMU or Special Make-Up, indicate the name and style number of the shoe and the special changes that should be made to the basic design. The following features can be customized on a Capezio pointe shoe:

Color. Black, white, and custom-dyed shoes to match a fabric sample are available as a special order.

Size. In addition to standard sizes and half sizes, pointe shoes can be ordered in three-quarter sizes as a special order. A shoe can also be ordered with a combination last, which means that the heel can be one size and the ball, or center area of the box, another. This custom feature is helpful for dancers with a narrow heel and wide ball who have difficulty finding a stock shoe to fit both ends of their feet. Shoes can also be ordered in different lengths for each foot.

Widths. Shoes can be ordered in AA as a special order, and shoes that are not made in EE as stock shoes can be ordered in that width as custom shoes. Shoes can be ordered in different widths for each foot.

Vamp length. Vamps can be made either $1/8''$, $1/4''$, $3/8''$, or $1/2''$ shorter or longer than the standard vamp length. A V-shaped vamp can also be ordered as opposed to the standard U-shaped vamp.

Back. The back of the pointe shoe can be cut $1/8''$ or $1/4''$ or higher or lower than the back of the standard shoe.

Sides. The sides of the pointe shoe can be cut from $1/8''$ to $1/2''$ higher or lower than the sides of the standard shoe.

Drawstring. The drawstring can be placed on the side to avoid pressure on the foot. An elastic drawstring can be specified.

Toe shape. A toe can be ordered squarer than the standard shoe, not as tapered as the standard shoe, or flatter than the standard shoe.

Pleats. Pleats can be ordered longer or shorter than the pleats in the standard shoe. A shoe made with longer pleats will have a shorter outer sole.

Boxing. A shoe can be custom ordered with a hard box. The "official" terminology for this change is a shoe with a double "C" toe. A shoe can be ordered with a lighter box. The terminology for this change is a shoe with no "C" piece. A shoe can be ordered with three-quarter boxing, which means that there is boxing three-quarters of the way to the drawstring, or half boxing, which means that there is boxing half of the way to the drawstring. The wings can be ordered strengthened and extended farther down the sides of the shoes for added support. This is called a wing block.

Shanks. Capezio shanks come in five strengths from #1, the weakest, to #5, the strongest. A shoe can be custom ordered with any of these five shank strengths. The term *double shank* means that the shoe is made with a shank twice the strength of the standard shank. A shoe can be ordered with a shank that is shorter than the standard shank. The correct terminology for this change is either a half shank (a shank that is half as long as the standard shank) or the more popular three-quarter shank (a shank that is three-quarters as long as the standard shank). A shank can be ordered with additional reinforcement.

Capezio shops may differ slightly in their SMU charges, but the average additional charge for an SMU order is $7.00 to $10.00 per pair. This one charge covers as many changes as the customer specifies on her order form.

Delivery is usually in five weeks. However, since lasts for SMU shoes are either custom made or temporarily customized to meet an order, filling orders for multiple pairs of special-order shoes can be a time-consuming process. Because shoes usually must dry for two days on their lasts, the shoemaker has to wait to begin the next pair until he gets the lasts back. Consequently, he can produce only three pairs of specials per one SMU customer each week.

NOTES

In addition to Judith Weiss, information about this most mysterious aspect of pointe shoes came from Bernard Kohler of Freed, Craig Coussins of Gamba, and the special make-up department at Capezio Ballet Makers in Totowa, New Jersey.

6

Profiles of Pointe
Shoe Makers and Sellers

AMERICAN MAKERS

Baryshnikov®

ASCO, Inc.
22–60 46th St.
Long Island City, NY 11105
phone: (718) 626–1900 or 800–272–6033
fax: (718) 626–0859
e-mail: ascoinc@aol.com

In early 1994, Mikhail Baryshnikov began working with Nadine Revene, director of design at New York-based ASCO, Inc. Together, they developed a line of professional quality pointe shoes and ballet slippers. Finally, after eighteen months of intensive research and development and hundreds of hours of testing with professional dancers, ASCO, in early 1996, introduced its new Baryshnikov line of pointe shoes.

By incorporating new and innovative materials, combined with a highly sophisticated method of fabrication, Baryshnikov and Revene have produced the Baryshnikov pointe shoes, beautifully designed and constructed to be extremely comfortable, allow freedom of movement, and reveal the beautiful, expressive line of the dancer's foot.

Baryshnikov pointe shoes are made in a pale peach matte finish satin and a soft peach blush canvas—colors that eliminate the need to use powder or pancake to create a matte look, while, at the same time, giving the illusion of lustrous silk. The shoes feature an unusual, diagonal stitching line that artificially connects the dancer's foot and its pointe shoe. This beautiful line, together with a delicate heel and a vamp line, make for an extremely flattering pointe shoe.

The Baryshnikov boxtoe has its own shape, one that allows room for the whole foot to spread, so that it can develop to its full potential. The boxtoe is made from an artificial, solution-activated material. It is designed with a modified wing shape, which facilitates easy and smooth demi-pointe roll-through and adds support on the side of the metatarsal. An innovative manufacturing method is used to create a firm, comfortable boxtoe which, with proper care, is durable and long-lasting.

Baryshnikov pointe shoes are available in three shank styles and strengths: *demi-strong, strong,* and *extra strong.* Although proper fitting depends on such factors as height, weight, shoe size and width, type of instep, strength of foot and flexibility of instep, the following categories should serve as rules of thumb in choosing the right shank:

Demi-strong is designed for dancers who require a softer roll-through, with a more "giving feel." It is perfect for dancers who have an average, nicely curved arch/instep. It can be adapted for strongly built dancers, from beginner through advanced.

Strong is excellent for dancers who need more resistance in the shank and in their roll-through. This shank is perfect for dancers with an average to high instep, who have a well-developed body. The strong shank is flexible, yet strong, and responds immediately to the demands of fast, brilliant footwork.

Extra Strong is a very strong-yet-flexible shank for dancers with high arches (banana feet) who need a strong uplift. It is perfect for dancers in need of a stronger shank strength, to support greater body weight and/or highly developed muscles. Rolling up and down is always smooth and easy.

Baryshnikov pointe shoes feature a soft, anti-slip suede leather outsole, for added traction, along with a most unusual anti-impact insole. The cushioned insole is made from reaction material, for added comfort, and carries the seal of acceptance from the American Podiatric Medical Association. An anti-impact insole can also be purchased separately and inserted into the shoe to fill voided spaces. The same reaction material can be used as a toe pad for dancers who want to add padding to the boxtoe.

When properly fitted, and after choosing the correct style shank, Baryshnikov pointe shoes can enhance all aspects of a dancer's class work and performance. The shoes are sized approximately two to two and a half sizes smaller than are street shoe sizes.

Because dancers' needs are highly individual, and because they often change due to personal development and different repertoires, ASCO accepts special orders. Dancers, however, may special-order one pair only. Turn-around time is typically between 10 and 15 days.

There is no minimum order amount; a special order fee runs between $10 and $15. The company has developed a special-order form for the Baryshnikov Collection, which can be obtained through dance specialty stores or through ASCO's customer service department. For quick turn-around, the special-order form can be faxed or mailed. In either case, a customer service representative will follow up with the store or the dancer concerning any additional questions the customer may have.

Capezio Ballet Makers
1 Campus Drive
Totowa, NJ 07512
phone: (201) 595-9000
fax: (201) 595-9120

Capezio is the largest manufacturer of pointe shoes. In addition to its dance products, the company creates special shoes for everyone, from the Pope, to dancers in Broadway shows, to midgets in the circus.

In 1887, when Cecchetti was making his debut in St. Petersburg, an Italian cobbler named Salvatore Capezio opened a small shop across the street from the old Metropolitan Opera House. Five years later, he became the Met's official shoemaker, making both costume shoes for the singers and dance footwear for the corps de ballet. Then, in 1915, Anna Pavlova endorsed his shoes; and at the Paris Exposition in 1925, Capezio dance slippers won the gold medal.

Capezio took up the challenge of making shoes for dancers. He was constantly dissecting ballet and pointe slippers and experimenting with new ways of constructing them. During his lifetime, he built his business from a tiny shoeshop in Manhattan's West Forties to an important manufacturing entity, with retail agencies in every major city. He died in January 1940, at the age of seventy.

After Capezio's death, leadership of the company passed to Ben Sommers. Later the founder of the Capezio Foundation and a prime mover in the development of American dance, Sommers had, at the age of fourteen, begun working for Capezio as an errand boy and shipping clerk. He was hired by Jimmy Salvaggio, later known as Jimmy Selva.

In recalling those early years, Ben Sommers remembers that the Capezio *fattorie* where the shoemakers worked in the 1920s consisted of two or three houses on West Thirty-ninth and West Fortieth streets. The factory included a cutting room, stitching room, and shoemaking room. At that time, shoes were stitched by hand (the Goodyear stitching machine had yet to be introduced).

After Jimmy Selva left Capezio in 1925, to form his own business,[1] Ben Sommers became more involved with both the dance and the theatrical aspects of the Capezio enterprise. Following Mr. Capezio's death, he served as president of the company from 1940 until 1976. Today, the president of Capezio is Alfred Terlizzi, a third-generation member of the Capezio family.

Capezio pointe shoes can be purchased in dance specialty stores and shoe stores throughout the United States. The company also has distribution in Japan, Hong Kong, and Europe.

Capezio offers a full line of pointe shoes designed to provide dancers and dance students with a wide variety of choices in the areas of shank and box strength, as well as basic shape. Capezio's goal in creating these choices is to make it unnecessary for customers to order custom shoes. Capezio's owners feel that the two major strengths of their shoes are that they are consistently made and long-lasting.

Shank strength is rated on a scale of 1 to 5; the higher the number, the stronger the shank. Strength #1, #2, and #3 are found in stock shoes; #4 and #5 must be special-ordered. Stock shoes in most sizes are available in widths A to EE. Narrower and wider shoes may be special-ordered.

The oldest shoe in the Capezio line is the *Duro-Toe* (105), which has a #3 shank. Originally made to be durable during the Depression, the *Duro-Toe* has a suede tip and reinforced box. In recent years, the shoe has largely been upstaged by Capezio's numerous innovative and updated designs.

All other pointe shoes in the line are hand-pleated and include:

103 Pavlowa Made with a #3 shank and reinforced box, this shoe is a classic, all-satin student shoe with a low vamp.

155 Nicolini Made with a #2 shank and box, this model is designed for advanced students and professionals; all satin.

172 Ultimo Made with a #2 shank and box; has a broad toe and flatter shape. Equal in strength to the Nicolini, it is for advanced students and professional dancers.

175 Contempora Built with a #2 shank and box, it has an extra-broad square toe. Capezio also makes the Contempora in Euro-Pink, a peachier shade of satin for matching European pointe shoes (176).

183 Infinita Made with a special shank engineered to make the shoe extremely flexible; comes in European pink satin and has a broader box, flat balancing surface, and comfortable fit.

185 Perfetta A professional pointe shoe in European pink satin, with a three-quarter shank. Softer and less "constructed," it provides a broad balancing surface and beautiful arch, and has an elastic drawstring and buffed, scored sole.

55X Assoluta A lightweight performance shoe, which is actually a lighter version of the Nicolini with a #1 flexible shank and box. It is still available to order as a special make-up.

191 Aerial Has a moderate light strength flat box with a #2 leatherboard shank. It gives extra width at the ball of the foot but has a narrow heel and an enhanced arch.

192 Odette Has a supple construction that molds to the dancer's foot. The box is light and wingless, and has a U-shaped throat. It is built with a redboard shank, elastic drawstring, narrow heel and buffed leather sole.

Fuzi International
749 Orlean Circle
Lexington, KY 40517
phone: 606–266–7347
fax: 606–266–7347

Xijun Fu, the owner and designer of the Fuzi shoes, was trained at the Beijing Dance Academy. He danced with the Central Ballet of China and the Santiago Ballet in Chile. Later, as a guest artist with companies in South America, Canada, and the United States, he wore shoes of his own design. Other dancers were so impressed that they asked him to make shoes for them. Those requests have resulted in yet another choice for dancers.

These new pointe shoes, which are made in China, have a different shape. Even though the box is not square, but pointed, the inside is wide enough for a comfortable fit. They are especially good for students because of the hard shank which guarantees long wear.

The shoes come in three widths—A, B, and C; lengths range from size 33 to 42, which correspond to European sizes. Upon request, Xijun Fu has a chart which shows the relationship between sizes of other well-known shoes. One of the most attractive aspects of the Fuzi shoe is the price, which is lower than others.

Xijun Fu, who is now artistic director of the Lexington Ballet, in Lexington, Kentucky, says his shoes are available in outlets in major cities in the East and Midwest.

Gaynor Minden
140 West 16th Street
New York, NY 10011
phone: 212 929–0087
fax: 212 929–4907
e-mail: minden@soho.ios.com

Although this classic peach pointe shoe may look traditional on the out-side, on the inside, it is all high tech. Designed with the idea that dancers are elite athletes as well as artists, Gaynor Minden is the first pointe shoe to utilize the same advanced materials that have revolution-ized athletic footwear.

Its patented design includes unbreakable shanks and boxes made from an elastomeric material—no cardboard, newspaper, burlap, or small nails. Shanks are available in a range of stiffnesses, from the extremely firm to the new, very supple "Feather-Flex." Because the shanks and boxes do not break in or deteriorate, it is important to select the appropriate shank right at the start.

Another unique feature of the Gaynor Minden is its adjustability. Using the heat from an ordinary blow dryer, a dancer can alter the shank's arch.

To minimize the pain, injury and noise that pointe shoes cause, Gaynor Mindens have shock-absorbing materials at areas where there is the greatest impact. The company also makes its own line of accessories, from state-of-the-art shock-absorbing materials, to a "Dynamic Box Liner" (patent pending) which helps dancers with fine-boned, compressible feet. In addition, special cushions are available for dancers with long second toes or sensitive big toes, heel grippers to keep the shoe on the foot, toe separators for dancers prone to bunions, and vamp elastic for dancers with extremely high arches.

Gaynor Mindens come in sizes corresponding to street shoe sizes 3 1/2 through 11 1/2. All lengths are available in a choice of at least three different shanks, two vamp heights, and three heel heights. Most lengths are available in a choice of widths and box styles ranging from narrow and tapered to wide and square. Though rarely needed, special orders are accepted.

La Mendola
1975 Express Drive North
Smithtown, New York 11787
phone: (516) 582-3230

Art Stone, a dance teacher and entrepreneur who created and administers Dance Olympus and DanceAmerica, purchased La Mendola when the former management fell on hard times. Long a respected maker of dance shoes, La Mendola has taken on a new, energetic character under Stone's direction. He has returned La Mendola to its former stature with a renewed emphasis on quality and product development for both student and professional dancers.

The revamped La Mendola pointe shoe line includes two shoes made to updated product standards and specifications. Each model can be ordered with customized features designed to meet the needs of individual dancers. One of the models is a suede-tip shoe with pleats; another is a lighter-weight, satin-tip shoe for students.

La Mendola has found that most of its student customers still begin their training in a shoe with a suede-block toe; this is true, even if they soon graduate to a shoe with a satin tip. The company prides itself on keeping its beginner's shoe lightweight, despite the suede-block toe.

Shoes are now manufactured in Jesup, Georgia, using the time-honored method of hand-lasting and hand-pleating. Although most La

Mendola veteran craftsmen are now retired, before they retired, they trained workers in Georgia with the old methods used for decades.

La Mendola pointe shoes are sold through the Art Stone Dance and Bodywear stores, as well as Nordstroms and dance supply stores located throughout the country.

Leo's Dancewear Inc.

1900 N. Narragansett
Chicago, IL 60639
phone: (312) 889-7700
fax: (312) 889-7593
e-mail: leo's@ix.netcom.com

Begun by Leo Harris in 1924, today, Leo's is managed by the family's second and third generations. The company's pointe shoes are sold in retail outlets throughout the United States.

Pointe shoes are cut at Leo's every two weeks. One employee oversees the complete manufacture of a pair of shoes. However, because the company's shoemaking process is extremely uniform, if necessary, one maker can complete work that was begun by another.

Leo's pointe shoe line includes the *Pas de Deux I*, a shoe for beginners; the *Pas de Deux III*, an intermediate-advanced shoe; and the *Roma*, a European-style professional shoe. Shoes can be customized by ordering double fiber shank, shorter or longer vamps, and higher or lower boxes.

All of Leo's shoes incorporate a rainbow-arch feature. The last on which the shoe is shaped is slightly arched; therefore, the shoe is slightly pre-arched when worn for the first time. Leo's pointe shoes have a felt lining in the back of the shoe, for comfort and to prevent heel slippage. The front of the shoe is lined with cloth, for absorbency and breathability. The shanks are made of fiberboard, which combines leather and artificial materials.

ENGLISH MAKERS

Dance Workshop 2000

1a Neptune Road, Harrow
Middlesex HA1 4HY
United Kingdom
phone: 0191 424 2200
fax: 0181 427 2330

Dance Workshop 2000 was formed in July 1995, by Bob and Pat Martin, with financial support from Derek Gandolfi. After working for Gamba for 35 years, Bob decided to move on and form his own company. His lifetime ambition is to develop what he calls the "ultimate" pointe shoe.

Bob Martin had already developed the famous *Turning Pointe* with his friend, Rodney Freed; but had wanted to go further. He feels that the *Innovation 2000* is the ultimate pointe shoe. It has a high vamp wing block with a V-shaped vamp (although it can be cut to any shape and height required). The insole or shank follows the line of the arch when en pointe and can be made of various materials, depending on the support required. The heel is tapered to give a closer fit. Sizes range from 8 to 13, with half sizes throughout. Fittings are N (narrow), X (medium), XX (wide), and XXX (extra wide).

Bob Martin has made shoes for Royal Ballet ballerinas Antoinette Sibley and Lesley Collier; now Dance Workshop continues to make shoes for many world famous dancers and companies. The company manufactures only pointe shoes. Besides the custom-made pointes which is 50 percent of production, DW also carries a full range of stock shoes.

Frederick Freed Ltd.
94 St. Martin's Lane
London WC2N 4AT
phone: 01–240–0432

or

922 7th Ave.
New York, NY 10019
phone: (212) 489-1055
fax: (212) 262-0041

Frederick Freed, founder of Frederick Freed Ltd., was the son of a sample shoemaker who opened his own shoe repair shop in England. Although young Frederick initially thought of becoming an engineer, at the age of sixteen, during World War I, he began making ballet shoes at a firm in London's West End. As Freed explained on his eightieth birthday in 1979, "I went into a room where I saw rolls of satin and bits of leather; and you know the old saying, if you see a girl you fall in love with, it clicks right away and you don't want to know anything else."

After observing veteran makers use seven to nine nails to pleat the toes of the shoes they were constructing, Freed invented a method of lasting-up that required only three nails. He developed a special sensitivity to the needs of dance customers, and his intense interest led him to open his own shop. Frederick Freed Ltd. was established in 1928, when Freed, his wife, and an assistant left Gamba to open a retail store in St. Martin's Lane, where they sewed shoes in the basement.

As his business prospered, Freed realized that many dancers stopped dancing because the traditional shoes of his day had a fixed width and were too narrow for some customers. So he began to concentrate on providing customized shoes, a skill and a service that remain Freed's special province. Today, Freeds are exported around the world.

After the death of Frederick Freed and his longtime friend and colleague Sam Thompson, who succeeded him as chairman of the board, the company was purchased by Chacott Ltd.[2] of Japan, a firm which also specializes in the manufacture of pointe shoes. While concerned with increasing productivity and service standards, the directors of Chacott have stated their firm's intention to maintain the unique integrity of the Freed line.

Bernard D. Kohler, managing director of Frederick Freed, Ltd. for well over forty years, was a key figure in guiding the company into this new era. Now that he has retired, Michelle Altfeld, a trained dancer and a director of the company, is the main spokesperson. They both see Freed's approach to serving the needs of individual dancers as starting with a basic stock shoe design and varying it to fit personal specifications. They believe this approach differs from Capezio's philosophy of creating a larger number of stock shoe choices and deemphasizing custom orders.

The Freed stock shoe is the FBT 102, a satin block pointe shoe which is all satin and has a sturdy arch. Stock widths are medium, wide (X), extra wide (XX), and extra extra wide (XXX). Narrow can also be ordered. Sizes range from 10 1/2 small to 9 large. Both regular and deep vamps are available from stock.

Freed's stock shoe has a standard blocking, a basic insole, and average-sized vamp sides and back. It is made in a heavy, cotton-backed corset satin. The glue used in Freed shoes is made of natural starches. A special paper is used for building the block.

Following are a few examples of the custom features that can be built into a Freed special-order shoe to meet a customer's needs:

Wings can be strengthened with newspaper, a stronger fabric, or with layers of glue.

Vamp lengths and styles can be altered.

Insoles can be varied in at least fifteen different ways, in terms of materials and construction. They can be cut from different strengths of board, the thinnest of which closely resembles posterboard.

The insole favored by Margot Fonteyn is called the Phillips insole. Flexible and suitable for a dancer with a high arch, it is named for a Miss Phillips, the first dancer who ordered one. Fonteyn's Phillips insole was only a half-inch wide in the middle. Insoles can also be cut wider for broader support.

Insoles can be made with or without a supporting shank (also called the centerpiece). Shanks are three-fourths as long as the insoles and can vary in terms of materials, shape, and size. They

are attached to the insole with glue and three nails.
Freed makes the last nail in the insole easy to remove, since many
  dancers do so.

There are supplemental charges over the stock shoe for custom changes.

Whereas all Freed makers use the same patterns and processes, each
has the artistic freedom to impose his own technique and style on the
work, on both stock and custom shoes. For instance, pleating style varies
from maker to maker. Each craftsman finds his own style and determines
whether his pleats will be narrow or wide, short or long.

Each maker has a personal symbol, which is used when the maker
begins to construct a pair of shoes. Initially the symbols were the letters
of the alphabet, but Freed became concerned that dancers were confusing the letters with widths. Consequently, they adopted other symbols
such as a circle, dot, square, split triangle, castle, the ace of spade, and
dead spider. Although Freed meant the symbols only as a means of
internal identification, dancers began ordering their shoes by them. To
avoid confusion, a symbol belonging to a retired shoemaker is not rein-
troduced for five or six years.

Although it is quite difficult to serve a dancer by mail or phone, Freed
will work tirelessly with a dancer thousands of miles away, to help her
find a satisfactory maker. They do their best to "second guess" the
dancer's physical needs and professional pressures and translate them
into structural and cosmetic shoe changes.

Perhaps the ideal pointe shoe-fitting situation exists when Freeds,
with the aid of the school's faculty, fits the students at the Royal Ballet
School. Starting with the earliest days of a Royal Ballet student's training, Freed analyzes the student's feet and adjusts her shoes accordingly
as she progresses. Fitters are able as well to suggest makers for individual students, since the latter are well aware of the special aspects of each
craftsman's style. This relationship often continues throughout a
dancer's career.

In addition to this honor, Freeds is now the official shoe of American
Ballet Theatre. The list of Russian dancers who now order Freeds
includes Semenyaka, Asylmuratove, Ananiashvilli, Nioradze, Jelonkina,
Makalina, Techstiakova, Schapchiz, Brissonskaya, and Rastorgueva.

Gamba Ltd.
3 Garrick Street
Covent Garden
London, WC2E 9AR
phone: 071–437–0704

Luigi Gamba, founder of the firm, arrived in London at the age of fourteen. After a stint as a waiter at the Savoy Hotel, which catered to a the-

atrical clientele, he opened a shoe shop. By 1912, he was making "Our special Toe Ballet Shoes, the exact make as the original shoes supplied to the famous Milan School." Prior to this time, all pointe shoes worn in England were imported from Italy. Gamba shoemaker Alfred Furse was the first Englishman to make pointe shoes for Anna Pavlova. Today, Gamba's theatrical division makes shoes for international companies of such major productions as *Les Miserables* and *Phantom of the Opera*. Gamba has eleven shops in the United Kingdom, with a flagship store on Garrick Street in Covent Garden.

The innovative *Turning Pointe*, which took seven years to develop, is currently considered Gamba's "prize" product. Featuring a wing block and V-shaped high vamp, it comes up higher on the foot, while providing mild support on the sides. Made in satin and canvas, the shoe has a three-quarter insole, as well as a square box and flat toe for balance and fit. The heel is cut to avoid pressure on the back of the feet.

Other interesting features of the *Turning Pointe* are a water-resistant, shredded-leather insole, which provides strength and flexibility. In addition, this insole material keeps the dancer's foot cool. The most unusual feature of the *Turning Pointe* is that it is made with a special paste that allows the dancer to "steam" the block into shape. Widths available are extra narrow (NN), narrow (N), medium (M), and extra wide (XW).

Gamba's other two best-sellers are models #92 and #93. The more current #93 features a flat and square box, a fiber-carbon shank that can be bent a thousand times without alteration. Resistant to heat and humidity, the shoe gives total consistency throughout its life. In addition, the *Pirouette*, Gamba's newest model, has numerous innovative features.

Recently, Gamba was acquired by Repetto, a French company.

OTHER INTERNATIONAL MAKERS

J. Bloch/Australia (USA) Inc
3895 Corsaire St. - Suite A
Reno, NV 89502
phone: (702) 824-2550 or 800–94BLOCH

Bloch's was founded in 1930 by Jacob Simon Bloch, whose three children, Bill, Bernard, and Betty, have all joined the business. The company is currently managed jointly by Betty's husband, Gerson Wilkenfeld, and their son, David Wilkenfeld. David and his brother and sister, Simon and Judy, work as a team within the company.

The arch support in a Bloch pointe shoe, which is available in both regular and strong weights, goes through a special shaping process, which enables the shoe to provide support where it is needed, as well as providing extra ease of movement and comfort where support is not required. The toe box is individually formed from many layers of natural fibers, combined with a paste made from natural materials. Drawstrings are thin but strong, to provide minimal bulking.

The current Bloch line includes:

Suprima A supportive shape with a tapered toe, for more advanced dancers. The Suprima provides particularly good balance when the dancer is standing flat. It is a slimline, soft-winged shoe.

Serenade A lightweight shoe with a wide, silent toe platform and low arch, which provide excellent lateral balance. This shoe has a wider, flatter box.

Signature The newest shoe that has two styles—*Rehearsal* and *Performance,* which are similar shoes. The *Performance* needs no breaking in.

Custom orders are accepted only from previous customers and require a minimum order of thirty-six pairs. Innumerable changes are possible, and special orders are customized to accommodate the needs of the individual dancer.

Bloch pointe shoes are available at the Capezio Dance Theatre Shop, at 1650 Broadway, in New York, as well as at dance and theater shops throughout the country.

Chacott Ltd. (Japan)

In 1951, a well-known Japanese ballerina asked Makoto Tsuchiya, a shoe salesman, to create a pair of pointe shoes for her. At that time, not long after World War II, there was a shortage of good pointe shoes in Japan. After analyzing the ballerina's European shoes, Tsuchiya decided to start his own pointe shoe company. Now the largest dancewear manufacturer in the world, Chacott has introduced machinery that accomplishes several major pointe shoe-construction steps traditionally performed by hand.

The Chacott *Coppelia II* pointe shoe is distributed in the United States through Freed of London. To offset the cost of importing directly from Japan, Chacott set up a special manufacturing facility in Spain to produce pointe shoes for export to the United States.

The *Coppelia* is a long-lasting, quiet shoe engineered to facilitate balance. It is available in B, C, D, and E widths in stock shoes, and EE on special order. Medium and hard insoles are available in stock shoes, and soft and supersoft insoles can be special-ordered. Changes in vamp height, size, and back of the shoe can also be special-ordered. Made in a rosy pink satin, the shoe is aimed at students and semiprofessional dancers; but it is also gaining acceptance among professionals. Chacott pointe shoes are made in sizes 30 to 41, the equivalent of American sizes 1 to 7.

Eva (Germany)

LaRay, 633 Alacci Way
New York, NY 10107 (showroom)
phone: 201-664-5882

or

250 W. 57th St., 2nd Floor
River Vale, NJ 07675

Eva shoes, manufactured in Germany twenty-five years ago by Karl Heinz Martin, are available in the United States only through Bruce Cohen, a distributor who has a showroom in New York City, along with a New Jersey warehouse. If a dancer is unable to visit the New York location for a fitting, it is possible to order Evas by mail or telephone based on current Capezio or Freed sizes and street shoe information.

Eva shoes are lightweight, yet durable, combining optimal support and flexibility. A flat platform gives excellent balance and makes the dancer feel lifted from the floor when on pointe.

The shoe is available in various vamp lengths and four different strength insoles, including three-quarter and half shanks. A unique toe-box and wing configuration ensure stability and allow the shoe to mold quickly to the foot. A hygienically safe paste formula limits the incidence of foot problems. Special orders are available for both advanced students and professionals.

Grishko

1655 Mount Pleasant Road
Villanova, PA 19085
phone: 610-527-9553
fax: 610-527-9579

Master cobblers, many formerly with the Bolshoi and Kirov ballet companies, create Grishko pointe shoes in Moscow. Made without a drawstring, to fit the natural curve of the foot, the shoes alleviate many of the problems associated with tendonitis.

Grishko pointe shoes come in three shapes. Each shape or last fits a certain shaped foot. If a student has been taught to "roll through" demi-pointe, she should be fitted with the *Ulanova I, Ulanova II, Elite,* or *Maya.* If, however, she has been instructed to use the Russian technique of going onto pointe, she should be fitted with the *Vaganova* or the *Fouette,* either of which enhances the dancer's ability to spring onto pointe.

> **Eleve models** Designed for "rolling-through" demi-pointe. All eleve models were improved in 1996, made quieter and lighter; they also feature their "super shank," which is reliable, resilient, and durable.

Ulanova I Has a regular vamp and comes in #UD (regular shank), #UDH (hard shank), and #UDS (soft shank).

Ulanova II Has a deep vamp and comes in the same shanks as the Ulanova I. This shoe features a deep vamp and the same shape as the Vaganova.

Elite Has a regular vamp and comes in #E (regular shank) and #ES (soft shank). This model features a broad, flat box and platform offering optimal stability.

Maya The newest style; has a regular vamp and comes in #M (medium shank), #MS (soft shank), #MH (hard shank). Grishko's lightest weight shoe, the Maya, fits like the Ulanova I but has a stitched sole and a suede bottom.

Releve models Accommodate the Russian technique of "springing" onto pointe.

Vaganova Has a deep vamp and comes in #VM (medium shank) and #V (hard shank). It has a tapered box like the Ulanova II.

Fouette Has a medium vamp, comes in #F (medium shank), #FH (hard shank) and has a broad box and wide platform, similar to the Ulanova I.

Sizes range from 1, which is equivalent to a street shoe size of 3 1/2, to 7.5, the equivalent of street shoe 10 1/2. Widths are X (narrow), XX (medium), XXX (wide), and XXXX (extra wide). Special orders are accepted; any changes or color requests are at an additional charge.

C. Porselli Ltd (Italy)

9 West Street
Cambridge Circus
London W.C.2
phone: 01-836-2862

Porselli pointe shoes are manufactured in Italy, where they dominate the market. Eugenio Porselli founded the company in Milan, in 1919. The company is still owned and directed by the Porselli family.

There is a Porselli shop in London, at Cambridge Circus; the shoes are also distributed to a hundred small retail dance shops throughout the United Kingdom. At the present time, there is no distribution through retail shops in the United States, although that may change in the future.

The ten styles the company used to stock can now be special-ordered. But its new *Gala*, as well as the *Colacrai* and the original *F* shoe, are the ones Porselli feels will best serve the needs of most dancers. Also, the color has been changed from sugary pink to the popular peach.

The *Gala* is a strong shoe, having a double back or shank and a wing. The company also produces a version with no wings, which makes it much easier to go through demi-pointe.

The *Colacrai,* designed by an Italian dancer from La Scala, has elasticated sides. It also allows the dancer to go through the foot easily.

The original *F* shoe uses a flexi-back. A light shoe, it is often used by beginners.

Gine Chant-Grostern, who manages the shop that has been owned by her family for about 15 years, takes mail orders worldwide, using the above address.

Repetto (France)

c/o Benedicte Marchois
Chef de Produit
22 Rue de la Paix, 75002
Paris, France
phone: (1) 44-71-83-10

or

215 Little Falls Rd.
Fairfield, NJ 07006
phone: (973) 785-9292 or (800) 858-5855
fax: (973) 785-1595

Repetto, the largest manufacturer of pointe shoes in France, makes several models of pointe shoes. The best sellers are the models #207, #215 and #211. Write to Repetto for current information detailing the qualities of these shoes.

Russian Class®

339 E. Liberty St.
Suite #330
Ann Arbor, MI 48104-2258
phone: 1-888-4 RCLASS or (734) 668-6545
fax: (734) 668-8552

Oleg Svintsitski, the executive director for Russian Class shoes, says that the president of the company, as well as the craftsmen who make their shoes, used to work for the Bolshoi. This new venture, which began in the summer of 1996, sells ballet and pointe shoes.

Russian Class offers five models of pointe shoes with the choice of two shanks in eleven strengths, four widths, and three vamp lengths. Dancers choose shoes models based on the structure of the "toe platform." Shoe width is based on the size of the dancer's foot from joint to the heel. All of these are available for special order, although they have in stock the sizes they consider the most frequently requested. The shoes come in pink. Special order colors, available for an additional charge with no returns accepted, are red, black, gray, and white. Standard models are as follows:

A Features a narrow toe platform and high instep. Recommended for dancers with narrow toes, or if the dancer's second toe is long.

B For dancers with medium width toes and toes of uneven length. The box offers support and comfort and fits many different types of feet.

C The same shape as Model A, but features a low instep. This is suitable for dancers with narrow toes and a "shallow" foot. Tapered toward the tip, the shoe enhances the elegance of the foot.

D Featuring a broad, flat box and low instep, this shoe is appropriate for dancers with wide toes and toes of even length. The shoe is slightly tapered toward the pointe.

E The same construction as Model B, it features a medium toe platform and low instep. Model E is pre-arched and provides additional support and a longer performance life for dancers with a strong arch.

"Standard" shanks are designed for dancers who prefer support in the toe area and spring up onto pointe. They are widely used in the Russian imperial style of ballet and are available in seven strengths. "Flexible" shanks offer dancers additional flexibility in working through demi-pointe, allowing roll-through because its sides are cut out in the toe area. They are available in four strengths ranging from from HLF (super hard demi-pointe) to MF (medium demi-pointe).

Mr. Svintsitski says the price is on the upper end because they believe that Russian Class is a superior product comparable to the best in the world.

A "souvenir pointe shoe," a precise copy of Russian Class pointe shoes, is approximately 4 1/2 inches long and available through the company.

Sansha Inc.
1717 Broadway
2nd Floor
New York, NY 10019
phone: 212-246-6212
fax: (212) 956-7052
e-mail: sansha@mail.usa.net

Sansha dancing shoes are designed by the Frenchman, Franc Raoul Duvall, originally from a French merchant family in Normandy. Mr. Duvall was nicknamed "Sansha" by his friends when he lived in Russia.

Following the success of his soft ballet shoes, he turned his attention to pointe shoes. He came up with a revolutionary idea for a replaceable shank, which allows the shoes to be worn even after the original shank is broken, thus offering a longer lasting shoe to professionals and students alike. He also developed the first "silent" pointe shoe which at last brought back the lightness and grace of the first pointe shoes as they appeared a century ago.

The shoes come in four widths, two heights of the vamp, and canvas or satin uppers. Customized orders are possible.

From Sansha's ideas has grown an international company based in Paris. Sansha provides shoes for dancers in more than 27 countries.

Sansha pointe shoes are available from Dansant Boutique, 1020 S. Wabash Ave. #50, Chicago, IL 60605   fax: (703) 847-9162.

Schachtner (Austria)
c/o Mary Price Boday
The Dance Works
719 W. Moss Street
Peoria, IL 61606
phone: 309-672-2114

Schachtner shoes, which are made in Vienna, Austria, can be purchased in the United States through the Dance Works, in Peoria, Illinois, which has an active mail-order department. Mary Price Boday, who runs the shop, discovered Schachtner shoes when she was dancing with the Zurich Ballet. At the time, she was going through four pairs of pointe shoes a day. Then she discovered that she could wear one pair of Schachtners for eight hours a day for seven days. When she returned to the United States and discovered that the shoes were not readily available, she began to import them.

Schachtner is currently run by Gerda Schachtner, whose father-in-law invented the shoes used by the dancers of the Vienna Opera Ballet. When her husband, who had taken over direction of the shoemaking process, died suddenly at the age of twenty-eight, Gerda Schachtner decided to carry on.

There are no "stock" Schachtner shoes; instead, shoes are made according to customer specifications from a broad set of choices. For instance, a dancer can order one width for the front of her shoes and a separate width for the back, as a standard option. Schachtner shoes are also available with a short, long, extra long, or regular vamp; a soft sole; and a regular, very soft, hard, or steel shank. Any of these shanks can be ordered three-quarters long. The shoes can also be ordered with a suede tip.

The width at the ball of the foot can be D (narrow), E (wider), F (wider), or G (wide). The width at the heel of the shoe can be N (narrow), B (regular), BB (wide). Any combination of ball and heel widths is possible. As a result, Schachtner offers much more variety in width than can be found in most pointe shoe lines.

In length, the shoes go up by half-centimeters, while American shoes go up in half inches or full inches, resulting in a much bigger jump between sizes. The dancer has the option of a three-quarter size, in addition to conventional half and whole sizes.

Pointe shoes can be made in canvas, leather, or satin in red, white, black, or pink.

To mail order Schachtners, a dancer simply outlines her feet on a piece of paper and provides written information about what kind of shoes she currently wears, what qualities and features she is looking for in a pointe shoe, the wear patterns of current pointe shoes (what breaks first, what kind of arch, etc.), and how much support she wants.

WHERE TO BUY POINTE SHOES: DANCE SHOPS AND MAIL ORDER

Check your local Yellow Pages under the listing "Dance Supplies"/"Shoes," and call the dealers listed to learn which brands of pointe shoes they stock and what styles and services they offer within those brands. You can also write to manufacturers to request catalogs and the names of stores carrying their products in your area. Refer to the above listings for information about the availability and sources of international brands. You can order Gaynor Minden from Capezio and Freed of London's New York store.

Capezio Mail Order
To receive a catalog and price list, write or call: Capezio Mail Order, 1650 Broadway, New York, NY 10019; or telephone 212-245-2235. When mail ordering, indicate quantity, style number, size, and price. Postage charges are $5 for the first item and 25 cents for each additional item. Dance companies, theater groups, schools, universities, and teachers are entitled to a 10 percent discount. New York State residents pay an 8 1/4 percent state tax.

Freed Mail Order
922 Seventh Avenue at 200 Central Park South
New York, NY 10019
phone: 212-489-1055

Mail and phone orders from the United States and Canada should be placed through the New York store. Write to Freed at the above address for a price list and catalog. In-stock items listed on the New York store's price list are shipped by UPS within seven days. Shipping can also be by U.S. mail parcel post, air mail, or Federal Express.

Special pointe shoe orders from England entail a ten- to fifteen-week delivery period. Approved studios, schools, and companies receive a discount of 10 percent. Basic fitting instructions are provided for mail-order shoes. A foot tracing is helpful, as is any information about a non-Freed shoe currently being worn. Payment for individuals may be by Visa, Mastercard, American Express, or COD.

Gaynor Minden Mail Order
140 West 16th Street
New York, NY 10011
phone: 212-929-0087

If a dancer cannot obtain Gaynor Mindens from her local dance shop, she can order them by phone, fax, mail, or e-mail directly from the company by writing to the above address. Careful foot tracings, showing both weight on and off the feet (to access compressibility), are recommended, as is extensive information on the dancer's feet, dancing history, and previous pointe shoe experience.

The company's fitters also operate a hotline (800-637-9240) for answering questions about shoes and accessories and to guide first-time users through the fitting.

Repetto Mail Order
215 Little Falls Road
Fairfield, NJ 07006
phone: 800-858-5855 or 201-785-9292

Write to the above address for information about mail order.

Capezio
1650 Broadway at 51st Street
New York, NY 10019
phone: 212-245-2130
fax: 212-757-7635
Open 7 days a week

Capezio has three shops in New York City. The largest, the Capezio Dance Theatre Shop, is an exciting, full-service dance supply center located in the heart of the Theater District. In addition to its full line of Capezio pointe shoes, this store stocks Bloch and Grishko pointe shoes. A full range of Capezio dance and character shoes, as well as Bloch ballet, jazz and character shoes, is also available. A wide variety of pointe shoe accessories can be found at this location. The staff are carefully trained and overseen by Judy Weiss.

Capezio East, at 136 East 61st Street, (212-758-8833), sell some Capezio pointe shoes, as well as dancewear, other dance shoes, and accessories.

Capezio East Uptown is located at 1651 Third Avenue, (212-348-7210). This new boutique specializes in children's dancewear, ballet shoes and accessories.

Freed of London, Ltd.
922 Seventh Avenue at 200 Central Park South
New York, NY 10019
phone: 212-489-1055

This is currently the only retail store owned by Freed of London Ltd. in the United States, although dance retailers around the country are stocking Freed shoes in their shops. The New York store is the "eyes and ears of Freed in America." They stock the basic Freed pointe shoe (FBT 102) in satin, with a regular or deep long vamp in sizes 13M to 7XXX. On orders for stock shoes, the maker may not be specified. Special orders can be placed through the store, with the advice of their trained fitting staff; these orders, however, must be in multiples of six and require a 50 percent deposit and a supplemental charge over the cost of a stock shoe. There is no minimum order on these shoes unless a maker is specified. All special orders must be sent to the factory in England and are shipped in approximately twelve weeks, depending on maker availability.

Gaynor Minden Boutique
140 West 16th Street
New York, NY 10011
phone: 212-929-0087

Gaynor Minden's boutique is a Victorian parlor in a brownstone in Manhattan's Chelsea district. Be warned: There is no sign on the front of the building. The company has created an atmosphere of discreet elegance that includes Tiffany lamps, Oriental carpets, carved mahogany furniture, lace curtains and Japanese prints, along with a barre, marley, and mirror and shelves of pointe shoes. Dancers are fitted by appointment so they can be sure of having the fitter's undivided attention. Samples of various styles with ribbon and elastic sewn on are available so dancers may evaluate and compare various shanks and styles by really working in them.

The Ballet Company
1887 Broadway between 62nd and 63rd Sts.
New York, NY 10023
phone: 212-246-6893 or 800-219-7335

This new shop is located directly across from Lincoln Center. Along with a variety of gift items, dancewear, ballet CDs, videos, books and autographed photographs and posters, Randy Cooper, the owner, stocks Capezio, Freeds, and Repetto pointe and ballet shoes. Specialty items such as the pointe shoes Margot Fonteyn wore in *Swan Lake* are available.

Write or call for a catalog or information about mail order.

NOTES

1. Selva and Sons, the company Jimmy Selva founded with his father and brothers, was a distinguished U.S. maker of pointe shoes for many years.
2. In 1990, Chacott and Freed of London Ltd. were sold to the Japanese company, Onward Kashiyama.

7

Basics of Teaching Pointe

THE BASIC ISSUE: WHEN IS A DANCER READY TO GO ON POINTE?

The most pressing question facing a teacher of pointe is how best to determine a student's readiness to begin pointe training. During our interviews with medical specialists and master teachers, we concluded that there is no simple answer to this question. There is agreement that the teacher must consider a combination of factors including the age, anatomy, bone development, strength, length of training, weight, and attitude of a student before making this judgment. Discovering consensus on a set of guidelines to use in evaluating these factors is quite another matter.

In his book *Dance Technique and Injury Prevention,* Dr. Justin Howse, orthopedist for the Royal Ballet School, says that for many years twelve was considered the age to begin pointe work. He feels that there is no particular age at which pointe work should begin. Dr. Howse states, "The only factor which matters is the state of the development of the child, and to be dogmatic about an age does not make any reference to the child's maturity or immaturity."[1]

Howse adds that there is no shame or disadvantage in beginning pointe work at a later age, while an early start before physical and technical readiness are present can be potentially harmful. A dancer who waits to go on pointe until the correct time for her particular body and skill development level will have less risk of injury, be able to achieve the correct technique with greater ease, and progress more speedily. He notes that a number of well-known dancers were not strong enough to start pointe work until they were teenagers, but found this no handicap to their careers.

In training situations where the only route to a professional career is through company schools, as in the Russian system, there would be no question of a student going on pointe who was not anatomically equipped to do so. The screening process for admission weeds out applicants with such limitations, or they are dropped from the school. However, a pointe teacher in the United States may very well be confronted with such cases since the only requirement for studying ballet may be a desire to dance.

This more democratic approach puts a great deal of additional responsibility on the teacher to decide when and if a student should go on pointe. The decision is one that can only be made on the basis of skill and knowledge and should not be subject to student or parental pressure. Dancing on pointe is serious business, and a teacher must protect her students from the risk of doing permanent damage to the bone and muscle structure of their bodies and feet. Such risks far outweigh the temporary disappointment a student may experience when told she is not ready or physically designed for pointe work.

It is entirely possible that some students may never "be ready" to go on pointe. If a teacher takes the course of least resistance and allows such a student to go on pointe, using the excuse that she will only find another teacher who will put her "up," that teacher is overlooking his or her responsibility for the student's current and future physical health. For this reason, it is important for teachers to develop strong rapport with parents. Once parents have confidence in a teacher's judgment, they are more likely to understand a thoroughly explained and scientifically supported discussion of why their child should not be placed on pointe.

It is also important that going on pointe not be made a key to studying ballet. If students who should not go on pointe or may not want to do so are made to feel a significant part of a studio program, they will be far more likely to remain on the roster.

Avoiding the concept of putting whole classes on pointe and thinking of readiness as an individual matter seems to be a good strategy. This is helpful both because children mature at different rates and because it takes some of the peer pressure off a child who is asked to wait or defer beginning pointe work. If a student appears in class who has been incorrectly placed on pointe at another school and shows evidence of such problems as bent knees or incorrect placement, she should be taken off pointe until her problems are resolved.

Too often the issue of when students will get pointe shoes overshadows the importance of adequate prepointe training. Great care needs to be taken to design a curriculum preceding pointe work that stresses the development of the needed strength and muscle tone. Particular emphasis must be placed on developing strength and suppleness in the feet and the strength of the postural muscles.

For this reason, students at the Royal Ballet School at White Lodge wear socks instead of tights during their prepointe training to enable teachers to watch the manner in which they are working their feet and legs. They wear elastic on their ballet shoes instead of ribbons to make the shoes easier to slip on and off. Teachers are concerned with checking the students' bare feet to be sure they are not clenching and gripping with their toes in tendu or forming other patterns that will have a negative impact on pointe work.

Christine Beckley, ballet teacher at the Royal Ballet School, stresses the importance of touching children as a teaching method rather than standing a distance off and demonstrating. The tactile element makes them aware of what they should be feeling. It is unlikely a child can fully comprehend the muscular actions related to pointe by merely imitating what she sees on someone else's body.

Students need to understand that "taking pointe" is not undertaking the study of a new technique. They are working on their pointe technique each time they do an exercise at the barre since these exercises are preparing them to be able to execute movements on their toes. The principles of classical ballet movement are the principles of pointe work as well.

Once a dancer has excellent placement, she can approach pointe work as a series of adjustments in weight distribution, areas of stress, and timing, not a new form of dance. Pointe work is an additional skill to be practiced and mastered.

Many teachers have convinced themselves that the only way to have a successful studio is automatically to allow every female student to go on pointe as soon as possible. Part of this practice is rooted in a lack of understanding of the anatomical and technical foundation of pointe work and part of it is based on poor logic. Putting every female student on pointe probably does as much to drive students away as to retain them. Many students who have gained reasonable proficiency in soft shoes find the reality of being on pointe so frustrating that they are discouraged from continuing their dance studies.

Some teachers take the position that children taking dance for enjoyment as opposed to preprofessional training should not go on pointe at all. They feel that a child should only begin pointe if she remains interested in dance at age thirteen or fourteen, and has a sound technical foundation with strong feet, legs, and back.

In *Anatomy and Ballet* Celia Sparger questions putting a student on pointe unless she is in a systematic, concentrated, professional training situation. Sparger explains that a once-a-week class can never be a suitable preparation for pointe work and carries with it the risk of lifelong disability. Teachers rarely see the results of poor pointe training, which may appear in later life in the form of foot, knee, or back trouble.

Clearly stated policies on pointe dancing that are explained upon entrance to a school program can go a long way to reducing the tensions surrounding this issue. One possibility is to offer a pointe preparation "option" requiring that children preparing for pointe take several classes a week for at least two years. Parents not choosing this option will be aware from the start that pointe is not a probability for their child.

Another strategy is to begin analyzing a child's anatomical problems from admission to prepare her and her parents to accept any possible unsuitability for pointe work. Capezio distributes copies of a free handout called "Why Can't I Go on My Toes?" through its retail stores; the handout is well written and ideal for distribution to parents.

Knowledge is the best weapon in successfully dealing with the issue of readiness. Teachers must know how to evaluate a child for pointe readiness and be able to clearly interpret the process for parents. Helpful guidance can be obtained by talking to podiatrists and orthopedists who work with dancers, attending seminars at conventions, and conferring with fitting specialists at dance shops. Many colleges offer courses in anatomy, and some are designed especially for dance majors. Taking such a course on a not-for-credit basis could provide a valuable base of knowledge. Outside support for a cautious approach to placing students on pointe can be gained by requiring that students have a consent form from their physicians indicating when they are at an appropriate stage in their growth and physical development to begin pointe.

Edith Royal, who with her husband Bill ran a successful dance school and company for more than thirty years, developed a method of teaching pointe that sought to maintain professional standards in a private studio setting. Her approach is a vivid demonstration that this is possible. Royal based her method on her own training at the Royal Ballet School in London, the Paris Opéra Ballet School, and with Robert Joffrey.

Royal gave a pointe test to students at her school when they reached age eleven to determine their readiness. Before taking the test, a student had to take classes for two years. The test examined pull-up in the legs, articulation of the feet, and back strength. Students who did not pass the test stayed in the same class as those who got their pointe shoes, but they did the pointe exercises on demi-pointe. In other words, pointe was a possibility and not an inevitability.

In surveying teachers around the country, we found that many tell students they cannot begin pointe work for the following reasons: improper placement; too young; not pulled up in body and feet; feet not arched enough; overweight; lack of strength in the torso; weak knees or ankles; basic stance on demi-pointe not strong and correct; and taking too few classes per week.

In determining a system for evaluating readiness for pointe, a teacher should consider the following areas.

Length and Intensity of Study

Time and preparation are needed for students to develop adequate strength and technique to begin pointe. It is essential that the student's musculature be strong enough to support her entire body. Much of the lift in pointe work depends on the two calf muscles which meet in the

Achilles tendon. Most of the teachers we interviewed require at least two or three years of serious ballet training and insist that a student be taking two or three classes a week. Many require four years of training.

In *Anatomy and Ballet,* Celia Sparger states, "The ability to do pointe work is the end result of slow and gradual training of the whole body, back, hips, thighs, legs, feet, coordination of movement and the placing of the body so that the weight is lifted upwards off the feet, with straight knees, perfect balance, a perfect demi-pointe and no tendency of the feet to sickle in or out or the toes to curl and clutch."[2]

Dr. William Hamilton, official doctor of the New York City Ballet, espouses George Balanchine's theory that a student should have studied ballet for four years before beginning pointe. It should be noted that Hamilton is not convinced by available research data that putting a child on pointe before a particular age is necessarily damaging. However, he does feel that a child with four years of training will have the strength and technique required to begin pointe. He adds that learning technique on demi-pointe puts no less strain on the foot than wearing pointe shoes since the weight is still bearing on the metatarsals.

Some teachers place the greatest emphasis on the training factor. For instance, Natalia Krassovska, former ballerina with Ballet Russe de Monte Carlo and the Ballet Marquis de Cuévas and now a teacher in Dallas, feels that training level and body development are more important than age. She believes that if a student takes class every day, she can develop strength very quickly and occasionally can go on pointe as early as eight after several years of intensive study. However, she would keep less serious dancers who take fewer classes off pointe until as late as age fourteen or fifteen. Krassovska insists that students come at least three times a week to be able to take pointe class.

Strength

Dr. James Garrick has stated that contrary to finding that going on pointe "too early" produces significant musculoskeletal problems, the Dance-medicine Division of his Center for Sports Medicine at St. Francis Hospital in San Francisco observes students who physically struggle with pointe because they lack the strength and technique necessary for "this demanding endeavor." He believes a student should be able to do a solid passé on demi-pointe with a straight, pulled-up knee. This requires that she put all her weight on one leg, with full knee extension and full relevé. He adds that if a dancer can go from a grand plié in center to standing with her knees straight, no wobbling, without altering foot positions, it may be time for pointe.

Dr. Richard Braver, medical consultant to Capezio, states that a student should be able to stand on demi-pointe for forty-five seconds on each foot, without faltering or wobbling.

Dr. Justin Howse says that strength must have been achieved in the feet and around the ankles, with full control of all relevant joints. Students should be able to hold turnout at the hips and be stable in the hip area when standing on both legs or one leg alone. There also needs to be strength and stability in the trunk. Inadequate control of the muscles of the trunk, hip, and thigh can make a student unstable and unsafe on pointe. If the feet and body are in any way soft, mobile, or floppy, pointe work must be delayed.

Age/Bone Development

Bones have different rates of ossification. The epiphyses are layers of cartilage or solid resilient cellular tissue present in bone that has not yet completed its growth. Some of these layers of cartilage do not totally ossify until humans reach their twenties. Bones harden gradually from the center outward. In the long bones, such as those of the leg, forefoot, and toes that bear the weight of the body when the dancer is on pointe, the shaft ossifies first. The epiphyses remain connected to the shaft by only cartilage until the early teens. There is great variation among children as to when the cartilage becomes bony; ossification may not begin until the age of fourteen. To compensate for this fact, the muscles must be particularly well developed to protect joint alignment. Otherwise, the pressure of body weight on feet and toes, which are still soft and growing, can cause malformation of the bones and joints. With correct training, the weight of the body should be held and distributed in such a way that a minimum falls on the toes.

Because of these developmental considerations, few of the teachers we interviewed think children should go on pointe before the age of ten, and many wait until students are eleven or twelve, regardless of how young they have begun their training. Joanna Kneeland, a noted dance teacher who has done extensive research in the field of dance movement, suggests sending children to a doctor and having the feet X-rayed to determine if the tips of the toes have changed from cartilage to bone. She suspects that the body may reach this stage of maturity faster in warm climates.

Even after determining that students are ready to go on pointe, some teachers carefully chart their growth spurts by keeping height charts at the studio. If a beginning pointe student experiences a growth spurt, she is taken off pointe for three or four months until her growth is stabilized. During growth spurts, weight distribution changes, the center of gravity changes, and the proportions of body parts change. Rapidly growing dancers run greater risks of injuries than others. Since muscles may not keep up with bone growth and grow tight, the resulting strain on the body can have a long-reaching impact. Students are kept in the same class structure, but work in flat shoes until the spurt ends. They might be given additional exercises to stretch the quadriceps, hamstrings, and calf muscles to keep them strong, stretched, and flexible.

Anatomy of the Foot and Ankle

A teacher must evaluate the structure of the student's foot and ankle. Although ideal feet are rarely found, extreme problems that may cause difficulties should be identified. The "ideal" foot for pointe is thought to be wide, with two or three toes of the same length and a strong ankle. This kind of foot provides a broad base for weight distribution. A student with a long big toe can do pointe work, but those with extremely long second toes find it more difficult. A narrow pointed foot with a high arch also signals potential problems.

The flexibility of the ankle and amount of natural arch in the instep should be examined. With limited flexibility and arch, a student may have problems aligning her ankle between knee and toes on pointe. A student with inflexible feet may experience Achilles tendon problems from pointe work because of the pressure created when the heel bone goes into the tendon.

A weak ankle and an instep with too much arch can also be limiting. When this kind of foot is placed on pointe, the toes usually curl under, forcing the front of the foot and instep down and forward from the ankle. The thigh and knee muscles are strained, and weight is not centered over the bones of the legs. The shoulders, neck, and whole upper torso can be adversely affected. Students with this problem need to do additional strengthening work before they begin pointe work.

A student with pronated feet or fallen arches that roll toward the inside, with more weight placed over the big toe and arch, should not go on pointe until the muscles around the ankle can be retrained to hold the ankle in the correct position. Pronation can cause bunions and longitudinal arch problems.

While the muscles of the ankle joint can adjust to changing positions, on pointe they are held in a fixed position and cannot move. Consequently, they must be strong enough to keep the foot from sickling out and causing the weight of the body to be shifted to the inside of the foot. When this happens, ligaments and muscles can be overly stretched and the additional weight that presses on the side of the big toe can cause it to become displaced. Sickling can make the ankle prone to sprains. A student with supinated or sickled feet that roll toward the outside, with the majority of weight placed over the fourth and fifth toes, should not go on pointe until the muscles of the ankle can be retrained.

A student with a weak instep who goes on pointe without correct preparation can cause lasting damage to the foot and ankle. The muscles of the foot and ankle need to be strengthened so that the foot is well controlled and able to be held in the correct rather than the overpointed position.

Weight

Overweight students should be encouraged to lose weight before risking damage by placing extra pressure on their toes.

Attitude

An enjoyment of dance is a definite prerequisite for pointe study. A negative attitude toward dance class before pointe training will only get worse once pointe shoes are introduced into the situation.

PREPARING A STUDENT FOR HER FIRST POINTE CLASS

At first students are often upset by how different pointe shoes feel than ballet slippers or street shoes. The teacher should spend time discussing the parts of the shoe and their function. Many stores that carry Capezio shoes have a display available that shows the inner structure of the pointe shoe. This display is often loaned as a courtesy to interested schools. The teacher should remember that first-time pointe students need careful directions on such matters as sewing and tying ribbons, toe protection, and shoe care.

THE LENGTH AND FORM OF POINTE CLASS

There is general consensus that pointe training must be slow and careful to give the bones and muscles a chance to develop properly. Individual attention is vital, since no small errors or sloppy movements can be overlooked. The student should not wear leg warmers during this early phase of pointe work to allow the teacher to carefully observe the knee, calf, and ankle.

Pointe training is scheduled in widely varying formats. Beginning students may wear their pointe shoes for ten to thirty minutes at the end of every ballet class, after they are fully warmed up, from one to five times a week. Or at first they may wear their shoes once a week, then twice a week, gradually building up to wearing their shoes for forty-five minutes. In some studios beginners take a separate one-hour pointe class. Many teachers mentioned preferring to teach beginning pointe at the end of the barre rather than the end of class, before students become too tired.

More advanced pointe students may take pointe classes for half an hour twice a week, or they may take half an hour of each hour and a half class on pointe. At some schools, students are slowly introduced to a full hour and fifteen minutes class on pointe on the theory that they will eventually dance almost entirely in pointe shoes and need to develop the endurance to do so early in their training. A more detailed description of how pointe education is integrated into the curricula of major training schools and private studios can be found in chapters 8 and 9.

SOME TIPS ON TEACHING POINTE

Dame Ninette de Valois once said, "When you are on your toes, keep off them." Failure to lift weight away from the hips results in toes being clenched and curled under instead of elongated and narrowed. Weight should be lifted out of the shoes and distributed throughout the body. Sinking down into the shoes causes stress and pain to foot joints and creates excessive wear on pointe shoes. (See chapter 9, "Sample Pointe Classes," for full notes on exercises for the first and second day on pointe and classes ranging from beginner to advanced levels.)

The teacher must guide the student to stand correctly on pointe, with the entire tip of the platform flatly touching the floor and the toes perpendicular to the floor. The foot should not be pushed back or pushed forward. The instep must be fully stretched to accomplish this. The teacher should be able to draw a straight line through the center of the hip, knee, ankle, and big toe joints when watching a student stand on pointe from a side view. From the front, the teacher should see a straight line from the hip, knee, and ankle joints through the box of the shoe between the second and third toes. Natalia Krassovska encourages beginning pointe students to look up and focus their eyes at eye level.

The teacher should stress working on both sides to avoid having students develop one foot more than another. This can be a particular problem with turns, where students tend to favor a "good" side. Remember that the way a student comes down from pointe is as important as the position she assumes on pointe.

A teacher should use correct language based on knowledge of the muscles, tendons, ligaments, and bones and how they operate. Do not try to teach pointe by using vague verbal images. Carefully educate the student about the mechanics of what they are learning. Encourage them to ask questions.

A teacher should look at each pointe student as an individual and not try to impose the same movement principles on everyone. If one student's foot structure is different than another's, she may need to carry her weight differently. Positions should not be forced; not all bodies can take it.

In *The Teaching of Classical Ballet,* Joan Lawson advocates teaching the student to find her own center of balance through the use of the spring. She explains that this center of balance falls between the first and second and sometimes third phalanges of the metatarsal arch.

After rising through quarter, half, and three-quarter pointe, the dancer makes a slight spring to reach the tips of her toes. If a dancer has long toes, this spring is taken sooner. It is a slightly backwards motion with toes going under the heel to cause the ankle and toes to stretch downward and outward so that the heel is not pulled backward into the Achilles tendon.

In · discussing the spring, Delores Lipinski of the Ruth Page Foundation School faculty points out that the English method of springing onto pointe by pulling the feet under is "nice and light" but does not work for students who have "banana feet" that lack strength. She feels that while springing tends to stretch out the foot and make it looser, rolling builds strength.

Advocates of rolling have students rise slowly to full pointe and roll back from the ball down through the heel, using the whole foot. The instep is developed as it raises and lowers the heel. Natalia Krassovska stresses the roll. She starts her students facing the barre and has them practice rolling up onto pointe. She does not teach beginners to spring. Joanna Kneeland also advocates the roll. She says the rise to pointe should require a minimal adjustment. It should be a smooth rather than jerky feeling. It is not a matter of springing and replacing the heel with the toe but of developing the strength needed to lower softly through the metatarsals. She says, "It is not the toes' job to jump under the body. The foot is the foundation and cannot be disturbed."

It is a good idea to videotape pointe classes so that students can observe their mistakes and also their progress. Tape allows students to see their feet in close-up. It also allows a teacher to see a mistake made by one student that might have been missed while attention was momentarily focused on another. Professionally made prerecorded tapes or those made with more advanced students at the studio can also be used to show students examples of a step being done correctly.

DAVID HOWARD'S PHILOSOPHY OF POINTE TRAINING

Master teacher David Howard's insights on pointe training are both provocative and informative.[3] The roots of Howard's movement philosophy are found in his study of kinesiology and twenty-two years spent observing dancers in the studio and in performance. He has his own syllabus which he has gleaned from various systems, incorporating the best features of all of them.

David Howard is particularly concerned with patterns of energy. He notes that while most people stand with two feet on the floor and pull the body up, he works from "up" first and thinks in terms of going through to a "down," then stretching away from the floor using the calf as a depressor rather than a pulling agent. He says the calf should push on the way up and push against the floor on the way down. It never changes its function as a muscle. According to Howard, if the calf is used as a pulling muscle, the knees lock and the natural coordination in the joint areas is gone. The calf must be thought of as a pushing muscle. When a person walks, he or she does not pull the calf but pushes through it every time.

This same dynamic must be applied to pointe. When it is, the dancer can achieve the quality of having pointe work appear to be an extension of the toe rather than a function of the box of the shoe. Most dancers resort to artistic camouflage to roll up and down on pointe. They roll up and down by pulling away from the floor instead of using the calf as a depressor to get them onto pointe. When the calf is used as a depressor on the way down, it offers great control since the muscles of the leg are being used as they were designed.

Howard believes that pointe work is an extension of natural movement. He feels that many teachers teach one thing at the barre and then expect their students to do something else in the center. They lock students into a different state at the barre and then scream at them when they do not move freely in the center. If bad patterns of energy are started at the barre, these patterns are inevitably going to be repeated in the center. But if the energy pattern is right, then the student will lift under the ankle, have a strong arch, and not knuckle.

The nature of pointe work is that it makes the body stiff. Howard finds that boys often progress in dance training more quickly than girls at the age when girls go on pointe. He thinks this is because traditional pointe training conspires to give a female dancer two straight stiff legs under a spastic body while boys are experiencing a greater range of motion. Although boys start later, they end up more coordinated.

Girls are always told their legs should be straight and pulled up, which they translate as stiff. Then when they move stiffly, they are "screamed at" to move. The emphasis should be on strong, stretched, and elongated rather than straight legs.

Howard observes that divers always have good feet because they stretch their feet instead of pointing them. They think of lengthening through the ankle and instep as much as possible, and a point is the result. Howard feels that "point your foot" is the right expression in terms of imagery but wrong in terms of teaching feelings. He explains that you don't point your feet. You lengthen them to the end of the extremity. You get energy to the end of extremity and then feel the stretch happen. Rather than pull and point, you push down to the end of your toes. Strength and length. It's not static. You need the energy flow. It's a circular action. It's straight in look but not in feeling. Demi-plié is down under and out and under up and through. It is a circular pattern in the knees and ankle joint. These areas have to sustain weight. They must go up to go down to stretch against the floor.

He cautions that a dancer should never go lower down than her calf can push in a demi-plié. She should feel as if she could thrust away from the floor without doing anything. The idea that the farther a dancer goes down, the farther she can go up is not valid according to his theory.

Howard stresses that he has not invented these concepts but is simply incorporating the way the body functions into ballet technique. He thinks ballet is trapped by its reliance on two-hundred-year-old ideas and is not taking advantage of contemporary knowledge about the body. He feels ballet has gone as far as it can go chained to these outdated practices. To reach another level, dancers and teachers have to be retrained to a different kind of understanding about body mechanics, with special stress on the pattern of energy that goes through the muscles. Without the proper pattern of energy, the dancer will struggle. Dancers have to turn away from learning by imitating and must deal with what they feel to gain strength and accomplish beautiful movement.

Howard sees gravity as the one obstacle to human movement, the "kiss of death" to a dancer. He says,

> if we use gravity as an aid rather than a harmful agent, we can use it to help us. If we push our energy down toward gravity and only stretch in the opposite direction, we are using gravity to help us. And if we are thrusting in a downward thrust to send the body away from the floor like a trampoline, then we are using gravity to help us. But if we are pulling the body away from the floor, we can never win. We can get certain height, but we cannot reach our fullest potential.

In other words, Howard suggests that we use rules of physics and nature to help us end up with much stronger, more elongated bodies and to accomplish things in the air. Otherwise we are relying on miracles, and as he observes, "sooner or later time runs out." Unless a dancer is working in harmony with nature, sooner or later something goes wrong.

He feels that Gelsey Kirkland and other dancers who have worked with him look different when they dance because their center of gravity is high. While their bone structure is up, their muscles are pushing down in opposition, resulting in a two-way energy pattern. Dancers using his method have the ability to release each area—the shoulders, the diaphragm, and stomach. They have flexibility in their hips and knees. Each of these factors contributes in taking the dancer onto pointe. The relevé comes from the torso to the foot. Pulling up in relevé produces hyperextension.

Howard notes that dancers are so determined and strong that they will find a way to stand on pointe even if their mothers glue their feet to the floor. Consequently, they continue to follow incorrect advice if that is what their teachers offer them. A few students survive in spite of teachers, by finding a way around what they are being taught in order to make things work.

To Howard, "pull up" is a look not a feel. In keeping with his philosophy of starting up and going down instead of starting down and going up, he begins pointe work with piqués at the barre rather than relevés. For the first two years he uses piqué plié rather than relevé plié.

Howard is not in favor of doing all classwork in pointe shoes because he thinks there is a lot of speed and flexibility to be gained from working on demi-pointe. He stresses that pointe work is only another level of ballet and not an individual discipline unto itself. Pointe work is a level the body can work from and not a matter of someone standing up on her toes.

Throughout his training process Howard creates exercises and combinations to build energy patterns, always stressing that energy must come from the torso through the bone structure to the ends of the extremities. He sees the body as an expressive instrument that has to act. Dance steps are not a series of frenzied movements but represent a need to communicate; they are a means of expression.

Howard feels that Katherine Healy is the purest realization of his training theory. Although Gelsey Kirkland, whom he describes as the greatest exponent of classical dance he has ever seen, was highly receptive to his concepts, Healy was much younger when she began working with him and reached an incredible level of technical and artistic achievement under his tutelage at a very early age. Howard believes that to train a dancer on pointe is to take something inherently artificial and transform it into genuine art.

POINTE TRAINING FOR ADULTS

The upper age limit for putting adults on pointe depends on how many hours a week they study, their general physical condition, muscular strength, and dedication. Patricia Klekovic, who teaches an adult pointe class at the Ruth Page School in Chicago, describes her students as "very brave ladies who have either had the dream of wanting to dance on pointe all their lives or have danced as children and wanted to experience the feeling again." She only allows them on pointe if they are taking a minimum of three classes a week and take a ballet class immediately before their pointe class. She never encourages adults to go on pointe and insists that it be completely their own decision. Klekovic notes that it is much easier for children to learn to work on pointe than it is for adults because adults have so much more weight on their ankles. Children also have less fear when confronting a challenge such as a pirouette on pointe.

Most of the women in the adult pointe class are fairly young, and few older women have made the request. However, one heavier older woman with big arches did express interest and was told she could go on pointe at her own risk. Klekovic insisted that this student do most of her work holding on to the barre. She feels that many of her adult pointe students cannot be injured because they are not exerting enough energy. Rather than trying to perfect their pointe technique, she allows them to move at their own pace.

Edith Royal also taught adult pointe in her studio in Orlando, Florida, and applied the same standards that she did to her beginning children's classes. Most of the students in these adult pointe classes were in their early twenties or thirties and were women who had studied dance until they attended college. They wanted to resume their ballet training both for physical conditioning and the satisfaction it afforded them. Royal insisted that they have the basic strength for pointe and take the same number of classes required for younger pointe students. Since these students were fairly skilled at basic technique from their past training, often they were able to become quite proficient at pointe.

POINTE TRAINING IN HIGHER EDUCATION

As dance becomes an ever-increasing presence in the college curriculum, the question of the role of pointe training at this level naturally arises. Since most serious female dance students have reached an advanced level by the age of fifteen and the average college graduate is twenty-one or twenty-two years of age, it is not reasonable to think of a college dance program as a likely training ground for major classical ballet companies.

Participants in college dance programs may range from serious majors undertaking the full dance curriculum as a preparation for performing or teaching careers to students who want to take several dance courses on an elective basis. They may arrive on campus with years of pointe training of varying quality or with no prior experience on pointe. The question of how best to serve these divergent populations in terms of pointe training is not a simple one to answer. A look at how pointe training is approached at the University of South Florida at Tampa under the direction of

Professors Gretchen Ward Warren and Sandra Robinson Waldrop offers some insight into how this issue may be handled.

Any student at the university who applies is admitted into the Fundamentals of Ballet course that meets twice a week for one semester. Students must audition for subsequent levels, Ballet I, II, III, or IV, and are placed according to their ability, regardless of their undergraduate status. They may remain at any level for three semesters, but cannot advance until judged ready.

Students in the performance track B.A. degree program are not formally accepted as dance majors until they have been placed in a level III (or IV) technique class. Once admitted to the program, either a ballet or modern emphasis is selected. The ballet major includes more pointe and variation requirements.

Pointe work is usually begun in Ballet II, a two-hour class that meets four times a week. For the last ten minutes of each class, the students work on simple exercises such as pliés and relevés facing the barre, échappés, bourrées, and, in the center, pas couru across the floor. Male students and students whose feet are deemed unsuitable for pointe work are excused from this part of class.

In Ballet III, which meets four times a week, more pointe work is part of the curriculum. Female students do a pointe barre twice a week and wear their pointe shoes for the last part of class on the other two days. The pointe exercises in the center alternate with men's work for the male students. In addition, many of the students in Ballet III also take a full pointe class on the fifth day of the week. The most advanced class, Ballet IV, meets five times a week with pointe work being integral to every class.

Warren and Robinson Waldrop created the program they are now following and established a syllabus designed to achieve their objectives. Their approach was influenced by their experiences at the Royal Ballet, American Ballet Theatre, North Carolina School of the Arts, and the Pennsylvania Ballet. They use the Vaganova system as a basis for their syllabus, but have added elements from the Bournonville, Balanchine, and Paris Opéra Ballet schools.

The University of South Florida approach offers a quick progression through the syllabus for the older dancer who is ready mentally as well as physically. A constant concern is balancing the students' physical readiness with their need to know the mechanics of the entire classical vocabulary.

Since students with professional body types are not generally attracted to college programs, the odds of producing professional dancers are not favorable. Warren and Robinson Waldrop estimate that they might see only three "good" bodies a year. The probability of producing accomplished pointe dancers is also unlikely, since few students have the "right" feet.

When a student with professional potential does appear, it is often only because his or her parents insisted on college before thinking about a professional career. Unfortunately, such students often spend four years without the stimulus of meaningful competition. There is also the rare possibility of a student with professional potential who is genuinely intellectually curious. One such academically gifted student was immediately hired after graduation as a soloist by Charleston Ballet Theatre, and another, who graduated with a minor in psychology, joined the Tampa Ballet.

When advising dance majors about their future potential, Warren and Robinson Waldrop try to point them in an honest direction. Depending on each individual's strength, they may suggest auditioning for a small company, teaching, or graduate school, for those who show talent as choreographers or writers.

They have found that some students who begin ballet in college may not advance at all due to lack of physical facility rather than age. On the other hand, many students learn to do the most with what they have. For instance, Warren and Robinson Waldrop had a student who lacked the necessary hyper-mobility in her ankle joints to allow her to stand fully vertical on pointe. She was a trained dancer who moved well and had nicely developed legs. They were able to help her learn to work her feet to their maximum potential, but there was little they could do to change the inherent limitations caused by the body structure of her feet.

The expense of pointe shoes is a real stumbling block for students in the program. Since many are working to pay for their educations, the added burden of paying for pointe shoes is a great strain. Consequently, they often work in broken shoes or cannot afford to experiment widely enough to find the right fit.

POINTE TRAINING FOR MEN

Whether it is useful for male students to study pointe is an area in which there is wide disagreement. Men may be interested in experimenting with pointe because they wish to strengthen their feet. Or they may plan on teaching pointe at some time in the future and want to have firsthand knowledge of the process. Or they may be part of a performing ensemble such as Les Ballets Trockadero de Monte Carlo, which requires pointe work.

Associate Professor Richard Sias, at Florida State University at Tallahassee, feels that pointe training offers male students a whole level of stretch not possible on demi-pointe or in ballet shoes. Rodney Irwin, who teaches pas de deux at the Ruth Page School in Chicago, thinks a male who has experienced pointe finds it easier to understand the problems of his female partner. He also believes it helps a male choreographer understand the limits of pointe work.

Mikhail Messerer, ballet master for the Royal Swedish Ballet and the Munich Opera Ballet at the time of our research, thinks pointe training for men is sensible if they can find pointe shoes that will not damage their feet. Messerer trained at the Bolshoi School, where men took pointe classes for strength and better balance. Joanna Kneeland, however, doubts that pointe shoes build strength in men that they cannot gain through other exercises. And a concern of those opposed to men's pointe training is that men may be heavier on their ankles and feet, which could result in injury.

One of the major drawbacks for American men who wish to experiment with pointe is the problem of finding shoes that fit properly. Since most stock shoes are not made above a woman's size 8 or 8 1/2 and are frequently not wide enough for men's feet, most men cannot find stock shoes that fit them. Consequently they have to order custom shoes, an uncertain, expensive, and time-consuming proposition.

Dancer Anton Wilson began pointe work to strengthen his feet while a student at Towson State University. He initially wore stock Capezio Pavlowas in size 8 1/2 D, and to give his feet extra support he elongated the vamp with pink denim. After finishing his education at the North Carolina School for the Arts, he joined Les Ballets Trockadero de Monte Carlo, the all-male ballet company that performs the classics and original works with men performing women's roles in female dress. The members of the Trockadero are classically trained dancers who perform on pointe and are also skilled comedians. Once in the company, Wilson had his shoes custom made and began wearing 8 1/4 E Contempora. The squarer box gave his toes more room.

However, he suffered from a large number of blisters when he began pointe and encountered a major problem with bruised toenails. He had a toenail removed and was in constant pain from the pressure of the shoes on his nails. Even the weight of a bed sheet became excruciating. His nails also hurt in flat shoes, and he dreaded the thought of performances because of this condition.

On the positive side, Wilson's performing experience on pointe gave him new respect for female pointe dancers and a more thorough understanding of partnering. He discovered new muscles in his calves and thighs when he danced on pointe and also learned valuable lessons about pulling up out of his legs.

NOTES

1. Howse, Justin. *Dance Technique and Injury Prevention.* (New York: Theatre Arts Books, 1988), p. 59.

2. Sparger, Celia. *Anatomy and Ballet.* (New York: Theatre Arts Books, 1970), p. 121.

3. Information attributed to David Howard in this chapter was gathered during an interview at his studio, May 19, 1989.

In addition to the teachers referred to throughout the chapter, material on the basics of teaching pointe was gathered by survey from teachers across the country. Teachers surveyed were asked at what age they placed students on pointe, what determined pointe readiness, which shoes they suggested, how they integrated pointe into their curriculum, how much time was spent on pointe per week, and what kinds of exercises they used in beginning pointe classes. Additional material was gathered on location at the schools profiled in chapter 8.

8

Profiles of Pointe Training Methods

POINTE TRAINING IN COMPANY SCHOOLS

The Royal Ballet School (London, England)

The Royal Ballet School, which celebrated its fiftieth birthday in 1981, consists of a Lower School for children between the ages of eleven and sixteen, housed in White Lodge in Richmond Park, Surrey, and an Upper School, for students aged sixteen and over, closer to central London at Barron's Court. Both White Lodge and the Upper School were under the direction of Katie Wade at the time of our research. The Royal Ballet School is not to be confused with the Royal Academy of Dance, which is a teacher-training institution with its own syllabus and system.

While the Royal Ballet School's graduates enter many ballet companies in Britain and Europe, the main purpose of the training program is to provide dancers for the Royal Ballet and the Sadler's Wells Royal Ballet. Entrance to the Lower School is by preliminary auditions held throughout Britain and a final London audition, which is highly competitive. Students must be eleven years old to be admitted, and they come from all over the world. Potential talent and physical suitability are both considered. While foreign students have to pay for their schooling, British students can be assisted with grants. No one who is eligible to attend has ever been turned away because they could not pay.

There are 125 male and female students at White Lodge, many of whom board at the school. While entering students take only one ballet class a day, by the time they leave the school they will be taking seventeen hours of dance classes a week. In addition to the dance syllabus, children also pursue their academic studies. Since many students drop out of the program along the way, the size of the classes decreases greatly by the end of the seven-year process. The school year runs from September to July.

While the Royal Ballet School students were formerly tested by outside

Cecchetti examiners, this is no longer the case. Individual teachers formulate their own classes, but the school tends to stress the Vaganova method. Accordingly, the first three years at the Lower School are spent in a slow training regimen that stresses repetition. Students go on pointe about halfway through their first term at White Lodge. Initially the girls wear their pointe shoes once or twice a week. Younger students often look to older students for advice about pointe work.

Christine Beckley is the ballet teacher who oversees the entire shoe-fitting process for every student in the Lower School. Beckley is deeply involved in helping each student select the proper shoe for his or her foot and determining what changes are needed in shoes as the student progresses. White Lodge students wear Freed pointe shoes and Gamba ballet shoes. Beckley teaches the students to darn their shoes and attach their ribbons. During their years at White Lodge, students wear lamb's wool. White Lodge students also wear uniforms for both their dance and academic classes. They are not allowed to wear makeup, jewelry, plastic pants, flashy colored leotards, or leg warmers.

The Upper School shares its studios with the Royal Ballet Company, and students are encouraged to observe the rehearsal process, which is helpful for those who eventually join the company. Graduates of White Lodge and students from other British and foreign schools complete their final training in a nonresidential setting. The curriculum includes classical ballet, character dance, pas de deux, contemporary dance, notation, singing, drama, stage makeup, variations from repertory, music appreciation, art appreciation, and dance composition. There are also student exchanges with the Paris Opéra School, the Royal Danish Ballet School, and the Peking Dance Academy.

When students transfer to the Upper School, they can wear any shoes they wish and are not limited to Freeds. Instead, they are encouraged to experiment. Students in the advanced classes at White Lodge and at the Upper School wear deshanked pointe shoes for ballet classes. Upper School students use floor wax instead of darning their shoes. Many of the students use newspaper instead of lamb's wool in their pointe shoes, and others use masking tape.

Paris Opéra Ballet School (Paris, France)

Claude Bessy, director of the Paris Opéra Ballet School since 1972, oversees a magnificent training facility that includes twelve dance studios, academic classrooms, and dormitories. The school, in existence since the reign of Louis XIV, is funded by a foundation.

Students are accepted into the school at the age of nine. They may be beginners or students who have studied elsewhere before applying to the Paris Opéra. Great emphasis is placed upon accepting students with perfect bodies. The school prefers students to have a long Achilles tendon to allow a very deep plié as well as a high instep with a flexible ankle. Successful candidates should also have natural turnout.

Once accepted at the school, students live there during the week and spend their weekends at home with parents. A typical school day finds them in academic classes in the morning and dance classes in the after-noon.

The majority of the students who enroll in the school complete six years of training there and then enter the Opéra Ballet. Exams are administered at the end of each year to determine which students are qualified to continue in the program. Those students who do not enter the Opéra Ballet may seek work in other countries or decide not to pur-sue professional careers.

Pointe is introduced into the curriculum in the second year, when the children are strong enough to work on demi-pointe and on one foot. At the beginning of the year, students have a full class off pointe, then put on pointe shoes and return to the barre. As students progress through the second year, they graduate to doing pointe exercises in the center.

No particular style or make of shoe is suggested, and each student is encouraged to find the shoe best suited to her foot. Shoes are fitted in dance shops and then brought to the school for final approval.

The use of elastic on pointe is frowned upon since the staff believes that correctly fitted shoes and adequately strong feet should provide enough support without it. Students use Kleenex and cotton in their shoes but are not allowed to wear anything synthetic.

The school requests that students use old pointe shoes for class rather than soft ballet slippers, which are called demi-pointe shoes. Demi-pointe shoes are only worn by very young students, or for occasional rehearsals, or in the event of injury.

Royal Swedish Ballet School (Stockholm, Sweden)

The Opera Ballet School was inaugurated in Sweden by King Gustav III in 1773 and until 1981 offered classes after regular school hours. However, in 1981 the school's traditions and resources were transferred to the municipal school system of Stockholm, under the authority of the Board of Education and renamed the Royal Swedish Ballet School. While the Royal Swedish Ballet School maintains close contact with the Royal Opera Theatre, it now integrates traditional academic studies with dance education, a goal achieved after years of planning and discussion.

Royal Swedish Ballet School provides professional dance training to the Royal Ballet and other ballet companies in Sweden and around the world as well as offering dance education to those interested in allied dance professions such as teaching and choreography.

The school, directed by Gosta Svalberg at the time of this research, offers a six-year comprehensive program and a two-year gymnasium (high school) program. It is located in an impressive facility which contains nine studios, academic classrooms, and a charming 260-seat theater.

Auditions are held every March for entry into the school, which strives to have an equal number of girls and boys. Boys currently make up about 45 percent of their enrollment of one hundred girls and eighty-five boys. Students can enter the school at the beginning of any year, but are encouraged to start at age nine or ten for the best results. Students entering during the first six years usually come from the Stockholm area, but those who enter during the final two gymnasium years may come from other parts of Sweden or outside the country. Such students live in dorm facilities, while most students live at home throughout their schooling. Due to illness, a shift in interest, or a family move, students drop out of the program and are replaced by others each fall. As a consequence, class size can fall to eight or nine students.

Most entering classes of nine- and ten-year-olds have about thirty-two students. Boys and girls study dance in separate classes. This is due to both technical and social considerations. The school is sensitive to the fact that boys may initially advance more slowly than girls and doesn't want to subject boys to feeling "silly" in a co-ed class. Also, a concerted effort is made to provide boys with challenging, male-oriented dance training and repertory.

Academic classes are taken with children from the dance program, and from other programs as well, broadening the children's social contacts. By the time the students are fifteen, they are taking nineteen hours of dance classes a week in addition to their academic load. However, their academic teachers are well aware of the nature of their special interest and are involved in the curriculum planning process. Issues such as rehearsal and performance schedules are discussed by the total faculty. The faculty finds that dance and academics seem to reinforce each other here, with both motivating students to care about their schooling.

Since the school is part of the Swedish public school system, tuition is free. Students wear standardized uniforms but must supply their own leotards and tights.

Shoes are provided free of charge. The school tries to find the right pointe shoes for each student and makes a variety of brands available, including Freed, Gamba, Capezio, and K.H. Martins. A staff member handles all shoe purchasing and distribution for the student body, which is a more difficult job than in a traditional ballet company because of constantly growing and changing feet.

Girls go on pointe at age nine or ten after three months in the school, beginning very slowly at the barre with both hands. Their rate of progress is determined by their individual strength.

Students have one teacher for their first two years, then usually stay with a teacher for one-year periods until their gymnasium years when they again stay with one teacher for two years. For the first two years, students take ballet class for one and a half hours, five times a week. They also take an improvisation class and a gymnastic-acrobatic class weekly. The acrobatic class is popular with the boys as well as the girls since it allows them freedom at a time when precise, limited movement is stressed in their ballet classes.

Character classes are introduced in the second year and are continued until graduation. Modern and jazz training are introduced in the fourth year and repertory classes start in the fifth year. Students are often taught repertory being performed by the Royal Swedish Ballet at the Opera House so they can substitute for corps members. In the sixth year, they begin pas de deux work once a week and then add an additional pas de deux class the last two years.

The school has its own syllabus that the staff created, but students are exposed to a variety of styles as they progress to an advanced level. Most of the teachers have been professional dancers in Sweden, although teachers from other professional backgrounds have taught at the school as well.

At the time of our research, Marianne Orlando, who was a prima ballerina with the Royal Swedish Ballet and also danced with American Ballet Theatre, taught the female students during their last two years at the school. Orlando trained at the Opera Ballet School from the age of eight and studied in Russia and Hungary. Consequently she is anchored by the Swedish tradition but is also able to enrich her students' training with her diverse experiences.

Orlando's students were sixteen years old and took class for an hour and a half, six times a week. At the beginning of the gymnasium year, she gave twenty to thirty minutes of pointe at the end of each class. As the year progressed, she built up to giving one full pointe class a week. She taught a combination of springing and rolling. Since Orlando believed that muscles should do the work for beginning dancers, she felt hard shoes dangerous and encouraged students to work in lighter footwear.

As Svalberg explained, some classes at the school are like fine wine from a particularly good vintage. Others are not as good. However, because of the public school setting, the teachers' mission is to treat every student with the same concern whether they appear destined for a professional career or not. The school believes that dance training is never wasted and offers extensive benefits in later life.

School of American Ballet (New York City)

Located at Lincoln Center Plaza, the School of American Ballet is financially supported by private and public sources. Nathalie Gleboff is executive director of SAB, and Peter Martins is chairman of the faculty. At the end of their SAB schooling, many students are taken into the New York City Ballet Company with which SAB is affiliated. Ninety percent of the dancers in the company are trained at SAB. The rest of the graduates are found in other major American and European companies.

Students are admitted to the school through auditions. General physical qualities sought are long legs, narrow knees, high insteps, long necks, small heads, and natural turnout.

The school has five children's divisions, and children are admitted between the ages of eight and nine. Students are placed on pointe in January of their first year of study. At that time they get fifteen minutes of pointe at the end of their regular three weekly hour-and-a-half technique classes. By the fifth year, they are taking four hour-and-a-half ballet classes a week and a one-hour pointe class a week.

There is a Parallel Division of ten- to twelve-year old beginners who start pointe classes during their third year with one hour a week. Stronger children in this division may start in their second year. In this program, students take three classes a week the first year and six classes a week the following year to allow them to catch up with the students in the Children's Division.

As the students enter the intermediate level, the Children's and Parallel divisions merge. In the intermediate level, the students take six ballet classes and two pointe classes a week. By the time they move to the Advanced Division they are taking a total of ten classes a week. Students are evaluated at the end of each year and after the age of fourteen may be encouraged to take as many as twelve classes a week or eighteen hours of class work plus rehearsals for a workshop performance in the spring.

SAB students wear a special shoe called the "Balanchine Shoe" that was originally manufactured for the school by Capezio at George Balanchine's request. It is softer than the typical student shoe and designed to encourage the dancer to work her feet. It has a very flexible shank, short pleats, and a slightly lower vamp with light boxing.

SAB also offers a summer program for gifted students twelve years of age and over from around the country at the intermediate and advanced levels. Regional auditions are held around the country for this summer course. A thorough knowledge of fundamental ballet positions and exercises is required. Applicants are expected to have well-proportioned, flexible, coordinated bodies, good turnout, and high insteps. They cannot be overweight and must be at a stage of technical advancement appropriate for their age. The summer course includes work in academic ballet, pointe, variations, adagio, and character.

School of Classical Ballet (New York City)

The School of Classical Ballet is an intensive training program instituted in 1988 by American Ballet Theatre at their headquarters on Broadway and Nineteenth Street to shape young talent to serve the company's specific stylistic demands. As artistic director of the company during the school's formative phase, Mikhail Baryshnikov was actively involved in the planning and development of the curriculum, which is strongly influenced by the teachings of Agrippina Vaganova, the Soviet ballet theorist who synthesized international ballet styles. Martha Rosenthal, a former administrator at SAB, serves as the school's director.

All students are on full or partial scholarship; half of the school's $550,000 annual budget is used for this purpose. Classes include technique, variations, and character dancing. The regular faculty includes four Russian-trained teachers who also teach company class for ABT.

Regional auditions are held around the country for a summer session and particularly gifted students are invited to join the year-round program. The school plans to maintain two class levels with a total of fifteen students.

Prospective students are required to have strong feet and legs and "potential." Current students range in age from thirteen to nineteen and come from thirteen states and Puerto Rico. They live at approved homes or share apartments. If they do not have a high school diploma, they must finish their schooling at the Professional Children's School. A combined academic-ballet class day typically lasts from 7:45 A.M. until 4:00 P.M.

Houston Ballet Academy (Houston, Texas)

The Houston Ballet Academy is housed in a large, two-story building which it shares with the Houston Ballet. Ben Stevenson serves as artistic director of both the Houston Ballet and the Houston Ballet Academy. Rosemary Miles, principal of the Ballet Academy at the time of our research, supervised the eight-level program. Students who reach levels 7 and 8 are judged by the school's staff to have the potential to function at a professional level either as dancers or choreographers. The school typically provides 75 percent of the Houston Ballet's company members.

Students begin in a class called Creative Dance and do not start Ballet 1 until they are seven years old. Ballet 1 and 2 meet once a week. Ballet 3 twice a week, Ballet 4 three times a week, and Ballet 5 and 6 four times a week. The students at the seventh and eighth levels take class every day. Ballet 8 students attend from 9 A.M. until 3:00 P.M. daily.

Throughout the training process, students proceed through the program on an individual basis. They are not automatically moved from level to level but are evaluated on the basis of physical and emotional readiness. Parents are encouraged to watch class twice a year to help them understand how their children are progressing. As a child matures, her body type may lessen her chances for a professional career. Such students are guided away from a performing career and steered toward other alternatives. Students with professional potential are advised to forgo a university education until they have established their professional careers.

Students go on pointe in level 4, where they have two half-hour pointe classes a week. In Ballet 5 and 6, the students have two forty-five minute pointe classes a week. Ballet 7 students add a pas de deux class to the schedule. Ballet 8 students have a daily hour and forty-five minute technique class plus three one-hour pointe classes a week and a one-hour pas de deux class. They also have four hour-and-a-half rehearsals for their graduation performance for which they wear pointe shoes.

Pointe classes generally follow technique classes. The upper levels have a fifteen-minute break between classes, but the younger classes do not. Older students can take whole technique classes on pointe, but younger students are not allowed to do this because of the potential for injury. Forcing is avoided throughout the program of study in favor of slow, careful progress toward using the body to its maximum capability.

Children beginning pointe are introduced to both the roll and spring since the staff feels that the roll (going up through the top of the foot and the top of the pointe shoe so that the instep is lifted and rolling through the foot) strengthens the foot and ankle, which allows the dancer to spring without wobble or give.

Teachers at the academy use a combination of Cecchetti and RAD methods but do not follow a set class syllabus. Since Rosemary Miles is English, she recommends that her students wear either Freeds or Gambas. Academy students are allowed to use elastic on their shoes.

San Francisco Ballet School (San Francisco, California)

Helgi Tomasson is the artistic director of the San Francisco Ballet and San Francisco Ballet School. Nancy Johnson Carter served as manager of the school at the time of our research. The school offers classes in technique, pointe, men's work, pas de deux, modern dance, and character dancing.

Students are accepted at age eight into a graduated curriculum with eight levels and must attend at least two classes a week. Progress is evaluated twice a year. Advanced students may be invited to join the company for one transitional year as apprentices. There is also an adult ballet program which does not offer pointe classes.

As a result of regional auditions, there are a large number of new students at the school each summer. San Francisco Ballet competes with SAB and other major schools for these students, whom they consider "the cream of the crop."

There are eight graded levels of ballet. Pointe usually starts at the third level, depending on individual readiness. By this level, students take six classes a week. Three of these are designated for pointe, but each teacher decides how much time students actually spend on pointe. Each level has a "homeroom" teacher; this teacher gives technique classes and other instructors teach special classes such as pas de deux and character. At level 8, students wear their pointe shoes for all technique classes, although some wear them de-shanked. Students at level 7 are encouraged to do the same.

Faculty member Jocelyn Vollmer described an advanced pointe class that would follow an hour-and-a-half technique class. The pointe class begins with a short barre including a few relevés, échappés, piqués, rolling up and rolling through the foot, and springing up. She keeps the class in the center most of the time to discourage reliance on the barre.

Fifty percent of the fifty-four dancers in the company come from the school. Six students a year are selected to serve as apprentices for one year, taking company class, rehearsing, and performing with the company. Following this year, they may be invited to join the company.

POINTE TRAINING IN PRIVATE STUDIOS

STEPS (New York City)

STEPS, a private dance studio located at Broadway and Seventy-fourth Street, offers classes in ballet for students ages six to adult. Pointe work is taught in the Children's Program, Young People's Program, and open classes.

Nancy Bielski taught STEPS' youngest students at the time of our 1998 research. Children start pointe at the age of ten and eleven in Ballet V, the highest Children's Ballet class, twice a week. Bielski begins with five minutes of exercises at the barre, such as holding onto the barre with two hands while slowly rising in both parallel and turned-out position. She also includes foot-stretching exercises like rolling up to pointe, or working with one knee over the other to stretch the ankle.

Through slow rises and demi-pointe work, emphasis is placed on the proper use of the foot—how to get up and down without jumping or dropping. Pliés and relevés are avoided because beginners tend to jump while trying these movements on pointe. Posture is also stressed because beginning pointe students tend to stick their stomachs out and bend their knees while looking at the floor. Pointe helps ballet students understand the importance of being pulled up and having stretched thighs and straight knees.

Bielski tries to do a complete pointe barre after six weeks, as long as the girls are strong enough. She includes preparation for bourrées early on and soon progresses to walking across the center on pointe and two-foot relevés in center. Students are also taught grands battements en pointe in the center, although few can execute them successfully at first. This gives students a chance to practice balancing without having to rely on relevé and requires that they hold their arms and backs correctly while trying to maneuver their legs. The movement might be done à la seconde, moving forward or en croix from fifth. Grands battements en pointe give the students a sense of where their bodies are in relationship to their legs. If a class is ready, students also do relevés, passés, and pirouettes in the center. These preparations lead to pas de bourées and both relevés and piqués (first at the barre, then in center).

Bielski suggests Capezios for her beginning students. Sometimes she suggests the Balanchine shoe that the School of American Ballet uses, but since these are a custom order, she allows the students to use other Capezio shoes. Freeds are considered unsuitable for beginners because students seem to have difficulty getting up straight on pointe in them. Bielski also teaches her students how to prepare and wear their shoes properly. Students at STEPS may wear lamb's wool and are encouraged to tape their toes with adhesive tape.

Daniel Catanach, Artistic Director of Catanach Ballet Theater who has been on the faculty of several New York studios, teaches in the teen intermediate and advanced ballet program at STEPS. He evaluates each student's skills before he allows them to go up on pointe during class. Catanach sees intermediate students twice a week for a 1 1/2-hour class with a 1/2-hour pointe class following.

Many advanced students at STEPS aspire to become professional dancers. They have a weekly, one-hour warm-up class followed by a one-hour choreography workshop on pointe. They also have a weekly, two-hour class which includes pointe and partnering, followed by a one-hour partnering choreography workshop on pointe.

Because a professional dancer might be required to do anything on pointe, Catanach feels that, with the exception of relevés and echappés at the barre, class becomes the same as a daily ballet class. He encourages advanced students to work in Freed pointe shoes, which force the muscles to develop to the strength needed for rehearsals and performances.

Kathryn Sullivan, a former dancer with Les Grands Ballets Canadiens and Boston Ballet, teaches pointe classes for the open professional and adult classes at STEPS. She focuses on pointe skills that are not usually a part of a regular ballet class on pointe. These include stretching and strengthening of the feet and specific pointe vocabulary such as bourrées, echappés, and piqués. There are three class levels—beginner (one-half hour), advanced beginner (one-half hour, twice/week), and intermediate (full hour class) focusing on pointe vocabulary.

Sullivan's students may include professional dancers seeking a clearer understanding of pointe work skills, musical theater dancers preparing for a specific audition, or adult dancers who did not have pointe as children. Dancers often take the pointe classes before ballet class to warm up their feet.

Sullivan recommends Capezio shoes for their range of styles, or Gaynor Minden, for durability and for students with very flexible feet.

Ruth Page Foundation School (Chicago, Illinois)

The Ruth Page Foundation School, directed by Larry Long, has as its goal the production of dancers who can easily assimilate the style of various major companies. Long describes the school's curriculum as an American application of a Russian approach.

Students start pointe work at the intermediate (Ballet 4) level, when they are taking four classes a week. Children are evaluated for pointe based on individual readiness and are not placed on pointe "en masse," but when each is mentally and physically ready to accept the challenge. No student is placed on pointe before age ten. The school feels that once a child is strong enough, progress on pointe will be rapid.

During the first year on pointe, students take one pointe class a week that follows a technique class. The staff finds an entire pointe class more useful to the student than relegating a portion of a technique class to pointe. During the second year, if they have not encountered any problems on pointe, students take one pointe class a week at a more advanced level. If they need to work on stretching their feet or gaining strength, they repeat beginning pointe and also take the second-year class. During the third year on pointe, students take a second-level and a third-level pointe class. When they enter the advanced class, they take an advanced pointe class and an intermediate pointe class. When the director feels they are strong enough, students take a pas de deux class. A special adult pointe class is also offered.

Beginning pointe students wear Capezios, with the staff favoring Contempora for those with wide feet and Nicolini for narrower feet. Suede-tipped shoes are not allowed, but extremely soft shoes are also avoided for beginners. Parents are oriented to expect to buy at least three pairs of shoes from September to June if their child is taking one pointe class a week. They are told they may have to buy more than three pairs if their child has a problem finding the correct shoes.

Neubert Ballet Institute (New York City)

The Neubert Ballet Institute, founded by Christine Neubert and now directed by Ellen Moran, offers classes for professional dancers and children in Studio 819 of Carnegie Hall. Students enter by audition and are rarely placed on pointe prior to their eleventh birthdays since it is the institute's belief that premature pointe work can be harmful.

Faculty members accompany students to their first fittings and teach the children how to prepare their shoes and take proper care of their feet. Students at the institute do not use lamb's wool, but protect sensitive areas with moleskin and a skin-hardening substance called New Skin that is available in drugstores. Students are allowed to sew elastic on their shoes since it is felt that a dancer can develop hammertoes trying to hold her shoes on with the toes.

Beginning pointe students work for fifteen minutes on pointe at the barre at the end of each of their three regular hour-and-a-half technique classes. Early exercises emphasize rolling up on pointe and simple tendus. During their second year on pointe, students are expected to take four classes a week. Two of these are two-hour classes that include thirty minutes of pointe, and two are regular hour-and-a-half technique classes. The Neubert Institute keeps class size as small as possible to ensure that all the students in each class are at the same level of development.

POINTE TRAINING IN RUSSIA

Since the collapse of the Soviet Union, dance training in Russia has both changed and remained the same.

There were no private dance studios in the Soviet Union. Early dance training was offered at local recreation centers called Palaces of the Pioneers whose teachers were usually former members of major Russian ballet companies or graduates of state-sponsored teacher-training programs. Dance classes at the palaces were generally offered three times a week and were part of a broad spectrum of classes in all the arts. They were for enjoyment and an understanding of the arts rather than for professional training.

Students with a special interest in dance were auditioned for major company schools at the age of ten. Entrance requirements were rigorous, and students had to show exceptional promise and meet exacting physical standards. Only those having what has been defined as a perfect dancer's body could be admitted.

These resident schools offered a combination of classical ballet training and academics. The first classes, which began early in the morning, were classical ballet and, as a student advanced, pointe, variations, and pas de deux. Academic courses were offered until seven or eight in the evening. Homework was done in the evenings. Ballet students also took classes in character, historical dance, acting, mime, piano, history of dance, theater and music, music appreciation, painting, sculpture, and stage makeup.

Yearly examinations were given in every subject from the third grade until graduation, and students had to pass all examinations in order to move on to the next grade. They could be dropped at the school's discretion, and few who were dismissed continued dancing.

Larisa Sklyanskaya, who was trained in the Bolshoi School and was a member of the company for fifteen years before emigrating to the United States and joining the San Francisco Ballet faculty (the position she held at the time of our initial research), suggested that many American training schools for serious classical ballet students suffer from a lack of this unity in professional and academic education. For example, she felt that students who arrived at the San Francisco Ballet School late in the afternoon after a full day of conventional academic schooling lacked the right kind of energy to derive the fullest benefit from their ballet classes.

Victoria Schneider completed the Methodology Program at the Vaganova Academy of Ballet in St. Petersburg from 1993-1995 and is now program coordinator and ballet faculty member at the Harid Conservatory in Boca Raton, Florida. She notes that dance studios owned by individuals now exist in Russia. The social/sports clubs called Cultural Institutes, where regular students study dance, continue as they had before the fall of communism.

Schneider explains that company schools still teach the syllabus and implement it as she has read they had historically. These company schools, however, have a much harder time economically because they are not sufficiently supported by the government. They are forced to find private and/or corporate funding, or form joint ventures with people interested in opening businesses in Russia.

According to Schneider, teachers at the company schools are still mostly graduates of pedagogy programs, but those programs are now four years long instead of two years. This change reflects their new academy status which enables a new quality of education for the teachers with a higher diploma status. (The Bolshoi had this status before the dissolution of the Soviet Union.) Most programs that included foreign teachers have been eliminated because it became too difficult for the schools to maintain them.

Agrippina Vaganova began training teachers in 1921 and graduated her first class in 1924. Since that time her system has been passed down and disseminated by teachers throughout Russia. The Vaganova method is stilled used uniformly throughout Russia, in some form, for training classical ballet dancers, according to Schneider.

Vaganova combined concepts from the Danish, French, Italian, and Russian schools and codified ballet movement into a basic system of uniform guidelines for executing each component. Although the Bolshoi and the Kirov schools produce dancers who are quite different stylistically, their underlying technique is based on the Vaganova system. While the Bolshoi's image is to project the technique in broader strokes with more emphasis on big movement, it has its roots in the same training method as that used by the drier, more conservative Kirov.

As a student of Bournonville and Cecchetti techniques, Vaganova became a funnel for their ideas, combining the best elements of each. Her goal was to develop a logical system based on a perfect body order that would build dancers who could evoke both strength and lightness. She emphasized the importance of the torso, not only the legs and feet.

In the Vaganova system there are seven pointe exercises in grade 1. They are learned at the barre and carried to the center. According to Sklyanskaya, the Vaganova system teaches both the roll and spring, but starts with the spring to build lightness and strength. The roll is not introduced as early on the theory that it can result in injury to the untrained muscles in the thigh.

Schneider, who began her study of the Vaganova system in 1987, feels she has only seen the spring up/spring down, taught—never the roll up as it is taught in the United States. She feels that what Russians consider a roll down is not the one taught elsewhere.

In Russia, after their early training years, students generally wear pointe shoes with the shank removed rather than soft ballet shoes for flat work, since many feel that soft slippers do not give adequate support. In interpreting that practice for her American students, Sklyanskaya thought beginners should wear soft ballet slippers until grade 4 and then switch over to de-shanked pointe shoes.

Sklyanskaya believed that as a result of increased contact between the United States and Russia, the Russians are starting to stress thin bodies, high extensions, and physical appearance. This shift may have an impact on the schools' values as well.

In recent years, a number of exponents of the Vaganova method have been offering workshops on the system in the United States. Sklyanskaya stressed the importance of carefully checking the credentials of anyone offering such a workshop. The method is quite complex and should only be taught by someone who has been through the full training program and gained a complete command of the mechanics involved.

9

Sample Pointe Classes

While traveling across the United States and to Europe to gather information for this book, we had the opportunity to observe many wonderful pointe classes. Each of these classes had something unique and important to offer.

Because many of the teachers we surveyed indicated an interest in knowing how other instructors teach the various levels of pointe classes, we thought we would choose a representative sampling of exercises offered in some of the schools we visited. These exercises were notated by Janice Barringer.

The following abbreviations are used throughout this chapter:

B+	Balanchine coined this phrase, meaning that the back foot is tendu derrière with both ankles touching.
bk	back
ft	foot
frt	front
L	left
pt	pointe
R	right
xs	number of times, with 4xs meaning four times

References to the fixed points of the practice room and term definitions have been drawn from the third edition of Gail Grant's *Technical Manual and Dictionary of Classical Ballet* (New York: Dover Books, 1982).

BEGINNER CLASSES

First Day on Pointe, School of American Ballet

This segment is typical of a first pointe class; it takes place the last fifteen minutes of an hour-and-a-half ballet class.

BARRE

Exercise 1

Standing in parallel or natural position with both hands on the barre: Roll slowly $\overset{1\,2\,3\,4}{}$ up through the metatarsal to full pointe, roll down. Repeat 4xs. $\overset{5\,6\,7\,8}{}$

Exercise 2

Same as above except in 1st position.

Exercise 3

From 1st position: Roll up slowly to pointe, plié pushing out the instep, straighten legs, roll back down to 1st. Repeat 4xs.

Exercise 4

From 1st position: Press up to full pointe, hold, roll down to 1st. Repeat 8xs. Can be repeated in 2d position.

Exercise 5

From 1st position: Tendu R ft à la seconde, bring back to 1st in demi-plié, tendu L à la seconde, demi-plié in 1st, tendu R à la seconde, hold, bring back to 1st in demi-plié. Repeat 4xs.

Exercise 6

4th position, R ft frt: Rise to full pointe, press heel forward and release, press forward and release, roll down to 4th. Repeat and then same with L ft frt.

Exercise 7

5th position, R ft frt: Rise to full pointe, pull legs closely together, roll down. Repeat 4xs. Same with L.

Exercise 8

1st position, L hand on barre: Rise to pointe and walk down length of barre, turn to barre and return.

Second Day on Pointe, School of American Ballet

During this fifteen-minute segment, the instructor repeated continually that students must have an "excellent" position of the feet, meaning a nicely turned-out position. She would say, "try to stretch the arch" as she took a foot in her hand and pressed the heel forward. Other instructions were, "don't look down; stretch all your toes; chin up; push your foot more, and more, more, more!"

BARRE

Exercise 1

1st position facing barre: Tendu R à la seconde, demi-plié in 1st, tendu L à la seconde, demi-plié in 1st, tendu R à la seconde, hold, demi-plié in 1st and straighten. Same to L and repeat.

Exercise 2

1st position facing barre: Rise to full pointe, hold, hold, roll down off pointe. Execute 8xs.

Exercise 3

Same as exercise 2, but in 2d position.

Exercise 4

Same as exercise 2, but in 4th position. R ft frt first, then L ft frt.
   The teacher took great care that the students pressed the heels forward.

Exercise 5

Same as exercise 2, but in 5th, and being sure to bring legs together into a tight 5th position in the rise. R ft frt first, then L ft frt.

CENTER

Exercise 1

Changement 16 xs.

Révérence.

   The teacher says, "Good-bye, girls," and they all reply, "Thank you."

Advanced Beginner Pointe Class, Ruth Page Foundation School

This class, inspired by Patricia Klekovic, is given at the end of the first year or beginning of the second and is done in ¾ time.

BARRE

Exercise 1

Facing barre, stand in parallel position: Step onto pointe in parallel position, R first, then L, holding barre with both hands. Roll off pointe slowly, demi-plié and straighten knees. Step back slightly and repeat starting with L ft. (Teacher emphasizes aligning body as this is executed). Repeat. Music continues. Step away from barre; R ft tendu devant, spring R L again, but this time into 5th en pointe, R ft frt. Bourrée down the barre to the R, passé L to place in frt, roll down into demi-plié, step back onto R and tendu L devant. Repeat starting with L. Repeat last 16 counts.

Exercise 2

Facing barre, stand in parallel position, both hands in barre: Demi-plié, relevé, plié, relevé, plié, relevé, roll down. Repeat 7xs.

Exercise 3

The stronger dancers place L hand on barre while the weaker ones use both hands on barre. Feet in 1st position: Demi-plié, relevé en pointe, plié, relevé, plié, relevé, roll down. Repeat 7xs.

Exercise 4

Facing barre, stand in parallel position, both hands on barre: Demi-plié, relevé en pointe, plié en pointe, straighten knees, roll down. Repeat 3xs.

The teacher tried to shape the feet correctly with her hands. She sat on the floor behind the dancer as she worked with the feet.

Exercise 5

Exercise 4 in 1st position.

Exercise 6

Facing barre, 1st position, both hands on barre. *One-half* of class begins. Demi-plié, échappé to 2d, return to 1st in plié. Continue for 2 counts of 8. *The second half* of the class executes the exercise while the first half rests. Now the first group executes the exercise from 5th position followed by the second group.

Exercise 7

Facing the barre, 5th position R ft frt, both hands on barre. *First half of class:* Demi-plié, sous-sus, plié, sous-sus. Continue through 8 counts.
Second half of class executes exercise.
First half repeats 8 counts with L ft frt. *Second half* repeats.

Exercise 8

The stronger dancers place L hand on barre while the weaker ones use both hands while facing the barre. 5th position, R ft frt: Demi-plié, sous-sus, plié,

2 & 3 & 4 &5 & 6 & 7 & 8
sous-sus, plié, sous-sus, plié, relevé passé R leg from frt to back. Same with L.
1–8
Repeat. *Second group* executes the same 2 counts of 8.

& 1 & 2 hold 3
First group: Demi-plié, relevé retiré devant, plié in 5th R ft frt, relevé passé close
4 5678 1–8 1–8
5th derrière. Same with L ft. Repeat.

Exercise 9

& 1
Facing barre, 5th position, R ft frt: *First group* starts: Demi-plié, relevé retiré
& 2 &
devant, plié in 5th R ft frt, relevé retiré devant, turn body slightly to L (as a small
3 4
windup to propel body in an en dehors turn), return body, roll down to 5th, R
5 6 7 8
ft bk. Repeat with L ft in frt. Repeat last 8 counts. *Second group:* Same.

Exercise 10

& 1
Facing barre, 5th position, R ft frt: *First group* starts: Demi-plié, relevé passé en
2 3 4
arrière to 4th position demi-plié, pirouette en pointe en dehors closing 5th en
5 6 7 8 1–8
arrière. Same with L ft in frt. Repeat. *Second group:* Same.

The teacher wants the students to hold the passé position for an extra half
count before closing in 5th en arrière.

Exercise 11

Repeat exercise 10 except the stronger students do it with one hand on the barre.

Exercise 12

& 1
Facing barre, 5th position, R ft frt. *First group* starts: Demi-plié, relevé on L with
& 2
R in Russian sur le cou-de-pied pointed position, demi-plié with R ft frt, relevé
&
on R with L in Russian sur le cou-de-pied pointed, demi-plié, continue
alternating 3 & 4 & 5 & 6 & 7, demi-plié on L, relevé on L (double relevé on &
7 & 8). Plié on both feet with R ft frt and reverse last 8 counts. *Second group:*
Repeat 1–16. *First group:* 1–16.

Second group: 1–16.

Exercise 13

L hand on barre, on the diagonal into the barre; standing on R ft, L in croisé
& a 1 & a 2
derrière. *First group* starts: Pas de bourrée en avant, pas de bourrée en arrière, pas
& a 3 & a 4
de bourrée en avant, pas de bourrée en tournant en dedans one-quarter turn
(toward barre—ending facing into barre). Now, with R hand on barre on
& a 5 &
diagonal, standing on R ft, L in croisé devant: Pas de bourrée en arrière, pas de
a 6 & a 7 & a 8
bourrée en avant, pas de bourrée en arrière, pas de bourrée en tournant en dehors

$$1-8$$

one-quarter turn (turning toward barre—ending in original position). Repeat.

Second group: 1–16.

Exercise 14

                                                                          &   1

Facing barre, 5th position, R ft frt. *First group* starts: Demi-plié, relevé onto L

                                                                      &

with R in Russian pointed sur le cou-de-pied devant, demi-plié with R ft frt in

2

5th, relevé onto R with L in Russian pointed sur le cou-de-pied derrière,

&

demi-plié with R ft frt in 5th. Continue alternating feet for the counts & 3 & 4
& 5 & 6 & 7. On the counts & 8 repeat the relevé on L (double relevé).

$$1-8$$

Demi-plié and begin by doing the relevé onto the R with the L in sur de
cou-de-pied derrière and continue for 8 counts.

                                  1–8 1–8 1–8 1–8

Second group: Same. *First* and *Second groups* each repeat.

Exercise 15

Facing barre, both hands on barre. *First group* starts: Demi-plié, sous-sus, pas de
bourrée suivi (Russian) or pas de bourrée couru en cinquième (French)—
commonly called bourrée—in place, slowly lifting only slightly off the ground.

1   2   3

Lift R to very low pointed sur le cou-de-pied position devant, close to 5th, lift L

   4   5   6   7   8   1   2   3   4   5

derrière, close to 5th, lift R, close, lift L, close, lift R, close, lift L, close, lift R,

 6   7   8   1   2

close, lift L, close; faster—lift R, step on R as L is lifted (simultaneously), step on

       4   5   6   7   8   12345678

L as R is lifted, lift L, lift R, lift L, lift R, lift L; even faster, typical quick bourrées
in place. *Second group:* Same. *First* and *Second groups* each repeat starting with L
ft in frt in 5th.

Exercise 16

Facing into the barre (croisé), L hand on barre, R ft frt in 5th position. *First*

                  & a

group starts: Quick pas de bourrée suivi (commonly called bourrée) in place,

1

demi-plié on L and dégagé the R foot to the fourth position devant en l'air à la
demi-hauteur. Bring the R foot to the 5th position devant, rising onto pointe

                                                                            2

       & a

and quickly bourrée in place. Immediately plié on the R ft and dégagé the L

                                        & a 3   &a4   &a5 &a6   &a7

derrière en l'air à la demi-hauteur. Continue front, back, front, back, front, and

&a8

back. *Second group:* Same. *First* and *Second groups* each repeat starting with the L
ft in frt in 5th with R hand on the barre in croisé.

Exercise 17

Facing barre, both hands on barre, R ft in frt in 5th position. *First group* starts:

&   1   &   2   &   3

Plié, sous-sus, plié in 5th, relevé on L with R in retiré devant, plié on L, take R

en relevé   &   4   en relevé   &   in plié

leg to attitude derrière, plié on L, extend to arabesque and quickly close to 5th
5 & 6 & 7 & 8   1–8
behind. Same with L leg. Repeat. *Second group:* Same: *First* and *Second groups*
each repeat two more times.

Exercise 18

Facing barre. *First group* starts: Piqué en pointe stepping back onto L with R in

retiré devant, coupé onto R, piqué onto L as R does ballonné à la seconde sur la

pointe, roll into plié (as R goes to sur le cou-de-pied derrière). Same in other

direction starting on L. Same R except close into 5th position plié on count 4,

sous-sus, roll down releasing back ft in cou-de-pied derrière. Repeat those 2
counts of 8 starting in other direction. *Second group:* Same.

Exercise 19

Repeat exercise 18 except the tempo is faster, which means the leg cannot go as
high.

Exercise 20

Facing barre, standing farther back than typical, standing on L ft, R behind in B

+. *First group* starts: Fondu on supporting leg (L), R does a piqué onto pointe

in arabesque, balancé en arrière (L, R, L), repeat, fondu on L, R does a piqué

onto pointe in arabesque and hold, roll off pointe, step back onto L, then R and

point L tendu devant to prepare to repeat the step starting on the L. Repeat

starting on L ft. Repeat on other side. *Second group:* Same.

Exercise 21

Similar to exercise 20, but with L hand on barre, R ft in 5th position frt. *First*

group starts: Fondu on supporting leg (L) as the R does a piqué onto pointe in

arabesque, balancé en arrière (L, R, L), repeat, fondu on L, R does a piqué onto

pointe in arabesque on R and holds—(now exercise changes)—turning toward

barre (en dehors), bring L leg into retiré devant as R hand takes barre, roll off

pointe into plié as left leg développés devant, close 5th. Repeat by stepping onto
L leg into arabesque. Repeat entire sequence. *Second group:* Same.

Exercise 22

The class lines up single file at the end of the barre. The girls start one at a time,

L hand on barre, R ft frt in 5th position: Fondu on supporting leg (L), step into

5th position en pointe. Roll into demi-plié on left as R goes to sur le cou-de-pied

        & 4 5   6   1 2 3 4 5   6

devant. Repeat last 2 counts. Hold and balance with arms in 1st, roll into demi-plié (or fondu) with R in sur le cou-de-pied devant. As there is room, the next girl follows the first and so on until the barre is filled with dancers. When they have gone the length of the barre, they turn around and go the other way.

CENTER

Exercise 1

One at a time, moving across the floor; this movement is exactly like a typical piqué turn en dedans except *without* the turn.

    The teacher emphasized moving the body in one piece as the dancer springs onto pointe. It is done slowly with typical arms.

Exercise 2

Dancers make several lines with their bodies facing wall 6 (Cecchetti method) and R shoulder to the mirror. They must be very far upstage so they have room to do chainé turns toward the mirror. Stand on L, with R leg tendu devant.

INTERMEDIATE CLASSES

Intermediate Pointe Class (Level V), Houston Ballet School

This class, inspired by Allyson Swenson, follows an hour-and-a-half ballet technique class.

BARRE

Exercise 1

Facing barre in parallel position: Roll through foot to ball, to pointe into arch, [1 ... 2]
roll back to ball, put heel down. Same with L foot. Repeat. Both feet press to [3 ... 4 ... 5 6 7 8 ... 1–8 ... 1]
pointe, R rolls down, both feet to pointe, L rolls down. Repeat 2xs. Repeat last [2 ... 3 ... 4 ... 5 6 7 8 ... 1 2 3 4]
part except from straight legs, roll down into the plié for same amount of time. [5 ... 6 7 8]
Turn out to 1st. R ft tendu à la seconde, flex, roll through foot to touch pointe [1 ... 2 ... 3 4]
on floor, press into arch bending R leg, straighten up, close to 1st. Same L. [5 6 ... 7 ... 8]
Tendu R, close in 1st with demi-plié, tendu L, close in 1st with demi-plié. Tendu [1 ... 2 ... 3 ... 4 ... 5]
R à la seconde, close 1st, press up in a rise with straight legs, lower heels into [6 ... 7 ... 8]
demi-plié. Same L. Repeat R and L. Demi-plié, staying in plié, lift the heels, [1 ... 2]
rolling onto pointe, staying en pointe straighten legs, lower heels to 1st. Reverse [3 ... 4]

by pressing up to pointe, demi-plié en pointe pressing into arches, lower heels to 1st while still in plié, straighten legs. Repeat.

Exercise 2

Facing barre in 1st: R leg tendu à la seconde, close 1st, L tendu à la seconde, close 1st, demi-plié, spring onto pointe in 1st, lower to plié, spring onto pointe, lower to plié. Straighten standing leg as the R leg tendus to side to repeat. Repeat exercise except plié on counts 2 and 4.

At this point the teacher saw one girl knuckling. She said to press out the elastic of the shoe—pull up in the upper part of the foot. The end of the shoe must be on the floor. Don't pull back on the foot. Also think of pressing the foot out where the ribbons cross. The teacher manually shaped their feet and checked to see how much of the shoe was dirty, which shows how much of the shoe is on the floor. The student should pull the heel "out of your shoe."

Exercise 3

Facing barre, R ft frt in 5th: Sous-sus, plié, sous-sus, plié, échappé to 2d, plié in 5th, échappé to 2d, plié in 5th. Sous-sus, plié, sous-sus, plié, échappé to 2d, plié in 5th, sous-sus, plié. Same with L ft frt. Repeat both sides.

Exercise 4

Facing barre, R ft frt in 5th: Échappé to 2d, plié in 5th, échappé to 2d, plié in 5th, passé R ft, plié, sous-sus, plié, passé L ft, plié, sous-sus, plié in 5th. Repeat. Same with L ft frt.

Exercise 5

Facing barre, R ft frt in 5th: Fondu on L, développé à la quatrième devant, demi-hauteur, piqué en avant to 5th sur la pointe. Pas de bourrèe suivi (commonly known as bourrée) in place. Passé R leg closing derrière while still en pointe (R arm comes off barre and moves to Russian 3rd or Cecchetti 5th on the passé; then as the leg closes behind, the arm goes to 2d and back onto the barre. The head turns to the L when the R leg and arm are moving and vice versa). Fondu on the R, and repeat using the other leg. Repeat both sides.

CENTER

Exercise 1

5th position, R ft frt. Preparation: arms move from preparation to 1st to 2d and back to preparation position as the R ft tendus à la seconde and closes to 1st

$$\overset{\&}{} \qquad \overset{1}{} \qquad \overset{\&}{} \quad \overset{2}{} \quad \overset{\&}{} \quad \overset{3}{} \quad \overset{\&}{}$$

position. Demi-plié, spring to relevé in 1st, plié, relevé, plié, relevé, plié,

$$\overset{4}{} \qquad \overset{\&}{}$$

straighten legs, plié. Repeat 3xs.

Exercise 2
Repeat previous exercise except with different timing. This time plié on *1* and spring up on &.

Exercise 3
Repeat center exercise 2 except on the last & 5 & 6 & 7 & 8 the front row splits in the middle and runs upstage to form the back line as the 2d line runs forward to form the 1st line.

Exercise 4

$$\overset{1}{} \qquad \overset{2}{}$$

Croisé, R ft frt in 5th. Same arm preparation as center exercise 1: Sous-sus, plié,

$$\overset{3}{} \qquad \overset{4}{} \quad \overset{5}{} \qquad \overset{6}{} \qquad \overset{7}{}$$

sous-sus, plié, sous-sus, plié, échappé changing directions to finish in plié facing

$$\overset{8}{} \quad \overset{1}{} \qquad \overset{2}{} \quad \overset{3}{} \qquad \overset{4}{} \quad \overset{5}{} \qquad \overset{6}{}$$

corner 1 with L ft frt in 5th, plié. Sous-sus, plié, sous-sus, plié, sous-sus, plié,

$$\overset{7}{} \qquad \overset{8}{} \quad \overset{1}{} \qquad \overset{2}{} \quad \overset{3}{} \qquad \overset{4}{}$$

échappé to croisé facing corner 2, plié. Sous-sus, plié, échappé (to corner 1), plié,

$$\overset{5}{} \qquad \overset{6}{} \quad \overset{7}{} \qquad \overset{8}{} \quad \overset{1}{} \qquad \overset{2}{} \quad \overset{3}{} \qquad \overset{4}{}$$

sous-sus, plié, échappé (corner 2), plié, sous-sus, plié, échappé (corner 1), plié,

$$\overset{5}{} \qquad \overset{6}{} \qquad \overset{7}{} \qquad \overset{8}{} \quad \overset{1\text{–}8}{} \quad \overset{1\text{–}8}{} \quad \overset{1\text{–}8}{} \quad \overset{1\text{–}8}{}$$

sous-sus, plié, and straighten legs plié. Repeat starting with L ft frt in 5th croisé facing corner 1. Repeat entire exercise, except on the last 8 counts, the students change lines as in center exercise 3.

COMMENTS ON LEVEL V POINTE BY ALLYSON SWENSON
Students usually spend two years in level IV pointe, which is the first pointe level, before progressing to level V. In level IV they do not actually do much work on pointe. In the level V class described here, the students stay mainly on two feet. They are just starting to work on one foot. They may spend two years in level V, more or less.

Level V is just starting to do single turns from 5th position. The students are ages 11 through 13. One girl is 14, but 12 is the average age. Level IV students are aged 10 through 12. They do not start on pointe until they are 10 and then only if they're ready.

At level IV students are given one-half hour of pointe a week. The level Vs get a half hour twice a week. The level IVs stay on two feet the whole time. They work entirely in first and second position. For example they do the same warm-ups as the level V students—the same 1st, 2d, and 3rd exercises. When they do the 1st exercise, I tell them not to stretch the foot over, but to place the foot on pointe so it will be exactly the way it would be if it was up on pointe. They are not standing on it yet; they are just placing the foot.

What I'm looking for is exactly where they would be on pointe. I don't want them to fold the toes over or anything like that. I want them to be straight up on the end of the shoe so they feel the shape of the foot before putting any weight on it. After that they go up on pointe and do the changeover from one foot to the other.

With the older classes, starting with the Vs and VIs, I'll take them into plié on pointe. Now there is more pressure on the foot, but they are still supposed to keep the foot's shape and not push the arch out yet. The plié makes it a little harder.

Also with the IVs, Vs, and VIs I'll do the flex through the demi-pointe to try to get them to use the shoe. And then the tendu and plié with the stretch and rise is the first time they have really gone on pointe; they've done it with their feet parallel, but not in a rotated position. And then with the VIs I'll have them do rise, plié, rise, plié, which the IVs and Vs don't do. I'll usually have them take a balance at the end of that.

Sometimes toward the end of level IV I'll throw in a few sous-sus in fifth, but most of their time is spent doing exercises like tendu side, plié in 1st, tendu, plié in 1st, échappé and plié in 1st. They might try sous-sus, plié, and stretch (straighten their legs), plié, sous-sus, plié, and stretch, plié, sous-sus, plié and stretch, plié échappé, plié and stretch plié. They repeat this on the other side. While level V can do continuous relevés from two feet to two feet, the IVs do better if they have a breather in between, whether it's a plié and straighten or a tendu.

I spend a lot of time correcting in level IV. I work with kids who can't make it all the way up and kids who are pushing over. They don't know how to work the feet on pointe yet. We also spend time learning to tie ribbons, how to cut them to the right length—they don't know to cut them on an angle, they don't know to turn the ribbon under when they sew it—they don't know how to put the shoes on.

I take new beginners to the center, and the first thing we do is turned in walking on pointe. Again, I always keep them on two feet. We might do the exercise described above in the center. After we get going along, we might do real simple bourrées. Sous-sus, bourrée in place, and change feet. I do that a lot with the level IVs to get them used to being on one foot. After they have been in class for a year, we'll do the bourrées and change feet in the center. Newer students change feet, but older ones change with a passé or retiré so they get used to coming into a position. Sometimes I'll take a separate group of the older kids and do a relevé on one foot at the barre, like jeté, relevé, hold, plié and pas de bourrée under. Just that one little relevé for the old kids because they have been doing the pointe work for two years. This gets them ready to move to level V because that's when they do more work on one foot.

In level V, the students don't do piqué turns across the floor. They do piqués across the floor without a turn. Instead I'll start them with turns from 5th position. Because there's a lot they have to hold on to with a piqué turn. There's a lot of placement that you can lose. Whereas from 5th, it's cleaner. It's harder for them to lose the position and placement of the body. We might do, for instance, a tendu side, a plié, half turn, roll down, tendu, plié, half-turn, roll down; and then the same with a full turn. When the kids move up to level VI, they do pirouettes in the center so they've got to have had a little bit of that in V. Then their teacher at level VI will start giving them double turns from 5th position; she starts things across the floor like piqué turns. Usually they can make the transition all right because they've had time to get used to the feeling from the exercises in IV and V. A lot of the time I spend, particularly with the IVs is just learning how to put the feet on pointe. You see every single foot is different and a teacher can't just say, " this is how you do it." I'll get them all to watch what I do with one person so they get an overall understanding, but each person is different. Some people I have to tell, if they have a low arch or instep, you'll have to work to get the foot over more. If they have a high arch, then they have to keep the foot stretched in the shoe so they don't break over. I spend a lot of time in IV just working on that kind of thing. By V, they've pretty well got it, but there are still some problems. Especially the kids with high arches and insteps. They need more special care. They go up more easily, but need help with breaking over. Sometimes they sew elastic across the top or get a high vamp for extra support. And then some of them need to break the shoe in one place, while other girls need another place. By the time they get to level VI, they should know what they're doing.

Intermediate Pointe Class (Level VI),
Houston Ballet School

Inspired by Swenson, this follows an hour-and-a-half technique class.

Exercise 1

Same as exercise 1 in level V.

Exercise 2

Same as exercise 2 in level V.

Exercise 3

L hand on barre; in 5th position, R ft in frt: Sous-sus^1, demi-plié^2, échappé to 2d^3, closing in 5th with^4 L ft in frt. Sous-sus^5, plié^6, échappé to 2d closing in 5th with^7 R ft in frt.^{8} Échappé to 4th with R ft in frt^1, return to 5th in plié^2 (arm goes from 2d to preparation position, 1st arabesque with palm facing floor, inclining head),

échappé changé to 2d taking arm to 2d, plié in 5th, R ft bk. Same with L ft in frt.
Repeat. Quickly turn to other side and repeat entire exercise.

Exercise 4

Facing barre with R ft in frt in 5th: Fondu on L with R in sur le cou-de-pied devant (pointed), développé R ft devant and piqué onto pointe to 5th with R ft frt. Small bourrées in place. Retiré R leg devant, take to attitude derrière, take R arm to high 5th, extending to arabesque as arm turns to allongé. Close R leg in 5th derrière, roll down to demi-plié. Same starting with L ft. Repeat both sides.

Exercise 5

R ft frt in 5th, L hand on barre: Développé en fondu à la quatrième devant à demi-hauteur, piqué to 5th position sur la pointe R ft frt, roll down off pointe to demi-plié. Repeat. R ft relevé passé en arrière, plié, relevé passé en avant, plié.

Repeat counts & 1 2 & 3 4 5 6, but on count 6 remain en pointe. Turning away from the barre (demi-détourné), simply bring L foot to close en pointe in 5th devant. Now R hand is on barre. Same starting with L ft. Repeat entire exercise.

CENTER

Exercise 1

Croisé, R ft frt in 5th: Sous-sus, plié, sous-sus, plié, sous-sus, plié, échappé changé, finishing in croisé with L ft frt in 5th (facing corner 1). Repeat with L ft frt in 5th. Sous-sus, plié, échappé changé (changing to face corner 1), sous-sus, plié, échappé changé (facing corner 2), sous-sus, plié, échappé changé (to corner 1), walk backward on the diagonal to corner 3, R, L, R, close L ft frt in 5th.
Repeat entire exercise starting with L ft frt in croisé.

The teacher wanted the students to rotate their legs by taking the seams of their tights and bringing them forward.

Exercise 2

Croisé, R ft frt in 5th: Hands on hips, plié, sous-sus, plié, passé R to bk (R arm opens from 1st to 2d and bk on hip on the plié), plié. Turn to face corner 1 on the passé. Same with L. En face passé R close bk plié (R arm opens from 1st to

2d), passé L to bk plié (L arm opens from 1st to 2d),⁵ passé R bk plié⁶ (R arm moves quickly through 1st to high 5th to 2d),⁷ passé L to bk plié⁸ (L arm moves quickly through 1st to high 5th to 2d). Repeat 3 more times.^(1–8 1–8 1–8 1–8 1–8 1–8) After executing 4xs, repeat with L ft frt.

The teacher's corrections were that when students do retiré or passé, they should lift from underneath their "rear." In the plié, they must lengthen out the body—not settle into the plié or sit into it. They must pull out of the hip flexor, not collapse it.

Exercise 3

Moving across the floor to the R: Piqué tour en dedans R 2xs,^(1 2 3 4) piqué on R with⁵ L sur le coup-de-pied derrière (making half turn to R), plié, piqué on L lifting R^(& 6) to sur le cou-de-pied devant (making half turn en dehors), plié, piqué en dedans^(& 7) R, plié on L.⁸ Continue across floor. Then to L across floor.

A Typical Vaganova Intermediate-Advanced Pointe Class

BARRE

Exercise 1

1st position, facing barre: Demi-plié, relevé to pointe, hold, roll down to plié.^(&   1   23   4) Execute 8xs.

Exercise 2

2d position, facing barre: Demi-plié, relevé to pointe, plié, relevé, plié, relevé,^(1   123   4   567   8   1) press in plié over the pointes, straighten knees, roll down.^(2 3 4   5 6   7 8) Execute 4xs.

Exercise 3

5th position, R ft frt facing barre: Plié, sous-sus, demi-plié, sous-sus, plié, relevé^(&   1 2 3   4   567   8   1 2) on L with R in sur le cou-de-pied, pointed devant, plié, relevé on L and low^(3 4   5) développé à la seconde with R, close bk in 5th.^(6 7   8) Same with L ft frt. Repeat 2xs.

Exercise 4

5th position, R ft frt, L hand on barre: Sous-sus, développé R ft devant,^(&1   2 3 4) demi-rond de jambe en l'air en dehors to 2d, bring to retiré devant.^(5 6   7 8) Demi-plié on^(1) L as R ft is brought to pointed sur le cou-de-pied devant, relevé on L as R goes^(2)

to attitude derrière while turning to face barre. Place R hand on barre making ³ ⁴
a quarter turn and stretch into 1st arabesque. Close to 5th and roll off pointe, ⁵ ⁶　　　　　　　　　　　　　⁷
demi-plié, and straighten. Same starting with L and repeat. &　 ⁸

Exercise 5

5th position, R ft frt, facing barre: Coupé dessous onto pointe on L, coupé ¹　　　　　　　　　　　　　　　　　　²
dessus to demi-plié on R, pas de bourrée dessous. Same other direction. Relevé ³ & ⁴　　　　　　　　　　 ⁵ ⁶ ⁷ & ⁸
onto L on pointe as R leg does double rond de jamb en l'air en dehors, close 5th ¹ &　　　　　　　　　　　　　　　　　²
derère demi-plíe; same relevé double rond de jamb en l'air but en dedans, and ³ & ⁴
again en dehors, close 5th derrière demi-plié, sous-sus, demi-plié. Repeat entire ⁵ &　　 ⁶　　　　　　　 ⁷　　　 ⁸
exercise to L.

Exercise 6

Reverse exercise 5.

Exercise 7

5th position, R ft frt, facing barre: Pas de bourrée suivi en pointe mving R. ¹ ² ³
Passé L ft from back to front closing in 5th remaining en pointe. Same moving &　　　　　　　　 ⁴
to L. Repeat.

CENTER

Exercise 1

5th position, R ft frt in croisé: Dévelopoppé à la quatrième devant à la &
demi-hauteur en fondu, turning en face, bourrée en avant (arms moving through ¹ ² ³
first to 2d position), passé R ft to 4th position derrièrre. Pirouette en dehors, ⁴　　　　　　　　　　　　　　　 ⁵ ⁶
finish in croisé in 4th, tendu R ft, close to 5th derrière. Same starting with L ft frt. ⁷　　　 ⁸

Exercise 2

Poser on L with R ft behind in B + in croisé: Moving en diagonale to Vaganova corner 2 ballonné devant sur la pointe en relevé in effacé, traveling forward.
Relevé, roll down, relevé, roll down, relevé, roll down, relevé while sweeping R ¹　 &　　　 ²　 &　　　 ³　 &　　　 ⁴
leg into attitude effacé derrière. Step on R ft and execute to L. &

Exercise 3

Croisé, 5th position, R ft frt: Développé écarté devant en relevé, close 5th in
demi-plié. Relevé to 2d arabesque on R, close L in plié 5th derriére. Développé
écarté devant en relevé with L, close in 5th devant sous-sus, plié. To R piqué tour
en dehors on L 3xs, close R ft derrière in 5th, sous-sus, lower to demi-plié. Same
to L. Repeat.

Exercise 4

Poser on L with R ft tendu in effacé devant: Moving toward corner 2 Vaganova
en diagonale, soutenu en tournant en dedans, step into original poser position.
Repeat continually across floor. When finished, travel across the floor to L.

Exercise 5

5th position, R ft frt, en face. Preparation, tendu R ft à la seconde, demi-rond de
jambe to 4th position derrière, demi-plié: Single or double pirouette en dehors
and then three fouettés rond de jambe en tournant en dehors (Russian school)
finishing in 4th position derrière, tendu R on straight leg, return to 4th position
preparation and continue with the fouettés. On the last set, tendu R and close in
5th derrière. Do the same combination to L.

Exercise 6

Croisé, R ft frt: Retiré devant en relevé, close 5th devant demi-plié, 3xs, relevé
passé closing in 5th derrière as body turns to croisé with L ft frt. Same with L ft
frt. Repeat.

ADVANCED CLASSES

Advanced Pointe Class (Level VIII),
Houston Ballet School

This class was inspired by Clara Cravey.

BARRE

Exercise 1

Facing barre, feet in parallel position: Standing on L, cross R leg over L and
place ft en pointe beside the heel of the L ft. Demi-plié on the L and push over
the pt of the R ft. The L knee bends and pushes into the R knee which is bent.

1 & 2 & 3 &
Push into the pointe, release back, into the pt, release back, into the pt, release,
4 & 5 & 6 7 &
into the pt, release, into the pt, release, into the pt, hold, release, step on R in
8 1–8
parallel position. Same with L ft crossed over. *Next,* with L ft in same place, put
1 2 3 4
R ft heel directly in front of the L toe and knees are bent as the hips push in
1 2 3 4
toward the barre to stretch the calf muscles. Change feet and do same. Next, the
1 2 3 4
R foot goes into same position, but with a space the length of a foot between the
5 6 7 8
R and L feet to get a bigger stretch of the calves. Same with L. *Next,* place both
1 2 3 4
legs together in parallel position with the legs straight, press the hips to the barre,
5 6 7 8 1 2 3 4
putting hips back on top of legs, lean forward on straight legs until back is flat
5 6 7
but head is up, arch back as head lowers and roll up through the spine to a
8
standing position. (The leaning forward and rolling up should stretch the arms
and the upper back.)

Exercise 2

1 2
Facing barre in 1st position: R ft sur le cou-de-pied, extend devant about two
3 4 5
inches off floor, flex ft and bring it back to 1st position. Tendu R à la seconde,
6 7 8
bring to 5th devant with demi-plié, tendu R à la seconde, and bring to 1st with
& 1–8
demi-plié and straighten legs. Same en dedans. Execute entire exercise starting
with L ft.

The teacher's corrections were that students must be sure that all five
metatarsals are on the floor in plié. They should not be all "clinched up." Let the
ligaments and tendons relax in the plié instead of holding or gripping.

Exercise 3

1 2
Facing barre, 5th position R ft frt: Tendu R à la seconde, roll down through
3 4 5 6 7 8
foot, point tendu again, close 5th derriere. Repeat, finishing cou-de-pied devant.
1 2 3 4 5 6 7 8 & 1 & a 2 & a
Frappé à la seconde 3xs, hold, frappé à la seconde 3xs, hold, battement frappé
3 & a 4 5 6 7
double 4xs à la seconde, tendu R ft à la seconde, demi-plié, straighten R and
8 &
tendu L, close L in 5th devant. Same starting to L. Repeat all.

Exercise 4

1 2
Facing barre, 1st position, both hands on barre: Take R hand off barre and
extend to seconde (looking into hand) as the body leans slightly in same
3 hold 4
direction. Bring arm to high 5th (same as Russian 3rd) as feet press up to pointe.

Leaving arm in 5th, lower [5] through the metatarsals to the balls of the feet, press [6] back up to full pointe, lower [7] down to demi-plié (as arm is placed back on the barre), [8] straighten legs. [1–8] Same with L arm. Repeat, [1–8 1–8] this time taking both arms off barre for a quick balance on count 4 before lowering through the metatarsals. Repeat all 4 counts of 8.

Exercise 5

Facing barre, 1st position, both hands on barre: Demi-plié, [&] spring into relevé, [1] down, [2] up, [3] down, [4] up, [5] down, [6] up, [&] down, [7] up, [&] down; [8] repeat two more times. [1–8 1–8] Pick [&] up L foot sur le cou-de-pied derrière, [1 2] pas de bourrée dessous ending in 5th. [3] Pick [4] up R foot to sur le cou-de-pied derrière, [5 6] pas de bourrée dessous ending in 5th en [7] pointe (pas de bourrées are done picking up feet), extend L foot with small [8] développé à la seconde and roll down gently to 1st position and plié. [&] Repeat [1–8] exercise, [1–8 1–8 1–8] but start the pas de bourrées with R foot. Repeat entire exercise. [8 counts of 8]

The teacher's corrections were to "lift" the body up as the dancer springs down so the body will not be heavy going down.

Exercise 6

Facing barre, L ft in frt in 5th. Échappé to 2d, [1] plié in 1st, [&] échappé to 2d, [2] plié in [&] 5th R ft frt, [3] échappé to 2d, [&] plié in 1st, [4] échappé to 2d, [&] plié in 5th L ft frt. [5 & 6] Pas de [7 & 8] bourrée dessous 2xs lifting feet as in Exercise 5, but closing in 5th in demi-plié [1 & 2 & 3 & 4 &] at the end. Repeat the échappés, [5] relevé on R with L in retiré devant, hold the [6] balance and passé the leg to close in 5th derrière, [7] demi-plié. [8] Repeat, but this time with the L leg closing 5th the first time.

The teacher's correction was that when students go up into the retiré for the balance, they make the adjustment to position themselves for the balance after they have arrived—that their body weight is too far to the center. On the spring they should pull the foot directly underneath themselves so they will be immediately on balance; no shifting of the weight should be necessary. Also, the teacher wants a beautiful cou-de-pied position—shape the foot beautifully, don't just let it hang.

Exercise 7

5th position, R ft frt, L hand on barre: Pas de cheval 3xs, [& 1 & 2 & 3] fondu on L (R is in [4] tendu devant), piqué onto pointe on R with L sur le cou-de-pied derrière, [5] plié, [6] relevé, [7] plié, [8] relevé, [1] turn into bare (put both hands on barre) and développé L leg [2] à la demi-hauteur à la seconde, petit battement alternating closing back and front

starting devant—frt, bk, frt, bk, frt, bk, frt, bk, frt, make a quarter turn placing
R hand on barre closing L ft frt in 5th. Same starting with L. Repeat exercise.
Teacher calls sur le cou-de-pied the "kissing heel" position.

Exercise 8

Repeat exercise 7 with ballonné simple.

Exercise 9

R ft frt in 5th position, L hand on barre: Chassé en avant, relevé into attitude
derrière, extend into arabesque, close 5th, roll down into demi-plié, repeat the
chassé relevé and extend. Then bring L leg into retiré devant as body turns to face
barre with R hand holding barre and L arm 5th en haut. Extend L leg into
arabesque (passer la jambe) as L hand does allongé. Make another quarter turn
en dehors bringing L leg into retiré and closing in 5th devant with R hand now
on barre. Demi-plié, relevé to retiré devant, close 5th L ft devant, demi-plié,
pirouette en dehors, close L ft 5th devant. Same starting to L. Repeat entire
exercise.
   The teacher explained that the heel, hip, and head all move together on the
chassé to attitude relevé.

CENTER

Exercise 1

Croisé, R ft frt: Échappé sur les pointes to 2d, closing 5th in croisé L ft frt.
Échappé again ending croisé R ft frt. Sous-sus en face R ft frt (arms in 5th en
haut), lift R ft sur le cou-de-pied pointed devant, place back into 5th en pointe,
lift L ft to sur le cou-de-pied pointed derrière, place back into 5th en pointe,
demi-plié returning to croisé R ft frt (arms open to 2d on counts 6 7 and arrive
in preparation position on 8). Repeat 2 more times. Repeat counts 1 2 3 4 and
execute one more échappé ending facing corner 1 (Cecchetti) or croisé L ft frt in
5th, sous-sus, plié. Same starting with L ft frt. Repeat entire exercise.

Exercise 2

Moving across the floor to the R. Preparation, standing on L, R ft tendu croisé
devant: Attitude turn R, step onto L in fondu as R ft does tendu croisé devant

to corner 2 and R arm extends back and L arm moves from 1st [2] position moving parallel with the leg as it stretches into allongé [3] (typical révérence). Bourrée to [123] corner 1 with arms extended in 2d allongé, piqué on R [123] (to corner 2) croisé en [123] avant 2xs, attitude croisé derrière on R, step back on L [123] into original preparation. Repeat the attitude turn [123] into the reverence posé [123] and the bourrée R [123] [123]. Pas de [123] bourrée dessous 2xs with lifted feet (LRL, RLR), ending with R ft 5th in frt. Pirouette en dehors [123] ending in 4th R ft behind, temps lié en arrière [1 2 3] ending with L ft tendu devant in croisé (to corner 1). Same to L. Repeat entire exercise.

The teacher suggested leading with the back foot in the bourrée, that the feet should "feel" they are touching. There should be no spaces between the feet. The back foot should feel that it is pushing away from the floor with lots of energy instead of "dragging." The dancer should allow the back foot to lead.

Exercise 3

This is done in a circle moving to the R first. Preparation, standing on R, L ft tendu croisé devant: Step onto L [8], glissade précipitée derrière [& a] (L ends in frt) R, développé à la seconde R [1] (going into the circle), R crosses in front of body and [2] does chassé croisé en avant [& a], same with L [3] with the développé going out of the [4 & a] circle, again with R [5 6], coupé under [&], piqué turn R 4xs [7 8] moving in a circle [1 2], double [3] piqué turn [4], chassé pas de bourrée dessous 2xs [5 & a 6] [7 & a 8]. Continue to R. Exercise moves only in one direction. When all have done it, start to the L.

The teacher's correction was to be more explicit with the feet after the 3rd développé in the chassé, not just to fall onto the R foot.

Advanced Pointe Class (Level VIII), Houston Ballet School

This class was inspired by Rosemary Miles, principal of the Houston Ballet School.

BARRE

Exercise 1

L hand on barre, 5th position, R ft frt: Tendu devant with R ft [1], roll thru foot to [2] 4th position with straight legs [3], tendu close to 5th [4]. Tendu devant [5], close 5th with [6] plié [7], tendu devant, close 5th with straight legs [8]. En croix. Same other side.

Exercise 2

Facing barre, feet in parallel position: Standing on L, R leg crosses over L and places ft en pointe beside the heel of the L ft. Demi-plié on the L and push over the pt of the R ft. The L knee bends and pushes into the R knee which is bent.

1 & 2 & 3 & 4
Push into the pt, release back, into the pt, release, into the pt, release, into the pt,

& 5 & 6 & 7 &
release, into the pt, release, push, release, push, release, step on R in parallel position. Same with L ft crossed over. Repeat both sides.

Exercise 3

1 2
Facing barre, feet in 1st position: Tendu R ft à la seconde, roll through foot to

3 4 5 6 7 8
2d position, roll through L ft to tendu, close L ft to 1st. Same starting with L ft.

1 2 3 4 &
Rise up onto pointe with straight legs, hold, roll down with straight legs, press

5 & 6 & 7 & 8
up, lower down, press up, lower down, press up, lower down, press up, lower down to 1st. Repeat.

Exercise 4

& 1 2
Facing barre, 5th position, R ft frt: Plié, sous-sus onto pt in 5th, spring down

3 4 5 6
into plié, échappé to 2d, spring down to 5th with L ft frt, sous-sus, spring down,

7 8
échappé to 2d, spring down to 5th with R ft frt, repeat counts 1, 2, 3, 4, and

5 6 7 8
sous-sus and hold and hold, spring down in plié to 5th with L ft frt. Repeat with L ft frt.

The relevés are executed with a spring, but the teacher reminded dancers that this exercise must be smooth and not bouncey, in spite of the spring. The exercise is repeated to capture this quality.

Exercise 5

1 2 3
Facing barre, 5th position, L ft frt: Jeté R, spring into relevé, spring down into

4 5 6 7 8 & 1 2 3 4 5 6
plié, relevé, plié, relevé, plié, relevé, plié, jeté L, relevé, plié, relevé, plié, relevé,

7 8 &
plié, relevé, plié. Repeat R and L.

CENTER

Exercise 1

1 & a
5th position, R ft in frt, en face: Tendu R ft à la seconde, demi-rond de jamb to

2 3
4th position derrière, plié (preparation for pirouette), double pirouette en

4 5 & 6 7 and
dehors, close R ft in 5th derrière. Sous-sus, demi-détourné, chassé pas de

a 8
bourrée dessous upstage toward wall 7 (Cecchetti) or wall 5 (Vaganova), 4th

position plié with L ft frt. Double pirouette en dehors, close R ft in 5th derrière, sous-sus, demi-détourné, roll down tendu R ft à la seconde, demi-rond de jamb to 4th position derrière, plié Pirouette en dehors, closing R ft derrière. Same starting with L ft.

Exercise 2

5th position, R ft frt, en face: Plié pirouette en dehors with a développé à la quatrième devant demi-hauteur, close 5th, R ft frt after one revolution. Port de bras: the arms go into Cecchetti 4th position en avant on the plié, the L arm comes in to meet the R as the turn starts, and the R arm goes (French 4th position) overhead as the body & head incline to the L and the dancer looks under the R arm. Landing in 5th, straighten the body and return arms to the preparation position. Do this pirouette 3 times, and then one double en dehors normally closing the R leg derrière in 5th. Repeat the pirouettes to the L. Repeat entire exercise.

The remainder of the class is spent with two groups dancing the Black Swan variation from *Swan Lake,* after watching it several times on the VCR and discussing its execution.

Advanced Pointe Class, Ruth Page Foundation School

This class was inspired by Larry Long, director of the Ruth Page Foundation School. The class starts in the center after an hour-and-a-half ballet class.

Exercise 1

R ft in frt in 5th: Tendu with R devant, close 5th, tendu à la seconde, close 5th derrière, tendu derrière, close 5th derrière, sous-sus, demi-plié. Same with L. Tendu L à la seconde, push into the pointe, straighten to tendu, close 5th devant. Same with R. Tendu R devant close 5th 2xs, tendu L derrière 2xs, fondu to the tendu à la seconde with L, soutenu with L ft frt, demi-plié. Repeat last 8 counts starting with R to back.

This exercise is repeated after a lecture by the teacher that students must really "work" the foot inside the pointe shoe.

Exercise 2

5th position, R ft frt: Échappé to second 4xs. Sous-sus, plié, sous-sus, plié, relevé on L with R sur le cou-de-pied pointed devant, plié in 5th, relevé passé with R passing to the back at the ankle, close 5th derrière.⁸ Same with L ft frt.¹⁻⁸ This exercise is repeated 3 more times.

Exercise 3

5th position, R ft frt: Échappé to 2d making quarter turn to R (ending with L¹²
ft 5th frt),³ bring L to retiré devant and demi-plié in 5th with L ft frt.⁴ Continue
with another quarter turn and retiré R,⁵⁶ to 5th plié (facing bk),⁷ another⁸ quarter¹²
turn (facing wall 6) and retiré L,³ to 5th plié,⁴ another quarter turn (now facing⁵⁶
front)⁷ and passé R ft bk ending in demi-plié L ft frt in 5th.⁸ Same going other way¹⁻⁸ ¹⁻⁸
with L ft frt. Repeat exercise.

Exercise 4

Exercise 3 is repeated except there is a half turn on the 3 retirés and 1 passé. That
is, quarter turn échappé (facing wall 8),¹² half turn retiré (facing wall 6),³⁴ quarter⁵
turn échappé (facing frt),⁶ half turn retiré (facing bk or wall 7),⁷⁸ quarter turn¹ ²
échappé (facing wall 6),³⁴ half turn retiré (facing wall 8),⁵⁶ quarter turn échappé
(facing bk),⁷⁸ half turn *passé* (facing front). Repeat going in other direction with L
ft frt to start.

Exercise 5

5th position, R ft frt: Échappé to second, but don't change feet,¹²³⁴ 2xs, relevé retiré⁵
devant,⁶ demi-plié in 5th R ft frt,⁷ pirouette en dehors close R ft in 5th derrière.⁸
Same with L foot. Repeat 3xs.¹⁻⁸

Exercise 6

Effacé devant, R ft pointing to corner 1: Piqué on R en avant,¹ step back on L,²
piqué R en avant,³ as body turns to effacé facing corner 2 the L does petit
battement derrière& and petit battement devant as R rolls down to fondu.⁴ Same⁵⁶
to the L.⁷&⁸ Step onto R and coupé L.& Do last 8 counts moving en arrière.¹²³&⁴⁵⁶⁷&⁸ Pas de¹²³
bourrée dessous, coupé under,⁴ bourrée en avant leading with L ft, bring R ft⁵⁶
forward in 4th position preparation (en face),⁷⁸ pirouette en dehors finishing with¹²
L ft bk in 4th demi-plié,³⁴ temps lié onto L⁵⁶ with R ft tendu croisé devant.⁷ Step⁸
onto R and execute exercise starting to the L.¹⁻⁸ ¹⁻⁸ ¹⁻⁸ Repeat both sides.

Exercise 7

Moving across the floor to the R en diagonale: Piqué arabesque R,¹ step on L,²
glissade précipitée derrière,&ª piqué to attitude derrière on R croisé derriére³
(facing corner 2), roll down to 4th with R ft frt.⁴ Relevé arabesque turn on R en⁵&ª
dedans, remaining en pointe place L ft down as R lifts for one half turn en dehors
and R does développé à la demi-hauteur effacé, chainé turn R.⁶ &⁷& ª⁸ Repeat to the R
across floor. When complete, do exercise moving across the floor to the L.

It is easier to do a chassé pas de bourrée before stepping into the piqué
arabesque for the flow of the step. The teacher said to get the attitude "up"
immediately. He also wanted a high arabesque since in modern times "long skirts
and lilies don't work anymore." Also he wanted the dancer to be on the leg in the
arabesque. The "rump" must be right up on top of the leg. Coming out of the
arabesque—as the L leg comes through, the R one rolls down—it doesn't all
collapse at once.

Exercise 8

Moving across the floor to the R en diagonale: Piqué turn R 3xs,¹²³⁴⁵⁶ relevé attitude&⁷⁸
croisé devant. Continue across floor to R. Then L.

Exercise 9

Preparation, standing on L, R ft tendu devant: Piqué turn R,¹² piqué arabesque R,³
step on L with R sur le cou-de-pied derrière,⁴ coupé dessous.⁵ Same to L.⁶⁷⁸¹² Same to³⁴⁵⁶⁷
R. Same to L except go into sous-sus instead of the sur le cou-de-pied and the⁸¹²³ ⁴ hold⁵⁶⁷⁸
coupé. Chainé turn R coming out of it¹²³⁴⁵⁶ with a quick pas de chat R.⁷⁸ This exercise
is easier to count as 12345 12345 12345 123 sous-sus 4 hold 5678.

Exercise 10

5th position, R ft frt: Demi-plié,& relevé retiré devant with R,¹ demi-plié,² relevé³
passé with R,⁴ plié.⁵⁶⁷⁸ Same with L.¹²³⁴ Again with R and L.⁵⁶⁷ On the last count of 8
coupé dessous.¹²³⁴⁵⁶⁷⁸ ¹²³⁴ Turning effacé, ballonné en relevé devant sur la pointe 7xs. On
the 7th one,⁵ do a slight fouetté to turn the body en face and leg à la seconde.
Close R leg in 5th derrière in demi-plié,⁶ sous-sus,⁷ demi-plié.⁸ ¹–⁸ ¹–⁸ ¹–⁸ Same starting with
L ft frt.¹–⁸ Repeat both sides.

On the ballonné devant sur la pointe, the teacher wanted the dancer to arrive
in the relevé immediately.

Exercise 11

Repeat the 1st two counts of 8 in exercise 10. Turning écarté, ballonné devant
sur la pointe 5xs¹²³⁴⁵⁶⁷⁸¹ moving downstage on the diagonal.hold² Step onto R and double

piqué tour on L en dehors (lame duck), close R ft derrière in 5th, demi-plié,
^{3 4 5} ⁶
sous-sus, demi-plié. Same starting with L. Repeat both sides.
⁷ ⁸

Advanced Pointe Class, American Ballet Theatre School

This class was inspired by Marina Stavitskaya. It follows an hour-and-a-half technique class. There is no barre.

Exercise 1

1st position, en face: Échappé to 2d, plié in 1st, échappé to 2d, plié in 1st, échappé to 2d, hold, plié in 1st; échappé to 2d, plié in 2d, rise in 2d, plié in 2d, rise in 2d, hold, plié in 5th, R ft frt. Échappé to 2d, plié in 2d, relevé on R with L in retiré devant, plié in 5th L ft frt, échappé to 2d, plié in 2d, relevé on L with R in retiré devant, plié in 5th with R ft frt, échappé to 2d, plié in 5th L ft frt, échappé to 2d, plié in 5th R ft frt, échappé to 2d hold, plié in 5th L ft frt. Same starting with L ft frt. Repeat R and L 4xs.

The teacher's corrections were that the movement should be more "special" —more exciting and lighter.

Exercise 2

Preparation, standing on L, R ft tendu à la quatrième derrière: Piqué on R sur la pointe, ballonné with L de côté, ending sur le cou-de-pied derrière in plié; same with R, same with L, same with R, but with R ending sur le cou-de-pied devant. 4xs ballonné devant sur la pointe effacé moving toward corner 2, tombé on R with L sur le cou-de-pied derrière, ballonné derrière sur la pointe effacé moving toward corner 6 2xs, tombé on L with R sur le cou-de-pied devant, ballonné devant sur la pointe 2xs, close R ft frt in 5th plié, échappé to 2d, plié in 4th L ft frt, double pirouette en dehors, close R ft 5th derrière. Same starting with piqué onto pt with R. Repeat both sides.

The teacher's corrections were that the leg should not be thrown away; it should feel as if it is being pulled.

Exercise 3

Preparation, standing on L, R ft tendu à la quatrième derrière: Turn body to face Vaganova corner 2, croisé derrière, piqué arabesque R (1st arabesque), failli L as R rolls off pointe and arms change to Russian 4th arabesque (now in a lunge in

4th position, L ft frt facing corner 2). En face glissade précipitée derrière R,

piqué R attitude croisé derrière (arms Vaganova 3rd), roll off pointe to 4th

position as arms open to 2d. Piqué L 1st arabesque, chassé with R to corner 8,

step R, from écarté derrière, grand rond de jambe en l'air relevé en dedans (arms

do a reverse circle from 2d to Vaganova 3rd), finishing with L ft tendu croisé

devant and R fondu (wrists are crossed in front of body). Contretemps and
repeat starting to the L. Repeat both sides.

   This is executed very slowly to gain strength and control. The teacher's corrections were that the back must be very expressive; it must be a "talking back." Also, stepping into the piqué arabesque, the foot must be *completely* stretched.

Exercise 4

Preparation, standing on L, R ft tendu croisé derrière: Moving on the diagonal toward corner 2 pas marché, (or in Vaganova, pas jeté fondu) sur la pointe with petit battement sur le cou-de-pied beating derrière and then devant—step R, L, same pas marché on R, but turning body to face corner 4 with L leg extending to corner 2, turn again and step on L with the R leg beating and extending to écarté devant. Piqué retiré devant en avant stepping toward corner 2 with body facing corner 8 2xs. Close 5th R ft frt, plié. Relevé double rond de jamb en l'air écarté devant, close R ft frt in 5th, plié. Moving backward toward corner 6, pas jeté fondu sur la pointe with petit battement sur le cou-de-pied beating devant and then derrière—step L, R, L. Piqué arabesque on R, close L devant in 5th plié. Assemblé soutenu sur les pointes en tournant en dehors, chainé turns on the diagonal toward corner 1. Finish in big posé effacé derrière. Step is executed moving L.

   The teacher's corrections were that dancers must be careful not to drop from the toe to the heel on the pas jeté fondu, but roll very carefully—lower gently through the foot. The feet must be very beautiful on the petit battement.

Exercise 5

Preparation, croisé, R ft frt in 5th facing corner 8: Fondu on L and développé croisé devant with R, close 5th plié, fondu on R and développé croisé derrière with L, close 5th plié, turning en face, double rond de jambe en l'air relevé en dehors on L, close 5th derrière plié, double rond de jambe en l'air relevé en dehors on R, close 5th derrière plié. Piqué on R to 1st arabesque, plié, relevé, plié, relevé to attitude derrière (changing to attitude arm), passer la jambe fondu on R with L in tendu croisé devant and wrists crossed in front of body. Moving to the L, bourrée in circle around self to finish facing corner 2 L ft frt in 5th, croisé devant. Same starting with L ft frt. Repeat both sides.

The teacher stated she did not want the circle to be a tight one—it should be a full circle with the front leg straighter than the back one to make it easier to get around in the circle. She also wanted the dancers to move very fast, "pushing" the back foot to allow for quick movement.

Exercise 6

Moving across the floor to the R. Preparation, standing on L, R ft tendu croisé devant: Emboîté en tournant en dedans sur les pointes, R L R, plié on L, piqué tour en dedans 2xs on R, repeat the emboîtés (R L R plié on L), piqué into chaîné turns to the R, plié on L. Continue across the floor to the R. Same to the L across floor.

The teacher's corrections were that she wants very strong and sharp feet; dancers should not get up to pointe slowly.

Exercise 7

Preparation, R ft frt in 5th, croisé devant: Entrechat quatre, passé R ft closing 5th derrière as body turns to face corner 2. Same with L ft starting front and turning on the passé to face corner 8. En face, 4 passés closing derrière. Turning en dehors in one complete revolution, passé R, close bk, passé R, close frt, passé R close bk, passé R close frt (now directly en face). En face retiré R devant, close 5th devant in plié, double pirouette in dehors, close 5th derrière plié. Same starting with L ft frt in 5th.

The teacher's corrections were that on the pirouette, dancers should bring the arms in to be smaller; if the arms are big, they make it difficult to turn. She wants them to stay for a moment in every relevé so she can see the position.

Every exercise in this class was extremely slow, which demanded tremendous strength and control. Following these 7 exercises, the class worked on two variations from *Sleeping Beauty*. The entire class lasted one hour.

ADULT CLASSES

Adult Pointe Class, Ruth Page Foundation School

This class was inspired by Patricia Klekovic.

BARRE

Exercise 1 (Plié)

L hand on barre, Demi-plié [1], straighten legs, tendu à la seconde [2] close 5th back [&], tendu à la seconde [&] close 5th front [4]. Demi-plié, straighten knees [5], rise to pointe [6], roll down [7]. Demi-plié and relevé [8], push out in plié en pointe over the pointes [1], straighten knees [2]. Demi-plié [3], relevé en pointe [4], lower heels through plié [&], relevé [5] and lower on straight legs [6]. Repeat to other side. [7] [8]

Exercise 2 (Dégagé or battement jeté)

L hand on barre, 5th position, R ft frt: Dégagé devant 2xs [& 1 & 2], dégagé derrière 2xs [& 3 & 4], échappé to 4th, plié in 5th 2xs [5 6 7 8]. Repeat starting to the back. Dégagé à la seconde [&] with R, close bk [1], same close frt [& 2], dégagé à la seconde with L [&], close frt [3], same close [& 4] bk, échappé to 2d [5], plié in 5th 2xs [6 7 8]. Repeat except starting with inside leg for dégagé à la seconde. Repeat to other side.

Exercise 3 (Tendu)

1st position, facing barre, both hands on barre: Tendu R à la seconde [1], flex ft [2], inside circle with ankle [3], touch floor [4], push over pointe to R (lunging to R) [5] [6], straighten up [7], close to 1st [8]. Repeat L, R, L.

Exercise 4 (Rond de jambe)

L hand on barre, 5th position, R ft frt: Tendu R devant [1], plié in 4th [&], relevé in 4th [2], plié, relevé in 4th [& 3], plié, straighten L pt frt [& 4], R close 5th [& 5]. Tendu L derrière [&], plié, relevé in 4th [6], plié, relevé in 4th [& 7], plié, straighten R pt back [& 8], L close 5th [& 1]. Rond de jambe en dehors with R, finishing with R frt tendu devant [2], plié in 4th [&], relevé [3], plié [& 4], straighten L and pt frt with R [5 6 7 8]. Repeat en dedans. Rond de jambe en dehors [1] [2] 2½xs finishing with R frt tendu devant [3], plié in 4th [&], relevé [4], lower L heel [&], cambré [5 6] forward with R ft still in tendu devant and both legs straight [7 8]. Repeat en dedans [1–8]. Close 5th. Repeat to other side.

Exercise 5 (Développé)

L hand on barre, 5th position, R ft frt: Demi-plié, sous-sus, retiré R leg to knee, then développé devant, close 5th. Same with inside leg to arabesque, same with R to à la seconde, hold in 2nd. Fouetté to face barre, balance in arabesque, close to 5th and turn to begin other side.

Exercise 6 (Rond de jamb en l'air en dedans)

Facing barre, R ft *behind* in 5th: Glissade derrière R, rond de jambe en l'air en relevé en dedans with R, close 5th frt. Same L. Passé R ft, close 5th frt. Passé R ft to 4th. Pirouette en dedans, close to 5th frt. Repeat to L.

Exercise 7 (Glissade précipitée with relevé)

Facing barre, R ft frt in 5th:Glissade précipitée devant 2xs R, relevé on R with L in retiré derrière, plié on R and relevé, plié passé with L ending in 5th in front. Repeat to L. Repeat exercise except instead of 2 relevé and 1 passé, do 4 relevés, hold a balance and then close L in 5th in front. Repeat to L.

Exercise 8 (Grand battement)

L hand on barre, R ft in 5th frt. Preparation, sous-sus: Grand battement devant 4xs. Développé R devant, fouetté to arabesque putting R hand on barre, close R in 5th bk and roll down. Sous-sus. Grand battement à la seconde 4xs closing bk, frt, bk, frt, développé L à la seconde, retiré derrière and close bk. Sous-sus. Grand battement derrière with L 4xs, développé L leg to arabesque, fouetté away from the barre, close 5th, roll down with L ft frt in 5th. Sous-sus. Grand battement à la seconde with R closing frt, bk, frt, bk, développé R a la seconde, retiré devant, close 5th in frt and roll down. Sous-sus. Grand battement derrière with inside leg (L) 4xs. Développé derrière to arabesque, fouetté toward the barre, close 5th and roll down with L ft in 5th frt. Repeat to Left.

Although it is atypical to have five sets of 8 counts, we feel this exercise is more complete with the five sets.

CENTER

Exercise 1

R ft in 5th frt: Relevé, plié, 3xs, hold the balance, roll down to 5th, 2xs. Repeat except in 4th position. Repeat to L.

Exercise 2

Moving across floor, R ft in 5th position frt: Chassé, pas de bourrée dessous $\overset{\&\ 1}{}$ $\overset{\&\ \ \ a\ \ \ 2}{}$ (under) to R (or tombé instead of chassé), to 4th position facing directly front (à la quatrième). Pirouette on L en dehors. Repeat across floor. Same to L. $\overset{3}{}$ $\overset{4}{}$

Exercise 3

R ft in 5th back: Glissade derrière R, rond de jambe en l'air en relevé en dedans $\overset{\&\ \ \ \ 1}{}$ $\overset{\&\ \ \ \ 2}{}$ with R. Same L. Pas de bourrée dessous en tournant to R, finish in 4th position, $\overset{\&\ 3\ \&\ 4}{}$ $\overset{5\ \&\ 6}{}$ R ft frt, facing corner 2. Pirouette en dedans finishing with L in 4th facing $\overset{\&}{}$ $\overset{7}{}$ corner 1. Pirouette en dedans ending with R ft in 5th frt facing directly front. $\overset{\&}{}$ $\overset{8}{}$ Repeat to L.

NOTES

Two excellent record albums (ST 810 and ST811) that detail Graded Pointe Technique are available from Stepping Tone Records, P.O. Box 35236, Los Angeles, California, 90035. A video including the exercises from both albums can also be ordered.

10

Pointe-related Injuries and Their Remedies

POINTE DANCING AND INJURY

In addition to natural ability, motivation, and dedication, a dancer must have a supple body and feet, natural turnout, healthy knees, and excellent training geared to developing proper technique in order to survive the rigors of pointe work.

As Dr. Justin Howse, orthopedic surgeon to the Royal Ballet School, explains in his book *Dance Technique and Injury Prevention,* no dance-related injury is an "act of God."[1] Variables such as the time spent dancing per day, week, or month; experience level; anatomical limitations; technical knowledge; quality of teaching and shoe fitting; history of previous injury; surfaces on which dancing is performed; and strength and conditioning level are among the factors that determine the likelihood of sustaining a pointe-related injury.

In his book *Dancer's Guide to Injuries of the Lower Extremities,* Stuart Wright, who has worked with students at the North Carolina School for the Arts as well as with many professional dancers, states, "virtually all dance injuries result from faulty technique."[2] Wright feels that incorrect line and improper weight-bearing are the principal factors that lead to injury and suggests that technical correction is the best means of prevention and treatment.

Even with optimum technique, dancers who wear pointe shoes are bound to experience wear and tear on their feet. Structural problems in pointe shoes, long strenuous classes and rehearsals, or poor placement caused by tired or weak muscles incapable of holding the feet in proper alignment may cause a variety of physical stresses and strains.

Injuries can also be the result of oversights by teachers or choreographers. Doctors expect a sharp increase in the number of ballet injuries each winter and spring during *Nutcracker* and concert and recital seasons. Rehearsal schedules suddenly multiply, resulting in overuse injuries which could be avoided by beginning rehearsals sooner and increasing them gradually.

Dr. William Hamilton notes that the injuries of professional and nonprofessional dancers are quite different. He finds a "tremendous Darwinism at work in ballet, or survival of the fittest." Most of the "wrong" bodies and less talented children are weeded out in the training process, leaving the "thoroughbred racehorses" to enter the profession. Many of the injuries he sees in nonprofessional patients result because their body types are not suited to ballet.

American pointe dancers are more subject to chronic injury than their Russian counterparts because they are less likely to be prescreened for physical limitations at the outset of their training. They are also more likely to experience overuse-abuse problems. Russian dancers have longer seasons and more consistent spacing between performances, allowing them more recovery time. A major American ballet company prepares for a season with six to eight intensive weeks of rehearsal; company members then continue to rehearse and take class during the season. Smaller companies often have very intense rehearsal periods leading to extremely short seasons and then may be inactive for months.

A major consideration in many injuries is that the average dancer often lacks even the most basic knowledge of the anatomy, kinesiology, and biomechanics of her own body. To meet the physical as well as the artistic demands of pointe dancing, such knowledge is vital.

FINDING MEDICAL CARE

Finding medical care for pointe-related injuries requires seeking out the services of a caregiver who has as much knowledge of dance as medicine. Needless to say, this remains a rare commodity. With the exception of the medical specialists who work with major dance companies, there are still few doctors who know much about dance injuries. Many dancers have to settle for a competent doctor who has little experience dealing with dancers or even athletes.

There are some muscular disorders unique to dancers which the average doctor may not know how to treat effectively. As chiropractor Janiz A. Minshew explains, the fact that dancers are so far beyond the norm in terms of physical conditioning makes them a mystery to "lay" doctors. A dancer can be out of commission as a dancer and still appear to be healthy by normal standards. Doctors who treat dancers quickly learn that what may be normal on a dancer's x-ray may not be normal for a nondancer.

Since dancers have a large range of motion, they must maintain exceptionally strong muscles and cannot be treated in the same manner as nondancers. Taking time off can lead to pain in noninjured areas where there was none before. The more in shape a dancer is, the faster she gets out of shape without exercise.

Often a dancer seeking care for a routine injury is told to stop dancing until it heals. This is usually not the correct advice for a dancer who knows she must make every effort to keep her training level up. In the time it takes for an injury to heal, the dancer can get out of shape. When she returns to dancing, she could reinjure herself as a result of the layoff. Realizing that they must stay active, dancers ignore the advice of doctors who try to tell them otherwise.

It is rare to find specialists like New York chiropractor Dr. Nathan Novick who says, "When a dancer tells me—I've got to go on—and I know they shouldn't, I just say good luck and I'll see you tomorrow. A dancer's emotional and mental health is just as important as his physical health. If you take away dance, he'll suffer in other ways."

While the fields of sports medicine and dance medicine are beginning to attract more interest, the simple economic facts are that few doctors can afford to specialize in treating dancers. In many areas there are few dancers to treat, and gaining the specific skill and background necessary to deal with their special problems requires a lot of time and knowledge of dance. Dance injuries are frequently far more subtle than sports injuries and demand an awareness of the intricate movement patterns that may have caused them. In addition, dancers often have limited incomes and no medical insurance.

Still, it is important for an injured dancer to do anything and everything possible to see a doctor with dance injury expertise. She should seek out sports medicine specialists to discover if they might also be familiar with dance, call the nearest ballet company or college dance department head for a suggestion, and ask other dancers. In the event of serious injury, a dancer might have to travel a great distance to get to the right doctor. The inconvenience and expense of traveling to find skilled care have to be weighed against the possibility of ending a career in dance.

Dr. James G. Garrick of the Center for Sports Medicine in San Francisco urges dancers to "shop" until they find someone who listens to their needs and offers informed help. He adds that it is important to avoid "quick and dirty one-shot treatments." Someone who will inject you with cortisone on request to keep you dancing today may not care what happens to you two years from now.

The adage "no pain, no gain" can be a dangerous one for a dancer to follow. Although there is a certain degree of healthy feel-good hurt that comes from a well-stretched muscle, there is a fine line dividing that feeling from the kind of pain resulting from incorrect stretching. Learning to differentiate between "good" pain and "bad" pain is vital if a dancer wants to avoid permanent damage to her body.

Dancers often wait too long to do something about an injury. They try to ignore small things that unnecessarily turn into major problems. This is a basic human tendency, but it is sometimes encouraged in dancers by unsympathetic responses from teachers, directors, and choreographers, and by pressure to keep dancing.

Dr. Garrick notes that professional dancers often have medical problems on the road, where local medical personnel may feel pressured to get them back on stage at the expense of their long-term well-being. He advises dancers to call for advice from a care center they trust and not to make a stupid decision under management pressure.

This problem is related to the fact that unlike dancers in other parts of the world, American dancers have no job security. A member of a major Russian or European company often has a job guaranteed for twenty years by contract. They are on salary during periods of medical injury, their medical expenses are covered, and helping them maintain their health and productivity is a direct concern of their employers. This is a far cry from the typical American dancer who is terrified of becoming injured because she cannot afford to pay the medical bills, fears losing her job, and cannot find a qualified specialist to treat her.

A dance specialist will approach a dancer's injury as a medical detective. As podiatrist Dr. Tom Novella explains, a dance specialist must look at everything in the dancer's history rather than a single injury. Everything is linked. The doctor needs to identify the original injury in a chain. He needs to treat the cause of a specific injury as well as cure it. Otherwise there is a strong possibility the injury will return.

Many female dancers' problems stem from the lack of mobility caused by pointe shoes, yet some problems that appear to be caused by shoes are actually technical or structural problems. On the other hand, sometimes what appears to be technical or structural could be the result of the shoe. Again, the doctor must be a sleuth.

In recent years dance medical specialists have noticed a disturbing trend among pointe dancers toward elective "cosmetic" surgery. For instance a dancer might want to have her arches made higher. Dr. Tom Novella had an inquiry from a dancer whose choreographer wanted her foot to have a more winged look; she wanted a surgically induced bunion. Noting that even the best surgeons have failure rates of one out of forty cases, Dr. Novella suggests that if a dancer is active and healthy, she should hold on to what she's got and work with it. In other words, if it doesn't hurt, leave it alone.

Chiropractor Janiz A. Minshew reminds dancers of another vital reason to pay careful attention to the treatment of any injuries they sustain. She says, "Age alone will not significantly alter performance and physical ability. However, age combined with injury combined with years of compensation cause ability to diminish rapidly. If you can fix problems rather than compensate for them throughout your dance life, this attrition will not be as sharp or as fast."

MEDICAL SPECIALISTS: WHO DOES WHAT?

When starting to look for medical assistance, it helps to have a clear idea of the role of each specialist.[3]

Podiatrists, or Doctors of Podiatric Medicine (D.P.M.s), treat feet exclusively. Podiatry school requires four years of training beyond college, and some podiatrists take additional training. Those certified by the American Board of Podiatric Surgery have additional practical experience.

Orthopedists are M.D.s who specialize in bones and muscles. After medical school, they complete a five- or six-year residency in orthopedic surgery. Although they are trained to treat any area of the body, a small but ever-growing number specialize in foot and ankle problems and many have completed postresidency fellowships in this field.

Osteopaths are physicians who diagnose, prescribe for, and treat bodily diseases and injuries. They are concerned with research into the causes, transmission, and control of disease and other ailments attributable to impairments in the musculoskeletal system and disorders of bones, muscles, nerves, and other body systems. They use X-ray, drugs, and other accepted methods of medical and surgical care. When deemed beneficial, they use manipulative therapy to treat and correct body impairments.

Chiropractors adjust the spinal column and other joints of the body to prevent disease and correct abnormalities believed caused by interference with the nervous system. Using X-ray and other instruments and equipment, they examine patients to determine the nature and extent of disorder present.

Physical therapists plan and administer medically prescribed physical therapy treatment programs that restore function, relieve pain, and prevent disability after disease or bodily injury. Physical therapists may work in private practice or be employed in hospitals and rehabilitation centers.

LEVELS OF INJURY

There are three major levels of dance-related injuries. First are acute injuries, which are injuries at the time they occur, such as a sprained ankle. Whether acute injuries are mild, moderate, or severe, they usually produce bleeding or hemorrhage into the surrounding soft-tissue structures. Treatment of these injuries is designed to lessen the initial injury to soft tissues since recovery is directly tied to the degree of original trauma and bleeding.

Dr. Hamilton suggests dancers remember the acronym RICE when confronting an acute injury—Rest, Immobilization, Cold, and Elevation. Rest means getting weight off the injury to avoid stirring up more bleeding and swelling. Immobilization means "splinting." In the case of a mild injury, the splint might be a simple Ace bandage applied loosely enough to avoid impairing circulation but tightly enough to restrict swelling. Elevation and ice also help keep swelling down. Ice should be wrapped in an ice bag or towel and not applied directly to the skin. An injury should be iced intermittently over the first twelve to twenty-four hours. Heat should not be applied during this period because it dilates the blood vessels and can cause excessive bleeding. Bleeding is no longer a factor after twenty-four to thirty-six hours, and heat can then increase circulation and have a positive impact on the healing process.

For acute injury, Dr. Hamilton tells his patients to get off the injured leg, elevate it, and ice it for twenty-four hours. Then keep weight off the leg as much as possible and keep it elevated for the next twenty-four hours, and start warm soaks after thirty-six hours.

Chronic injuries—the second level of dance-related injury—are those that have never healed or from which the patient has not completely recovered. If an acute injury is incorrectly treated or receives inadequate rest, it may develop into a chronic injury. Tendonitis, overuse strains, stress fractures that have never healed due to lack of rest, or pulled hamstring muscles that have become chronically tight and developed painful scar tissue are examples. Chronic problems require prolonged activity reduction to heal and can limit the dancer for as long as several months.

Third are recurring injuries—those that do heal but return again. For instance, a sprained ankle may heal but still be weak. Therefore it may be reinjured a month later. This cycle can only be broken through strengthening and rehabilitation. Some of these injuries may be due to such external factors as hard floors or errors in technique, placement, or alignment.

Dr. Hamilton observes that chronic injuries are the most common among professional dancers and that the specific injuries differ in frequency from company to company. This is the result of different choreographic styles as well as the floors different companies dance on, how much they travel, and the body types the company seeks.

POINTE-RELATED INJURIES OF THE FOOT AND ANKLE

In 1986, Dr. James Garrick reported the results of a five-year study in which he analyzed 1,055 injuries to dancers from two professional ballet companies and a large professional school. The dancers studied ranged in age from five to over forty. He observed that 9 percent of these injuries occurred to the spine, 3.8 percent to the upper extremities, 9.7 percent to the hip, 22.3 percent to the knee, 11.4 percent to the leg, 16.6 percent to the ankle, and 21.6 percent to the feet.[4]

While pointe shoes and pointe work have implications for a variety of injuries to the knee, leg, hip, and spine, we have chosen to stress the sites where the strain of dancing on pointe has the most immediate impact, the foot and ankle. Most injuries start from the bottom up, with problems such as feet that sickle or roll in or out, weak ankles, lax ligaments, and exceedingly high or low arches that are aggravated by flawed technique. On the other hand, Dr. Novella suggests that if a dancer is prone to foot injuries, the cause could be weakness in the hips or back, which brings stress to the feet. Without adequate strength in the upper torso, the dancer can land too hard and injure her feet.

The following review of foot and ankle injuries and conditions is a compilation of information and suggestions received from the medical personnel we interviewed. These brief summaries should help the dancer identify an injury. They are not intended to supplant the advice of a properly qualified medical specialist. Diabetics should not self-treat even the most minor foot problems without the supervision of a physician.

The Foot

In Dr. Garrick's study of ballet injuries, foot injuries were the second most often seen injury. Dancing on pointe adds a new list of demands to an already challenged foot. Not only does the dancer have to bear her weight on the tips of the toes, but she has to adjust to the nonanatomically designed aspects of pointe shoes.

When injuries of the foot and ankle force the dancer to keep weight off her lower extremities, Dr. Novella suggests doing floor barres and other excercises not involving the feet to keep the rest of the body stretched.

PROBLEMS ON THE EXTERNAL SURFACE OF THE FOOT

Athlete's Foot Athlete's foot is a fungal infection that thrives in a moist, dark environment. Tight, closed shoes and perspiring feet provide the ideal environment for athlete's foot. To prevent athlete's foot, the dancer should wash her feet at least once a day, being careful to dry the skin between her toes. If she develops the condition, over-the-counter remedies should cure it, or a doctor can prescribe a strong antifungal drug. She needs to continue preventive steps once the condition clears up, since it can readily return. Athlete's foot is contagious and can be contracted by not wearing shoes in the dressing room or shower room.

Blisters Blisters are caused by continuous friction when tender skin is rubbed back and forth against the inside of the shoe. This friction separates skin layers, and one layer slides over the other. The resulting pocket fills up with fluid that is either clear or contains blood. Many blisters caused by pointe shoes are blood blisters. Blisters may result from shoes that fit incorrectly, or they may develop during the breaking-in process. Seams in tights or socks that are too snug or wrinkles in those that are too loose can be responsible.

Using a drying powder can reduce moisture and the chances of getting blisters. Blister-prone dancers sometimes routinely tape their problem toes or lubricate them with petroleum jelly and wrap them in lamb's wool. In the days of czarist Russia, ballerinas reportedly put thin slices of veal in their shoes to prevent blisters.

It is best to catch blisters before they form. The warning sign is a warm red "hot spot." As soon as the dancer sees the skin is irritated, she should use a friction-proof substance such as petroleum jelly or cover the spot with a Band-Aid or moleskin. Another good protectant is Spenco Second Skin, a slippery friction-absorbing pad that can be purchased in pharmacies.

Once caused, a blister can be a small annoyance or a serious infection. The dancer needs to deal with blisters before they pop open and bleed; once the blister opens, the dancer must find a way to prevent infection from occurring while she continues to dance. When the raw skin is exposed, the pain of dancing with a large blister can be extreme. In such cases it may be necessary to give the blister time to heal rather than risk deepening or infecting the area by applying more friction. The exposed skin can be treated with Merthiolate.

A blood blister requires immediate consultation with a medical specialist since there is a greater risk of infection, but a dancer can treat an "unpopped" blister filled with clear fluid herself. First sterilize the blistered area with alcohol and then sterilize a needle with alcohol or flame. Using the needle, puncture the blister in several spots around the edge. Carefully push on the blister with a sterile pad to release the fluid.

Dancers used to be told to cut away the dead skin, but they are now advised to allow it to remain to cut down the risk of infection. Then apply an over-the-counter antibiotic ointment to the blister and cover it with moleskin. Repeat this complete procedure three more times within twenty-four hours. After three or four days, the dead skin comes off naturally. Try covering the tender new skin with a product like Spenco Second Skin or New Skin until it has time to toughen up.

Expose the blister to fresh air whenever possible, being careful to keep it sterilized. If dancing on pointe is painful before the blister has healed, try surrounding it with several circular layers of moleskin.

Calluses Calluses are thick, hard mounds of skin that appear on the bottom or side of the foot. They are caused by the friction and pressure of rubbing the skin of the feet against supportive surfaces. They usually occur on the knuckles and tops of the toes and on the Achilles tendon where the shoe rubs the heel. Dancers with flat feet or exceptionally high arches tend to develop a lot of callus. Excessive callus also frequently forms on one side of a tilted heel or imbalanced big toe.

Calluses appear as reddened areas that may be tender following pointe work, but will harden later. While some callus formation is useful for dancers in "toughening" the feet, a lot of callus may also indicate poor posture and weight-bearing or poorly fitting pointe shoes.

Callus that has grown too thick can produce pain and a burning sensation. It can also crack and bleed, and infections can result. Thickened callus that has lost its elasticity tends to move as a mass and can actually tear.

A painful blister can form under a callus. If such a blister breaks, the callus may fall off, resulting in a very sore foot and a long, painful healing process. A callus under the second metatarsal sometimes forms a hard core, which is another source of considerable pain. Calluses under the second metatarsal are a common problem for dancers with bunions.

To keep callus under control, soak the feet in a bowl of warm water and several tablespoons of mild soap for ten to fifteen minutes. Then gently file off excess callus accumulation with an emery file and massage the area with a small amount of olive oil. Do not try to remove the entire callus buildup in one treatment, but be sure to keep any remaining callus level with the skin around it. Finally, smooth the area with the finer side of the emery board. Repeat this procedure after bathing or showering, being careful never to file away too much callus. The area can be protected by applying moleskin before dancing.

Corns Corns are the result of abnormal pressure from incorrectly fitting shoes and can be quite painful. Unlike calluses, corns form in places that do not bear weight or they develop between the toes. Dancers with high arches are susceptible to corns because their toes tend to buckle.

There are two kinds of corns—hard and soft. Both types result from shoes pressing on the top layer of tissue, causing the tissue to be pressed inward. Since corns press on nerve endings and cause inflammation, they can be painful and incapacitating.

A hard corn is most often found on the side or the top of the little toe and can be caused by short pointe shoes. The most logical way to get rid of a hard corn is to remove the friction that is causing it. In other words, pad the spots where corns are forming with moleskin and look closely at the way the fit of pointe shoes may be causing the problem.

Surgically removing corns is not an option open to dancers. Chemical corn pads should also be avoided because of the risk of infection from a burn to the skin. If a dancer insists on using such pads, she should read the directions with care and be aware of any signs of infection, such as redness (particularly red streaks running up the leg), heat, pain, or swelling. She should seek medical care immediately if these signs persist because she could have blood poisoning and might need antibiotics.

To safely reduce the size of hard corns, soak the feet in warm, soapy water for five or ten minutes. Dry the feet and massage the toes with olive oil. Carefully rub the corn with the coarse side of an emery board and smooth the area with the finer side of the emery board. Do not go too far with this first effort. Repeat this routine whenever corns are softened with a shower or bath, until the corn is even with the skin. Only a podiatrist should cut away a corn.

Soft corns, which develop in the moist environment between the toes, have a mushier appearance than hard corns. They are gray-white in color and often appear between the fourth and fifth toes, resulting from pointe shoes that are too tight across the metatarsal area. Soft corns may signal that wearing a pointe shoe with a broader box is indicated. Soft corns thrive in warm, wet conditions, so feet must be kept as dry as possible with an antiseptic powder.

To treat soft corns, the dancer has to separate the toes involved to eliminate the pressure point. Once the pressure is gone and the area is kept dry, soft corns should disappear. The toes can be separated with lamb's wool, cotton, or a commercial toe spacer. Without this cushioning, bone spurs can rub away the tissue and cause an ulcer which is very painful and can become dangerously infected. If this separating strategy is unsuccessful, consult a doctor about the possibility of removing the blisterlike covering over the corn. Again, surgical removal of soft corns is not an alternative for dancers, and the use of medicated corn pads with soft corns should be avoided.

Dr. Novella warns that a thick soft corn can almost become an abscess without the dancer's feeling it if it is masking a pinched nerve. Novella often sees this happen between the third and fourth toes. A doctor should check to see if the sensitivity in the area of the soft corn is the same as it is in the rest of the foot. If not, he or she can try to discover the cause before it leads to infection.

Dermatitis Dermatitis is a skin irritation that occurs in reaction to something—usually an allergen or stress. The feet are often afflicted with itching, burning, or reddened areas. Reddish bumps or blisters may appear. Contact dermatitis usually results from skin contact with a substance to which one is allergic. Sometimes shoe leathers are processed with strong chemicals that are highly allergenic. If necessary, a test can be performed to determine the nature of the allergy. Neurodermatitis is stress related.

PROBLEMS WITH TOENAILS

Toenails are far more complicated structures than they appear. Each nail has six parts, starting from the inside and working to the tip—the matrix, the lunula, the cuticle, the root, the nail bed, and the tip. Toenails are made of the protein keratin, similar to the protein that makes up hair. To avoid problems, nails should be kept properly trimmed and cleaned.

Ingrown Toenails Ingrown toenails occur when the side edge of the toenail curls and pushes down into the soft skin of the toe, causing irritation or infection. Ingrown nails can be caused by abnormal pressure from pointe shoes that are too short or narrow, by incorrectly trimmed toenails, and by thickened nails caused by pointe work.

Redness is the first sign of an ingrown toenail. Sharp pain and swelling can follow. If any pus or infection is present, see a doctor immediately. If pain occurs, soak the foot in hot water and antibacterial soap several times a day and place a thin bit of alcohol-soaked cotton under the edge of the nail to push the skin away while the nail grows. By lifting the nail away from the nail bed, the cotton should provide relief from pain.

If the ingrown nail has reached a point where it must be clipped away, it is wise to see a doctor. Podiatrist Dr. Steven Baff treats serious cases by cutting away the ingrown nail so the tissue around the nail does not become inflamed or by permanently removing the ingrown portion of the nail down to the root using a chemical or laser beam.

Dancers can help avoid the problem by trimming the toenail straight, with only a slight rounding at the corners. The nail should never be rounded enough to come into contact with the skin on either side of the nail bed. Some dancers cut the nail a little shorter in the middle, giving the nail the shape of a letter U or V, and then pack a tiny bit of lamb's wool in the corners of the nail plate. Investing in a good pair of nail clippers is an essential for toenail maintenance.

Bruised Toenails The toes take a beating every day in pointe shoes and may show evidence of bruises and bleeding under the nails. This is particularly true if pointe shoes are too short or too narrow as well as if toenails are too long. When the blood vessels under the toes rupture, this blood cannot escape, causing a clot under the nail. This condition can also be caused by dropping something on the toe.

If the nail is iced as soon as the trauma has happened and kept iced periodically, the blood clot may be kept from forming. If the clot does form, the toenail can be saved if it is treated within two days after the blood has entered the space between the nail and the nail bed.

To treat the nail, Dr. James Garrick suggests heating a paper clip in a flame until it is red hot and pushing it through the nail to release the blood. The clip may have to be reheated a few times to complete the procedure, and additional pressure may have to be applied to the sides of the nail as well. This method should bring instant relief. After performing this procedure, soak the foot three times a day in warm water and Epsom salts and keep the nail painted with Merthiolate. Keep the nail covered with a Band-Aid.

If not treated soon enough, the nail will probably be lost within a month. If the nail does start to detach itself and there is no sign of infection, secure the nail in place with adhesive tape to protect the tissue underneath. It will take the new toenail about six months to grow back.

Thickened Toenails   A thickened toenail is grayish black or brown in color and occurs when the toe is constantly jammed by a pointe shoe. The pressure produces an additional layer of nail that in turn creates more pressure against the bed of the nail. Consult a podiatrist for treatment of thickened toenails.

Fungus Nails   A thick nail that becomes yellow-brown and has spongy growths underneath might be a sign of a fungus infection. A fungus infection can be a very serious condition and may spread to other toes. See a doctor immediately for a suspected fungus infection.

PROBLEMS WITH TOES

Toes of Various Lengths   Dr. Richard Braver estimates that one-third of the population has a second toe longer than the first toe, one-third has a first toe longer than the second, and one-third has both toes the same length. A second or third toe is not meant to function as the pressure-taking toe, so pain in the ball of the foot as well as stress fractures can result. While feet with longer second or third toes are not designed to be subjected to pointe shoes, recently introduced orthotic devices (see p. 157) may help by elevating or repositioning the toes to avoid undue pressure.

Bunions (Hallux Valgus)   Dr. Tom Novella feels that almost all dancers have a bunion or bunions in some stage of development. A bunion is a bony knob on the outside of the big toe that forms when the toe is forced to angle inward toward the smaller ones. The projection is caused by the deviation or drifting out of joint of one of the bones of the big toe. Pressure on the projection causes the skin around it to thicken, adding to the pressure. A portion of the bunion is made up of a bursa between the skin and the bone. This fluid-filled sac may feel bone-hard. A red, swollen bunion is the result of an inflamed bursa.

A hallux valgus is present when the first metatarsal deviates in the direction of the other foot and forms a knob on the side of the foot. This condition is often inherited and is usually seen on feet where the second toe is longer than the first, the first metatarsal is short, and the ball of the foot is overflexible. Dancing on pointe and rolling in to increase turnout can cause a mild case of hallux valgus due to stretching the ligaments on the inside of the foot.

While some bunions do not produce pain while dancing, in some cases shoe pressure on the jutting joint can cause bursitis or inflammation of the joint, causing it to become painful, swollen, and tender. In the case of either a bunion or a hallux valgus, the stress and friction of tight pointe shoes can create such problems.

When bunions are painful, a toe spacer can be worn between the big and second toes, which properly positions the big toe and prevents its being crushed into the other toes at an angle. A toe spacer can be made out of lamb's wool or a one-inch strip of paper towel folded into a small rectangle and placed between the toes. Moleskin pads and commercially made bunion cushions can also be used.

Care should be taken to see that pointe shoes (and street shoes) are wide enough across the metatarsal joints to avoid undue pressure and that the foot is placed properly on pointe. Padding around the bunion is helpful, and latex bunion shields or Dr. Scholl's Bunion Splints may provide relief from pressure. Try cutting slits in the side or back of pointe shoes to cut down on pressure or cut wedges out of these areas and fill them in with elastic or moleskin.

When the bunion projections are sore and inflamed, treat them with icing and contrast baths. Anti-inflammatories may also be helpful. Often, as the result of a bunion, other parts of the foot may start to hurt. The dancer might have pain under a second toe or develop a hammertoe. A soft corn could form between the first and second toe.

Most doctors agree that the hazards of bunion surgery outweigh the benefits for dancers. While the cosmetic result may be more attractive, such surgery may result in limited motion of the joint, sharply reduced technique range on demi-pointe, and chronic pain.

Bunionette A bunionette (sometimes called a tailor's bunion) is an enlargement of the head of the fifth metatarsal. This congenital condition causes the foot to be exposed to abnormal pressure, so a bursa may form over the joint to protect it. When this bursa fills with fluid and becomes inflamed, a burning sensation, swelling, and pain can result. Taking anti-inflammatories and applying ice help reduce the pain and swelling. The bunionette should be padded with felt or moleskin or covered with a commercially produced bunion shield to protect it from the pressure of the pointe shoe.

Hammertoes Hammertoes are toes that curl or hook downward. The condition can be either inherited or aggravated by wearing shoes that are too tight and too short, thus forcing toe joints and the extensor tendon to contract. Eventually the toes become locked and the tendon is permanently shortened. Hammertoes may accompany a bunion. They frequently occur in individuals whose second toes are longer than the first or who have a high arch.

Protective U-shaped pads can keep bent-up hammertoes from rubbing against the inside of the shoe and causing corns. These corns on the tip of the toes or the spot where the joints buckle are the actual source of pain from hammertoes. Treat a hard corn on a hammertoe as if it were a hard corn in any other location. A podiatrist can cut off a portion of the corn if it becomes excessive.

A hammertoe can be strapped with half-inch adhesive tape to the toes on either side during rehearsal or performance to take weight off of it. A podiatrist can guide you in strapping the toe. A hammertoe can only be corrected by surgery, an option not suggested for dancers.

Hallux Limitus and Rigidus Stiffness of the big toe joint is common among teenage dancers and comes from shock and forceful pressure on the joint. Repeated strain causes the toe joint to become inflamed and stiff in the hallus limitus phase. Since the range of motion in the big toe is limited, body weight shifts to the outside of the foot when the dancer is on demi-pointe, which may cause outer ankle strain, weak foot muscles, and pain in the outer leg. Unless the causes are controlled, the toe can become totally rigid, at which point the condition is called hallux rigidus. The key symptom is extreme pain in the joint of the first metatarsal when the dancer goes from demi-point to full pointe. The tendency is to shift weight to the outside of the foot to avoid this pain in the big toe.

The dancer should take anti-inflammatories, cushion street shoes, and pad the area under and immediately behind the joint. Several weeks of rest may be required. Consult a doctor for advice on this condition since, in its extreme form, hallux rigidus may require surgery to restore movement, leading to permanent weakening of this important joint.

Jammed Big Toes As the result of many consecutive hours of pointe work, the ligaments of the toe joint may be sprained, the cartilage may be bruised, or the joint capsule may be stretched and torn. Any of these injuries can be extremely limiting. Treat them by taking anti-inflammatories and massaging with ice three times a day for fifteen minutes.

Neuromas Morton's neuroma is a knotting of nerve fibers marked by shooting pains extending from the ball of the foot between the metatarsals into the toes. These enlarged, inflamed nerves in the ball of the foot usually occur between the third and fourth toes, but sometimes between the fourth and fifth.

At first a Morton's neuroma may appear as a burning feeling that spreads from the heads of the metatarsals toward the heel, initially noticed when weight is borne on the foot. Eventually, the feeling is present at other times too. Then it begins to resemble an electric shock that shoots from the ball of the foot into the toes. Numbness and cramping may be present as well. The pain usually goes away when shoes are removed. If ignored, the involved nerve may become more swollen and permanently scarred. The condition is usually caused by pointe shoes that are excessively tight and jam the heads of the metatarsals together.

The nerve returns to normal if the pressure is eliminated. Treat it with ice three times a day for twenty minutes and take anti-inflammatories. Be sure to ice after class, rehearsal, or performance. Also look in drugstores for special toe pads that separate the affected toes. Keep a pad behind the area that hurts to reduce pressure on the nerve. With luck, relief will arrive in several weeks. Before returning to pointe, see a shoe-fitting expert and experiment with shoes that have wider boxes. If these efforts fail to provide relief, see an orthopedist for advice. Since surgical removal of neuromas involves no joints or bones, this procedure is not out of the question for dancers.

PROBLEMS ON THE TOP AND BOTTOM OF THE FOOT

Extensor Tendonitis This injury involves pain on the top of the foot, accompanied by swelling and redness that can be caused when pointe shoes are too tight and do not allow enough room over this area. As a result of pressure and friction, the extensor tendons are inflamed. The top of the foot appears puffy, and lifting the toes causes discomfort.

Protect tendons by covering the foot or the inside of the pointe shoe with moleskin. As soon as possible, work with a skilled shoe fitter to find a style of pointe shoe that allows more room over the top of the foot.

Dorsal Exostosis This bony bump on the top of the foot may be congenital or caused by constant jamming of the big toe. The friction caused by pointe shoes aggravates the bump, making it inflamed and swollen. Flat or pronated feet are particularly liable to experience these bumps. Treat a swollen, aggravated bony bump by icing it several times a day for twenty minutes and taking anti-inflammatories. Surround the bump with moleskin to relieve pressure.

Plantar Fascitis The plantar fascia is a dense bundle of fibrous tissue strands that starts at the heel and connects with the metatarsal bones at the base of the toes. It stretches and contracts each time the foot is used. If it stretches so far that it loses its flexibility, it tears and causes an overuse condition called plantar fascitis. The key symptom is pain in the bottom of the foot, which may become bruised or swollen. Dancers with high arches and tight fasciae are prime candidates for this injury.

Treat the injury with rest from those movements that cause pain and with anti-inflammatories, ice, and contrast baths. Visit a podiatrist to discuss ways to reduce the pressure on the fascia.

Plantar Warts These virus-caused growths on the soles of the feet can make a dancer feel as if there is something in her shoe. Plantar warts grow in rather than out and appear under the heel, on the ball of the foot, or on the side of the big toe. Normal skin ridges, which continue across the surface of a callus, encircle a plantar wart, leaving only the growth surface smooth. Sometimes the warts appear in groups. If left alone, plantar warts eventually leave of their own accord. If they grow larger or cause discomfort, see a podiatrist about removing them.

Plantar warts are contagious, so wear shoes in the dressing room and shower room. If a classmate or fellow company member who shares such facilities discovers a plantar wart, disinfect the area with undiluted Clorox.

Sesamoiditis If pain is experienced at the base of the big toe where it joins the ball of the foot when pushing off the toe, the sesamoid bones may be irritated. The sesamoids are very small bones in the tendons connected to the big toe. They serve a pulleylike function and can be strained or even fractured. Sesamoids are particularly vulnerable when a bunion or hallux valgus is present. Bony feet and working on a hard dancing surface are also risk factors. Sesamoid trouble is recognized as pain experienced under the metatarsal in the demi-pointe position. Swelling will also be present.

Rest, ice, and anti-inflammatories should be used as treatment. Continue resting until the area is pain-free; then slowly resume activity. Padding beneath the sesamoids can reduce the impact of pounding. If pain is still fairly intense after two weeks, see an orthopedist to determine if there has been a fracture of a sesamoid and a cast is needed.

Stress Fractures Stress fractures, which can occur in any bone, are ranked by Dr. James Garrick as the fifth most frequent dancer's injury. They usually result from big changes in activity levels. Stress fractures can happen in any area of the foot that contacts the ground in a stressful way. They can happen in the sesamoids under the ball of the foot or in the metatarsal shafts. In experienced dancers, stress fractures are common in the base of the second metatarsal. The bone may thicken like the bark of a tree from work and exercise. In novice dancers they are common in the middle of the second metatarsal.

A stress fracture is evidence of the body's attempt to become stronger by removing calcium from one area and laying it down in another area. The stress fracture is a "too much, too soon" injury that happens during this process of removing and laying down calcium. A stress fracture occurs when a bone bends almost to the breaking point. The physical evidence appears in the form of a hairline crack that may not show up on an X-ray. As a result, with rest, a stress fracture may heal before it is diagnosed. Dr. Garrick uses radioisotope bone scans to confirm the diagnosis of a stress fracture early in its history.

Since a stress fracture develops over a period of time, the area around it usually feels tender before any pain is present. This area may not be any larger than the diameter of a penny. Eventually the pain becomes more intense and a burning sensation surrounds the fracture. The area involved becomes very painful to touch and will probably be swollen. Weight-bearing often becomes excruciating when a stress fracture is present.

When treating stress fractures in an early stage, a pain-free state can often be reached after a day or two of complete rest. Anti-inflammatories may be useful during this period, and ice can be applied if there is swelling. Resting a more serious stress fracture might require as long as a week on crutches.

When it is possible to resume dancing, find a level of activity that stops short of causing pain. Wear a thin layer of absorbent padding in the pointe shoe at this stage of the process. When discomfort is experienced, drop back to a lighter activity level. Keep increasing and decreasing the activity level until normalcy returns. Then watch for the warning sign of a tender area the size of a penny to avoid future fractures.

It is important to identify stress factures as early as possible because if ignored they can work all the way through the bone, actually causing it to snap in two. The resulting advanced fracture can require splints or casts, immobilization, and a long recovery period. Dr. Steven Baff uses a surgical shoe, which is a compression type of bandage, when treating advanced stress fractures. This is an anti-inflammatory, wet-type of bandage that hardens on the foot, contouring it to the shape of the foot and locking it into a normal position for function.

Stress fractures may be avoided if the dancer is sensitive to the possibility of developing them during increased periods of activity. The body is most vulnerable to stress fractures about three weeks into an intensified activity period; therefore, it is a good idea to pull back for eight or ten days during this period when bone removal is at its peak.

Dr. Tom Novella has a theory that adolescent dancers who are exremely active with a heavy class load and who get their menstrual periods very late in their teen years may be prone to stress fractures because they have a lack of circulating estrogen needed to make strong bones. If a young, very active dancer has not had her period yet and is getting stress fractures, a medical specialist should be asked about the possible need to take extra calcium. This connection between injury, menstrual function, and nutrient intake was the subject of a research study reported in an article in the *Journal of the American Dietetic Association* in January 1989.[5]

Some stress fractures are caused when a dancer works for speed and to accomplish this does not put the heels down between steps. Since the calf muscle is a spring, without a plié it does not open completely. Then it retains shock instead of absorbing it. Making the heels touch the ground uses muscular energy and takes the stress off the ball of the foot. Stress fractures can also be caused by the impact of repeated jumps and leaps. The lack of shock-absorbing materials in pointe shoes and unresilient dance floors are also factors.

A dancer can also develop a stress fracture when she works in soft shoes or bare feet if she is used to working in a rigid pointe shoe. The toes may not be able to withstand contact with the floor after being shielded in a hard block. On the other hand, a pointe shoe that is too short can cause the toes to curl under or compress or knuckle forward; as a result, the toes do not work properly when a dancer lands from relevés and jumps, so she may get stress fractures on the ball of the foot.

PROBLEMS WITH THE HEEL

Bursitis A bursa is a pocket of fluid wrapped in fibrous tissue that is found in areas of the body exposed to friction. A bursa's walls are moist and lubricated so they can slide. By easing friction where ligaments and tendons cross over bones, bursas make it possible for us to move. When too much pressure irritates a bursa, it can develop thickened walls and become inflamed. Fluid forms, making the bursal sac larger and causing more irritation. An inflamed bursa may be spongy at first, but gradually hardens as it grows, causing more pain. Bursitis can also be caused by a direct blow to the foot that ruptures tiny blood vessels in the bursas.

Bursitis can occur in a number of locations on the foot as a result of shoes that are too narrow, too pointed, or too tight. Dancers who roll in irritate the bursas on the inside of the foot. Pointe dancers often suffer from either a metatarsal bursitis or a bursitis of the heel. In the case of metatarsal bursitis, tight pointe shoes and jumping and leaping on hard, uneven surfaces can cause pain to streak across the ball of the foot, particularly during plié, jumps, and leaps, because the bursas at the heads of the metatarsals are bruised and inflamed.

The inflammation of metatarsal bursitis can be helped by taking anti-inflammatories and icing the area three times a day for three days. Then follow with warm soaks or contrast baths. This problem, however, is best solved with a period of complete rest from weigh-bearing; recovery can take from one to three months. High heels should be avoided, and extra cushioning should be added to street shoes. This pain can also be confused with other problems that plague the metatarsals such as stress fractures and should be reported to a medical specialist.

Bursitis at the heel can be either congenital or caused by pressure on the heel from a tight drawstring or a too-stiff shoe back. Posterior calcaneal bursitis is found at the center of the heel and is an inflammation of a bursa between the tendon and the skin. Another type of bursitis, Haglund's deformity, is located to the side of the heel and takes the form of a raised, hard formation. Bursitis at the heel is often seen in dancers with very low or high arches.

Skin blisters can be a warning sign that too much shoe pressure is present. A burning or aching sensation may precede intense pain. Once pressure is removed from the area, swelling can be reduced in several weeks by icing the heels for twenty minutes twice a day and taking anti-inflammatories. Avoid closed-heeled shoes or pad the backs of shoes with moleskin and elevate the heel with a lift. Some dancers cut the heel of their pointe shoes and sew in an elastic insert to get relief.

Contusions Contusions are bruises that often occur in the foot region; the skin or heel of the foot is especially sensitive to contusions. A contusion produces a pool of blood that has nowhere to go so remains trapped under the skin. Mild contusions produce little inflammation, and most of the discomfort comes from muscle spasms. Apply cold and pressure to avoid swelling, followed by a gradual stretch to relieve muscle spasms. If discomfort persists for more than five or ten minutes, wear an elastic bandage for the rest of the day. If symptoms are present the second day, try contrast baths. More serious contusions result from a hard blow to a muscle or bone and produce a great deal of pain and tenderness when touched. Ice the area and apply an elastic wrap intermittently for twenty-four hours. Elevate the injury. Following a serious contusion, it is wise to see a medical specialist to discount the possibility of fracture.

Dancer's Heel Sometimes too much pointe work on nonresilient floor surfaces creates inflammation in the dancer's foot above the heel bone. It seems to be a reaction to an injury to the joint where the ankle is connected to the foot. Pain is experienced deep in the area of the Achilles tendon each time the foot is pointed.

Treatment should include icing three times a day for three days and taking anti-inflammatories. Pointe work will be very uncomfortable so the dancer should try to limit her time on pointe until the pain has subsided or flex the knee slightly while working on the injured pointe. If the pain does not diminish greatly in ten days, see an orthopedist since the symtoms of dancer's heel can also signal the presence of an extra bone, the os trigonum, in the back of the foot.

Heel Bruises Calcaneal periostitis is one of the worst acute injuries a dancer can experience. It is caused by repeated compression of the tissue covering the bottom of the heel bone or its bursa. Dancers with bony feet or irregularly shaped heel bones are particularly subject to this injury, which can be induced by coming down incorrectly from a jump or by overuse. It can also be caused by stepping on a small object. The injury causes sharp pain under the back middle portion of the heel, which intensifies after leaping or jumping. This injury also makes it extremely painful for the heel to contact the floor.

Ice should be applied at once, and icing should continue three times a day; an anti-inflammatory should also be taken. Dr. Garrick suggests wearing a rigid heel cup in street shoes to cup the heel and re-form it to its original shape. A dancer can also strap and pad the heel to take painful pressure off the bruise.

Heel Spurs Heel spurs are bony growths on the bottom of the heel bone; dancers with flat feet are prone to develop them. Plantar fascitis (see p. 147) can also cause heel spurs by pulling a piece of bone loose at the heel. Upon arising in the morning and after extended periods of weight-bearing, pain is felt when pressure is applied to the front of the heel bone. Treatment involves removing the pressure and reducing inflammation. Anti-inflammatories can be helpful, and an application of ice for fifteen or twenty minutes at a time is suggested. Rest, contrast baths, and added support in street shoes may also be useful. If the symptoms do not ease after a few days, see a podiatrist for help.

The Ankle

In Dr. Garrick's study of ballet injuries, he found the ankle was the third most involved anatomic region. Acute injuries in this area were more common than overuse injuries. Sprains involved the ankle more than any other joint. Many of these sprains result from missteps and faulty landings during the acquisition of technical skills in dancers thirteen to eighteen years of age. A dancer with a hyperflexible high instep, whose muscles, tendons and cartilage are stretched beyond their maximum capacity, often lacks the strength in her ligaments to prevent ankle strains and fractures.

Achilles Tendonitis The Achilles tendon, the largest tendon in the body, extends down the back of the leg connecting the muscles of the calf to the heel bone. The Achilles tendon allows the dancer to rise onto pointe. Achilles tendonitis can be caused by overwork or a bruised heel. Some dancers try to protect their heels by not putting them down and as a result strain the Achilles tendon. Pressure from the back of an incorrectly fit shoe, the elastic, or a ribbon knot can cause problems with the Achilles tendon.

In Dr. Garrick's study of ballet injuries, most instances of Achilles tendonitis beyond the midteen years were the result of overuse or inadequate rehabilitation of calf muscles after an ankle or foot injury. In older dancers he found that the problem could result from microtears from repeated injuries over the years.

Symptoms of Achilles tendonitis include soreness along the length of the tendon, swelling, and severe pain, particularly in relevé. A slight noise may be heard in the rear of the heel when the ankle is moved. The pain is usually at its worst upon rising in the morning.

Tendonitis starts as tears in the individual tiny fibers that make up the Achilles rub against the sheath that surrounds it, causing the sheath to swell as well. At the first signs of Achilles tendonitis, it is wise to consult a medical specialist to determine a proper course of action. The specialist might suggest a combination of stretches, anti-inflammatories, and ice therapy for a mild case or complete cessation of dance activity for as long as three weeks in more serious cases.

When advised that it is safe to return to dancing, the dancer should begin barre work cautiously, stretching the tendon carefully. At first, all relevés, pointe work, and jumps should be avoided. Add only a few exercises at a time if no pain is present. If any pain develops, the dancer needs to stop immediately and give the area more rest, elevation, and ice. If allowed to persist, Achilles tendonitis can become very difficult to cure. Strengthening the calf muscles is a good insurance policy against Achilles tendonitis.

Sprained Ankle Dr. Tom Novella finds that sprained ankles are the most common injury he sees in pointe dancers. The ankle bone is able to roll toward the inside of the joint more easily than it is able to roll to the outside. If a traumatic event forces it to roll too far to the inside, the ligaments on the outside of the ankle bear the brunt of the sudden movement and can stretch, strain, or tear. This type of sprain is called a lateral sprain and results in pain and swelling on the outside of the ankle. Medial ankle sprains, which are much less common, occur when the foot rolls away from the body and causes pain to the inside of the ankle. Sprains can occur because of ankle muscle weaknesses or a structural problem such as a short fifth metatarsal. If the midfoot is loose, it can sickle in the center and give way during demi-pointe or relevé.

When testing an injured ankle to determine the extent of damage, the dancer will find that she can put weight on a sprain and twist it with some pain. However, if she feels anything grinding in the ankle, experiences numbness or a sensation of cold, or is concerned that the injury might be more than a sprain, she should see a medical specialist right away. If the pain is on the inside of the ankle, indicating a medial fracture, it is especially important to seek medical advice.

The initial swelling of a sprained ankle stems from internal bleeding resulting from torn ligaments and the surrounding soft tissues. This swelling makes the ankle stiff. To control swelling, wrap a sock around the injured ankle bone and then wrap the ankle area with an Ace bandage. Keep the area wrapped for twenty-four hours. Also intermittently apply ice over a layer of bandage. Do not use heat immediately after sustaining a sprained ankle. If swelling remains after the first day and/or if any discoloration is present, see a medical specialist to be X-rayed and checked for fractures.

After the swelling has subsided, try contrast baths, alternating between warm and cold soaks to increase circulation. Also begin moving the ankle to keep the muscle from wasting. Increase the ankle's range of motion and the overall activity level, with pain as a guide. Do as much as you can as soon as you can do it without pain. At night keep the injured leg elevated on several pillows, and use an Ace bandage if swelling intermittently returns.

Dr. Hamilton suggests that swimming can be helpful as form of substitute conditioning until a dancer can resume dancing. As ankle motion returns, he suggests doing a barre in chest-deep water after swimming twenty-five laps. Working on relevé, plié, tendu, and frappé in the buoyancy of the water helps restore strength and motion. When the dancer is ready to try a barre in the studio, at first it should be a "flat-footed" barre on both feet and without relevé.

A dancer working to avoid future sprains needs to think in terms of building strength and balance in both the ankle and midfoot. Sometimes balance training that makes use of such devices as balance boards and tennis balls can help.

Most experts in dance medicine agree that a dancer's sprained ankle should be healed with exercise and treatment rather than a cast since when it is removed the dancer is weaker, causing her to be more susceptible to future injury. If the nature of a sprain demands a cast, an air cast might be useful. This type of cast allows the foot to pointe and flex but not roll in and out. It can be taken on and off with a Velcro fastener. In the instance of severe sprains, an air cast can reduce healing time from the usual three to six months to six to eight weeks.

Posterier Impingement Syndrome Dr. Garrick's study found that working on pointe is often responsible for this common overuse problem. Impingement is a condition of the ankle that results from pressure applied while the dancer is in plié. The skin and soft tissue surrounding the bones of the ankle compress and wrinkle like an accordion. Some ankle bones react by developing ridges that cause the tissues to swell, reducing flexibility. As a result of this buildup of soft tissue and bone in the front or back of the ankle, plié or rising to pointe become impossible. Temporary relief is obtained by reducing the swelling and inflamation of soft tissues. But when a serious dance student spends more and more time dancing, with fewer opportunities for rest, the soft tissues stay swollen and permanently thicken. This adds another obstruction to an already crowded rear ankle.

Strong calf muscles can help ward off this problem, and dancers can attempt to take pressure off the ankle by technique adjustments. Surgery to remove the extra tissue and bone is the only cure for the problem. However, some dancers have had to repeat the surgery several times since the tissue and bone may thicken again. In Dr. Garrick's study, dancers undergoing this surgery were most often in their late teens.[6]

TOOLS FOR TREATING
AND PREVENTING
POINTE-RELATED INJURIES

Adhesive tape. Use special lightweight cloth athletic tape. Prepare the skin before applying tape by removing perspiration, dirt, and hair. Commercial tape adherents such as Tuf-Skin can be sprayed on the skin to help the tape stick. Use one-half-inch to one-inch tape in short strips instead of one long piece, to avoid wrapping it too tightly.

Antiseptic liquid bandages. Commercial preparations such as New Skin put a protective coating over a raw spot until the skin can grow back over it. They are waterproof, but allow the skin to breathe. Liquid bandages dry rapidly to form tough-but-flexible coverings to screen wounds from dirts and germs. They are used to prevent and protect blisters, protect cuts and scrapes, and help prevent callus formation. To use, clean and dry the broken skin area and spray from six inches away until coated. Allow the preparation to dry. Apply a second coat for added protection. Keep knuckles bent when applying and drying. Liquid bandages can be removed by applying a fresh coat of the product and rubbing off quickly with disposable wipe. Read the cautions on the package before using. The product is available in pharmacies.

Anti-inflammatories. Nonprescription pain relievers contain ibuprofen, such as Advil or Nuprin, and pure unbuffered aspirins are anti-inflammatories. Buffered aspirin and aspirin substitutes like Tylenol provide relief from pain, but do not act to reduce inflammation. To reduce the inflammation of a tendon or joint, two five-grain aspirins every four hours for up to seventy-two hours is considered a minimum dose. During this critical period immediately after an injury, some experts suggest taking this increased dosage and also to determine if any other medications currently prescribed should not be taken with aspirin. Take anti-inflammatories with a full eight-ounce glass of water to reduce the risk of side effects such as gastrointestinal problems and dizziness. While standard ibuprofen-containing anti-inflammatories and aspirin are available over the counter, stronger anti-inflammatories are also available by prescription.

Blister kits. Spenco has packaged a convenient mix of products to help protect against blisters. Call Spenco's toll-free number (1-800-433-3334) for the name of a local dealer.

Blister, corn, and callus padding. Commercial pads designed to help protect against corns, calluses, and blisters are available in pharmacies. Avoid using medicated pads because of the danger of infection.

Exercise bands. These rubber devices are six inches wide and vary in length from two- to three-and-a-half feet and come in a variety of colors. They are excellent for strengthening or warming up the feet and are easy to transport. A dancer with calf problems puts the center of an exercise band over the ball of the foot, flexes the foot, and pulls on the band by holding both ends. The band can also be used to warm up and strengthen feet when a dancer pulls on it for resistance while pointing her feet. Overuse of exercise bands can lead to tendonitis, so it's best to have their use prescribed by a professional therapist with a regimen of specific exercises. They are available under the brand names Theraband and Stretch-Ease Band and may be found at dance shops and sporting goods stores. They are also dispensed by physical therapists.

Elevation. When elevating an injured foot or ankle, keep it above the level of the heart. If you lie down and prop up the injured foot or ankle on several plump pillows, it should be at the right height.

Foot soaks. Burrow's solution is a popular foot soak. It acts as an antiseptic and anesthetic as it gives off a sensation of heat. Since overuse of such solutions can cause the skin to crack, Burrow's solution should be diluted and used in a footbath. Hot-water soaks with soap flakes can also be soothing and effective.

Heat.   Heat speeds up circulation and metabolism and encourages drainage. Superficial heating works on the skin's surface; deep heating acts within body tissues. Superficial heat can be applied by the dancer herself, but deep heat treatments must be taken under the supervision of a professional therapist or other medical specialist.

Heat is never applied immediately after an acute injury and is often not prescribed for as long as three days after an injury. When superficial heat is used, it should be applied to the injured area when getting up in the morning and before starting an activity. Superficial heat can take the form of an electric heating pad or a shower or bath. Moist heating pads are a popular option. An electric heating pad should not be applied for longer than twenty minutes.

Warm-water baths can be started at lower temperature and gradually made hotter, depending on the skin's tolerance. A good starting temperature is ninety degrees. Warm-water baths should last from ten to twenty minutes and be repeated several times a day. Hot wraps such as the Spenco Hot Wrap are reusable sources of soothing moist heat. They come in sizes ranging from small to extra large.

Contrast baths.   Alternating hot- and cold-water soaks relieve swelling and muscle spasm. For a contrast bath, prepare two tubs of water—one with a temperature of 105 degrees and one with a temperature of 60 degrees. Soak in hot water for five minutes and then in cold water for two minutes, then in hot water for four minutes and then in cold water for two minutes. Repeat the four-minute (hot) and two-minute (cold) cycles for sixteen more minutes, ending in the hot water. In a pinch, Dr. James Garrick suggests running hot water in the tub for the hot soak and sticking the foot in the toilet for the cold.

Heat rubs.   Heat rubs or analgesic balms such as Ben-Gay and Absorbine Jr. work by irritating the skin and causing a dilation of the small blood vessels, thus bringing a flood of blood and a feeling of warmth to the area. Once the acute phase of an injury is over, heat rubs are useful to provide relief from discomfort while a dancer is in motion. Heat rubs can be applied directly to the skin or to a cloth which is covered with plastic wrap and secured with an Ace bandage.

Heat rubs can burn if overused or used with strong heat from a lamp or electric heating pad. Avoid rubbing the eyes when heat rub is on the fingers. Some of the ingredients used in heat rubs are oil of wintergreen, red pepper, and menthol.

Cold.   When cold is indicated as a therapy it must be applied immediately after an injury. However, it should be used only for as long a period of time as advised by your medical specialist, usually twenty-four to forty hours. Later, cold may be part of longer-term therapy.

Cold works by restricting blood vessels and reducing spasms. After twenty minutes of cold application, an increase of circulation in the deeper tissues results. Stick the foot in a basin of cold water with ice cubes or ice an injury by using a plastic bag filled with ice held in place by an Ace bandage. (A cloth that has been soaked in water can be frozen and placed in a plastic bag to use in the same fashion.) If no ice is available, a chemical cold pack can be purchased that will become cold when mixed with water and last for about thirty minutes. Reusable cold wraps such as the Spenco Cold Wrap are available in pharmacies. These stay soft and flexible for greater comfort and come in small, medium, and large sizes.

Ice massage is often used in treating muscle injuries. The following regimen is repeated several times a day: freeze water in a paper or styrofoam cup and tear off the paper to produce a cylinder of ice. Wrap a cloth around the ice and rub the injured area with small circular movements until the skin feels cold and numb. Then stretch the injured area gradually, maintaining the stretch for one to two minutes.

Hydrogel dressings. Dressings such as Spenco Second Skin are helpful for covering abrasions and blisters. They held to reduce the friction on the skin.

Moleskin or molefoam. This felt or foam has an adhesive backing that can be used as padding on the foot and ankle.

Orthotics. Orthotics are custom-made devices created with negative plaster casts which work to counteract the impact of structural limitations and injury on the foot. Often the materials used in making orthotics are similar to those employed to support the frame of an aircraft. In an orthotic, these materials support the frame of the foot. Orthotics tend to be extremely long-wearing.

An orthotic locks the foot in normal position so it can function optimally. Whatever the foot's predisposition, the orthotic is made to hold it in a way that avoids the development of what would otherwise be a certain problem. Dr. Steven Baff believes that orthotics can slow down the advent of such problems by as much as 95 percent. In other words, if a dancer has a predisposition for a bunion, wearing an orthotic can slow down its development to that extent.

Orthotics absorb a tremendous amount of shock and extend from the heel to the end of the metatarsal heads, but not the length of the toes. While there are many such devices on the market geared toward foot problems related to walking, until recently there have been few designed for dancers. Orthotics are not yet widely embraced as effective for dancers, but they have enthusiastic supporters who claim they help the feet function properly with less trauma, just as glasses make eyes function properly.

Dancers interested in learning more about orthotics may want to investigate the Braver Ballet Device made by the Allied Orthotics Lab in Indianapolis, Indiana. Working with lab technicians, Dr. Richard T. Braver has developed an orthotic device that can be worn with pointe shoes. His goal was to make pointe dancing more possible for those who may not have the "right" feet.

This device slips onto the bottom of the foot and limits excessive rolling in and rolling out. It also corrects for the mechanical disadvantages imposed by enlarged and extra bones. It works by repositioning the joints of the foot to alleviate stretch on the muscles and tendons, thereby reducing fatigue and strain.

The device is designed to be a benefit when the dancer is in relevé, which is when the most destructive forces are acting on the foot and when most control is needed. It differs from a traditional orthotic because it gives the most support under the ball of the foot rather than under the arch. The amount and type of correction in the above device are determined only after performing an individual podiatric biomechanical evaluation that includes the structural relationships and movements of the dancer's foot, ankle, knee, and hip joints.

The orthotic is made of a flexible rubber and costs anywhere from $250 to $400, the average cost of a street-shoe orthotic. Each is completely customized by Dr. Braver for the individual dancer and is made from plaster of paris casts of the foot. When the cast is taken, the foot is positioned correctly so that the finished orthotic can realign the foot into the correct position.

Pilates mat and apparatus work. Developed in the early 1900s by exercise expert Joseph Pilates, the Pilates technique of body conditioning has been a dancer's tool for many years. Pilates brought the technique to the United States in the 1930s and operated a studio in New York for over forty years. The Pilates technique has been integrated into dance training by George Balanchine and other major figures in the world of ballet.

The technique revolves around a series of exercises done on a mat in conjunction with related exercises done on various types of apparatus. The key piece of equipment is the Reformer, a horizontal platform with a moveable carriage on which the dancer reclines, sits, or stands. Apparatus work and mat work educate the dancer in the "recentering" of body alignment.

Surgical or Metholated Spirit. This product is popular in Great Britain for deadening the top layers of epidermis, which helps dancers with tender feet to toughen their skin and get used to wearing pointe shoes. Surgical spirit must not be used if a dancer develops blisters.

Toe Caps. Dancers have tried to correct for toes of differing lengths by adding various types of padding material, such as cardboard, wadded-up tissue paper, and lamb's wool, to the boxes of their pointe shoes. We spoke to one dancer in Dallas, Texas, who out of desperation had created her own toe cap. By a lengthy process of experimentation, Alicia Hicks, a hand therapist, fashioned a toe cap from materials used in her profession to compensate for the fact that her second toe is almost two joints longer than her first. This device made it possible for her to dance with less pain.

While a dancer without Hicks's therapy background would find it difficult to make a safe and effective device for herself, we have learned about custom-made toe caps that are now available for dancers. These toe caps are made to fit each dancer's foot and can be worn with pointe shoes. They are created by a podiatrist, Alan S. Woodle, D.P.M., who specializes in sports medicine and is the company podiatrist for the Pacific Northwest Ballet in Seattle, Washington. Dr. Woodle's toe caps are molded to the dancer's foot while she alternates standing on pointe and flat in her pointe shoes under Dr. Woodle's supervision.

Dr. Woodle works with the dancer to make numerous finely crafted adjustments in the toe cap for maximum comfort and effectiveness. When the toe cap is worn, it is placed on the foot first; then the shoe is put on. A change to another brand or style of pointe shoe may require modifications to the toe cap. Dr. Woodle reports that after the toe cap has been "tuned" to the dancer's specific needs, it assists weight-bearing balance as well as reducing pain and compensating mechanisms.

Dancers who have problems with toes that are much shorter or longer than other toes, have painful bunions, sickle in or out, or place excessive stress on one or two toes on pointe may be interested in contacting Dr. Woodle about his toe caps. He can be reached at Greenwood Foot and Ankle Center, 8111 Greenwood Ave. N., Seattle, WA 98103, Tel: (206) 784-3144.

SHOES AND INJURY

Pointe shoe manufacturers are becoming more involved in the concept of designing shoes with medical considerations in mind. Dr. Richard T. Braver had been hired as a consultant to Capezio Ballet Makers. Capezio questioned dancers through survey forms to discover what features they would like to see in new shoes. Then they asked Dr. Braver to react to these suggestions from a medical viewpoint. He also made suggestions to the company about the kinds of materials used in shoes. He lectured to Capezio employees on the nature of dance injuries and possible improvements in dance shoes that could help prevent injuries. Capezio's association with consultants like Dr. Braver is a positive sign of the company's concern for its customers. Other evidence of growing concern over the health aspects of pointe shoes includes Gamba's research and development of their Turning Pointe shoe.

ENVIRONMENTAL CAUSES OF INJURY

Temperatures in which dancers take class, rehearse, or perform can have an impact on injury. Muscle injuries in particular are far more likely to occur when a dancer is not adequately warmed up. Therefore temperatures should not be allowed to fall below sixty-eight to seventy degrees. On the other hand, overly high temperatures can induce excessive sweating, leading to loss of water and electrolytes such as salt. Inadequate replacement of lost fluid can result in muscle cramps and spasms.

Floors are an extremely important factor in environmentally caused injuries. The problems encountered with floors fall into three areas—the actual construction of the floor, the angle of the floor, and its surface.

The actual construction of the floor is of the greatest importance to the dancer. Chiropractor Dr. Nathan Novick feels that dance floors that do not breathe and rebound are responsible for many dance injuries. An ideal floor surface for dance must be resilient and nonslip; it must also absorb significant impact and provide lateral foot support. Unfortunately, the floors on which dancers often take class, rehearse, and perform were often not constructed for dance and have reinforced concrete as their underlying foundation. The ideal dance floor is a "sprung" or "floating" wooden floor. Such a floor features crossbars, padded "sleepers," slats, runners, or risers placed at intervals under the subflooring and flooring to provide air pockets.

As chairman of the Dance Department at Towson State University in Maryland, Helen Breazeale designed and supervised the installation of new studio floors at her institution. Working with Jay Seals of Robbins Inc., she designed a floor featuring spring coils measuring one-and-three-quarter inches in height, mounted to wood blocks on one end and fastened to two-by-four inch sleepers on the other end. The sleepers are covered with three-quarter inch plywood subfloor, and the floor surface is the T&G Northern Hard Maple flooring. Each studio has fifteen hundred coil springs under the 1,870-square-foot surface.

Towson State faculty member Edward Stewart, who teaches advanced ballet students, observes that the number of major and minor injuries normally attributed to poor surfaces, such as sprains, tears, tendonitis, shin splints, back problems and knee problems, have come to a halt. Breazeale says, "the hefty price tab of $25,000 for each floor is a small price to pay for the years of pain-free productive work for any dancer who is fortunate enough to study in such a facility."

A wooden floor surface should not mislead a dancer into assuming the wood has been sprung. It may have been placed directly over concrete or rolled steel joists. The resulting lack of spring can cause many injuries. To determine whether a wooden floor is "sprung," rap on it with your knuckles or the heel of a shoe. A resilient sprung floor will sound a hollow drumlike retort since the sound of your rapping will be amplified by the air space. A sharp click will be heard when you tap a floor with a concrete base since there is no air space to create resonance.

Robbins Inc. (4777 Eastern Avenue, Cincinnati, Ohio 45226) offers a generation of "user friendly" wood floor products to the dance community. After being subjected to extensive dynamic testing at the Otto-Graf Institut of Stuttgart and subjectively evaluated by dancers, these new floors appear to have exciting potential for reducing dance injuries. Special emphasis has been placed on reducing impact loads to the dancer by altering dance component designs in unique ways. Robbins Inc. will provide information on these floors to interested dancers and teachers.

While nothing can take the place of a properly sprung floor, the strain of dancing on a concrete floor appears to be lessened when it is covered with layers of special cushioned vinyl. Although this is a possible alternative for occasional performances, the dancer should do everything within her power to find a situation that offers a resilient well-sprung floor for class and rehearsal, avoiding tile and cement.[8]

Dr. Novick suggests that dancers try to select shoes that will help protect their bodies from concussions caused by floors. According to Dr. Braver, if a dancer is forced to dance on a hard floor, she may want to experiment with switching to a softer pointe shoe.

The problem of floor angle refers to the fact that many performing surfaces around the world are raked. A raked stage gives the audience a better view but can both cause dance injuries and prolong them. Dancing on even a slight incline puts a severe strain on the body because the dancer has to readjust throughout the entire dance or performance. A raked stage forces a dancer to throw her weight back and is also difficult to move across.

Finally, the actual surface is important. Rosin overuse can be a problem. Floors that are heavily rosined must be cleaned regularly to prevent buildup in irregular and uneven patches; otherwise a dancer may find her foot sticking to the floor, with potentially disastrous consequences to the ankle or knee.

Margret Kaufman, who has danced in the United States, London, Germany, Holland, Sweden, and Finland, found not only that the raked stages of Europe were difficult, but also that the painted floor carpets were extremely slippery and unsuitable for pirouettes.

Deborah Allton, who dances with the Metropolitan Opera Ballet, says the members of that company endure a variety of floor problems. The stage is wood over cement and equipped with multiple hydraulic devices, turntables, and elevators. Consequently, there are high ridges in the surface, places where the floor sections do not meet, and even trap doors. Since the floor is covered with a floor cloth, these hazards are masked from the dancers' view. She recalled dancing in the opera *Macbeth* which had a forty-five degree raked stage and a floor covering hiding numerous holes and uneven seams. She did hops on pointe in front attitude going downhill on a raked floor and hopped into a pothole.

When American Ballet Theatre performs at the Met, they bring their own floor to surmount these problems. Before New York City Ballet acquired their current floor, they could only perform at the Kennedy

Center in Washington for two weeks at a time to prevent becoming "hamburger" from the knee down.

Rosin and Slip NoMor concentrate are the two best solutions to slip-proofing dance surfaces. Rosin is the brittle resin left after distilling turpentine from pine pitch. It is also used in the manufacture of varnish and ink and for rubbing on violin bows. Rosin can be purchased in rock and powdered form. Rock rosin, which is placed in a container large enough for a dancer to step into, is preferable. If a local dance store does not carry rosin, it can be ordered by mail from the Capezio Dance-Theatre Shop, Freed of London Ltd. in Manhattan, or the Dance Works in Erie, PA. Suitable rosin may also be found in a sporting goods store or music store.

Slip NoMor concentrate is a nonslip solution that adds a slip-resistant surface to all floor surfaces including wood, vinyl, and linoleum. It is a good substitute for rosin on vinyl floors and does not damage floor surfaces. It can be ordered from Stagestep, 2000 Hamilton St., Suite C200, Philadelphia, PA 19103.

SPECIAL CARE FACILITIES

Although medical care specifically tailored for dancers is still in dramatically short supply across the country, there are now several excellent facilities specializing in this field. Hopefully, they will serve as models for more centers that emphasize dance medicine.

Dancemedicine Division
Center for Sports Medicine, Francis Memorial Hospital,
900 Hyde Street, San Francisco, California 94109

The Center for Sports Medicine is headed by Dr. James G. Garrick, an orthopedic surgeon who specializes in working with skaters, dancers, and gymnasts. At the time of our research, he was assisted in the Dancemedicine Division by Patrice L. Whiteside, a former dancer with the Oakland Ballet who has a master's degree in movement analysis from Ohio State. Dr. Garrick felt that her ability to evaluate a dancer's physical problems by observing the nuances in an individual's technique was vital to the success of the center. The Dancemedicine Division, specializing in dance injury rehabilitation and general conditioning, offers Pilates-based apparatus and mat techniques and affords the dancer an opportunity to refine strength, flexibility, centering, and quality of coordination.

While many of the same injuries are seen on a daily basis, each dancer's specific problems in dealing with his or her injuries are unique. As the result of evaluation at the Dancemedicine Division, a physician or therapist may detect a dancer's technical error that is contributing to, if not causing, an injury.

After a client receives a preliminary physical exam, Garrick's assistant watches the individual go through a simulated class at the barre from both a lateral and a forward view and notes technique flaws. Dr. Garrick says that this level of symptom evaluation cannot be accomplished by a doctor or by a teacher who is trying to watch an entire class or rehearsal. He feels it is safe to assume that the dancer is unaware of the usage problems or the injury might not have happened. Armed with the knowledge gained by the team at Dancemedicine, a dancer may be able to keep the injury from recurring.

The rehabilitation work at Dancemedicine is then structured to adapt to each dancer's particular needs. Often after the rehabilitation process is complete, dancers continue with the program for general conditioning and centering work in conjunction with their training or performing. Clients of Dancemedicine also have access to the Physical Therapy Division, where whirlpools, friction massage, ultrasound, bikes, EGS, weights, and therabands are available. Also six universal reformers or plié machines and two trap tables are available at the center for Pilates work.

Dr. Garrick believes that it is possible to do the best job for the dancer when the entire treatment process is under one roof. Doctors, trainers, and physical therapists are able to look at the patient together and practice more effective medicine as a result, since they do not have to communicate by telephone or in written form. He mentions that there is "no hiding from the patient" in this kind of environment. Contact is maintained with members of the team, and feedback is much more efficient. He feels that patients often get lost in the shuffle when they have to be sent to a variety of locations, from physician to physical therapist to conditioning studio. The cost of multilocation treatment is also often greater than "one-stop" medicine. Dr. Garrick feels that the division must help each dancer find a way to be rehabilitated to dancing "full steam." He finds that of the dancers he sees, fully 80 percent of their problems are fairly common complaints, while the remaining 20 percent are unusual instances. When treating these, he frequently consults Dr. Justin Howse in London and Dr. William Hamilton.

The Dancemedicine Division treats all kinds of dancers, from recreational enthusiasts to professionals and from any dance discipline. The income from recreational dancers helps support the costs of treating professionals. Many company-affiliated dancers are treated under worker's compensation plans.

Westside Dance Physical Therapy
2109 Broadway, #204, New York, New York 10023

Administered by Director Marika Molnar, Assistant Director Liz Henry, and Senior Staff member Katy Keller, Westside Dance Physical Therapy specializes in preventing and rehabilitating the injuries of performing artists. Treatment incorporates evaluation of the neuromusculoskeletal system and development of individualized rehabilitation programs.

Services include evaluation of alignment, flexibility, strength, and proprioception; manual therapy technique, including soft tissue and joint mobilization, myofacscial release, and neuromuscular reeducation; craniosacral therapy; biomechanical assessment of the spine and lower extremities; dance technique analysis and modification; and instruction in home exercise programs and preventive measures.

Marika Molnar has worked with New York City Ballet as a physical therapist since 1980. She was a dance teacher and has a master's degree in dance and physical therapy.

The majority of pointe shoe-related problems seen at the center are foot and ankle injuries and some back injuries. Many problems experienced by professional dancers are related to the choreography they are working on at any given moment. Since learning a new role or rehearsing intensively involves repeating the same movement over and over, injuries are often the result of overuse. They can be a direct result of cooling down while standing around waiting for a choreographer to make a decision.

Molnar finds it particularly challenging to work with professional dancers to find a way to help them go on performing within the framework of their physical problems. This often involves helping them find a new way of moving.

Irene Dowd
Neuro-Muscular Therapist, 14 East 4th Street, Suite 607, New York, New York 10012, Tel: 212-420-8782

Irene Dowd takes a functional approach to treating dance injuries. She observes the dancer in action to determine minimal technique corrections that can correct problems. She was the protégé and assistant of Dr. Lulu Sweigard, who taught Anatomy for Dancers at Juilliard. Dowd is a member of the faculty at the Teacher's College at Columbia University. In addition to treating individual neuromuscular problems, she teaches anatomy classes at her studio.

Pilates Studio®
890 Broadway, New York, New York 10003

The studio, founded by Joseph Pilates, also the founder of the Pilates® method, offers individually supervised programs administered by instructors who have trained in this system of body conditioning. While teachers trained in the Pilates method offer programs around the country, this studio was founded by Joseph Pilates in 1923 and offers the only patented teacher-training courses. Romana Kryzanowska, who directs the Pilates Studio's teacher training program, was one of Pilates's first students.

The key aspects of the Pilates method are control and centering of the body, precision movement, flow of motion, proper breathing, and relaxation. This work is concerned with both adjusting the entire body and training the muscles to support the correction. All Pilates exercises start on a flat back and gradually change positions. The body is toned without pressure on the ankles, legs, and lower back.

Many of the studio's clients dance with New York City Ballet and American Ballet Theatre. They come to the Pilates Studio for alignment and corrective work, not exercise. After an injury, dancers work out there to reestablish alignment before returning to class. They also use the Pilates method to help them prevent injury. This method is a particular benefit to the pointe dancer because it strengthens the back and stomach, keeping weight off the feet and knees. Foot problems are often solved by working on the body at the Pilates Studio.

White Cloud Studio
50 W. 65th Street, New York, New York 10023

The White Cloud Studio bases its philosophy of exercise on Juliu Horvath's Gyrotonic Expansion System. Horvath, who developed his own method of teaching yoga, trained as an Olympic gymnast and was a professional dancer and competitive swimmer.

The goal of the Horvath system is to work in a nonstressful and organically natural way to develop and maintain maximum performance levels for professionals as well as anyone interested in caring for the body as a high-quality instrument. Clients begin with a basic series of exercises and progress to the most complex skills, incorporating a unique breathing technique.

Observing that there was no existing machine that enhanced bodily awareness of musculature, strength and flexibility for dancers, Horvath build his exercise machinery using the key principles of his yoga technique, through which major muscle groups are worked independently and in an integrated manner. The exercises are intended to develop a combination of coordination, dexterity, and rhythm. The system builds flexibility and movement without building extra bulk.

Devoid of gimmicks, Horvath's exercises are individually powerful and sequenced to allow a warming up of the muscles and joints as well as stimulating and massaging the internal organs. Unlike Nautilus equipment, the machines are not limited to one function. As the dancer progresses, so does the machinery. The Horvath Perpetual Gyrotonic utilizes 120 combinations of movement and works three-dimensionally, while most exercise equipment is two-dimensional in nature.

The Horvath approach is tailored to each individual's personality and physical needs. The equipment allows dancers to discover for themselves the bodily mechanics of turnout and alignment. They are guided into understanding their bodies and lose the sense that they are overpowered by their physiology. Their stronger and weaker sides are brought into balance; weaknesses are discovered where they are least suspected, resulting in both improved muscle tone and more evenness in movements such as jumping. The emphasis is on elongating muscles without joint compression and the avoidance of forcing. Many of the exercises are directly concerned with the foot and knee.

White Cloud offers teacher training courses and anticipates the opening of closely supervised Horvath-based studios across the country.

Houston Body Conditioning Studio
1916 West Gray Street, Houston, Texas 77019

The Houston Body Conditioning Studio has a twenty-five-year association with the Houston Ballet—testimony to the Houston Ballet's philosophy of responsiveness to their dancers' physical needs and its interest in making them "last." It was established initially as an aid to dancers recovering from injuries or working to prevent them.

The Pilates-based method used at the studio seeks to balance the body for any physical activity. Once imbalances are detected, weaker areas can be strengthened through isolation. The staff closely supervises a general program of stretching and strengthening and seeks to identify potential problems, arresting them before they can cause injuries. The studio's body conditioning retrains the body. Muscles elongate and joints are freed to achieve natural alignment. By conditioning muscles to support the spine's natural curve, lower back pain is alleviated and shoulders relax and fall into place.

The studio is a tool to help a dancer find answers to problems and enhance his or her natural coordination. Company members and upper level students use the studio for warmup and rehabilitation for free, while other students at the Houston Ballet Academy are charged a nominal fee.

Kathryn and Gilbert Miller Health Care Institute for Performing Artists
425 W. 59th Street, New York, New York 10019
Tel: 212-523-6200

The Miller Health Care Institute is a multispecialty ambulatory care center associated with St. Luke's—Roosevelt Hospital Center. Founded in 1985 with a grant from the Kathryn and Gilbert Miller Fund, this unique institute offers general and specialized health care for performers and those in associated trades such as teachers, production crews, designers, directors, and choreographers. It occupies custom-designed facilities that include a performance-evaluation studio with a sprung floor, barre and mirrors, and video equipment.

In the primary care area, the institute's physicians perform checkups, physicals, and women's health examinations. They administer diagnostic tests and treat illness and injury. In addition, specialists treat injuries and disorders that result from rehearsal and performance. Fees are competitive, but these specialists understand the performance environment and their diagnostic skills are fine-tuned to the exacting standards required by top professionals.

Artists can find treatment at the institute for everything from sprained ankles to chronic tendonitis, and from colds and flu to more performance-related problems and injuries. The institute's Three-Stage Preparation Program involves a physical examination to determine state of health and muscle condition, a videotape analysis of performance technique, and graduated series of muscle strengthening and conditioning under the guidance of a physical therapist, while institute doctors monitor the performer anatomically. Treatment is also offered for illness such as anorexia and bulimia. Both mental and physical health are addressed.

Under the Michael Fokine Fund, administered by the New York Community Trust, low- or no-cost care may be available for serious students or professional dancers with demonstrable financial need who are ill or injured and need medical care in order to dance. To find our more about this program, contact the social work supervisor at the institute.

PREVENTION OF INJURY

The following is a list of ways to help prevent unnecessary pointe-related physical problems.

Don't wear ribbons too tight. Tight ribbons cut off circulation and mask shoe-fitting problems.

Don't allow ribbon knots or tight elastic to apply undue pressure to the Achilles tendon.

Don't blame foot problems on pointe shoes if they are being caused by a poor choice of street shoes. When walking on concrete, wear well-cushioned athletic shoes, not skimpy sneakers.

Be aware of how feet are used when they are not dancing. A habit like wrapping feet around the legs of a couch while watching television can be the actual cause of what appears to be a dance-induced injury.

When starting to knuckle forward, look for weaknesses in muscles. Hip alignment could be off or an arabesque could be too far forward. If the problem is not a technical fault, try changing to a pointe shoe with a square box instead of a round one.

Look at the whole body on pointe when trying on shoes. Don't buy a shoe that changes the center of gravity. Observe how the shoe affects the rest of the body. Beware of shoes that thrust hips forward.

Never skimp on warming up and stretching. When the body is not warm enough or does not have enough range of motion to fit into a particular stance or position, something is going to strain or pull. Warming up and cooling down are crucial to the longevity of a dance career, no matter how limber or resilient the dancer thinks she is.

Whenever possible take a regular technique class before a full pointe class. Avoid dancing on pointe without warming up since this is a frequent cause of tendonitis.

Check the wear pattern on the heel of pointe shoes. If there is evidence of foot contact a half inch or longer on the satin at the heel of the shoe, the size may be too short.

Wear tights in natural fibers such as cotton and silk that allow legs to breathe. Lycra tights and plastic pants may be bad for circulation. These fabrics encourage "cold perspiration" and make it difficult for perspiration to evaporate. As one dance teacher commented, "If you put plastic pants over your head and try to breathe, you'll get a good idea of what you're doing to your lower extremities by wearing them."

Remember that leg warmers warm from the outside and not the inside. So it's a good idea to put them on after warming up to preserve the warmth, rather than wearing them to warm up and then removing them.

Don't try to force the foot into a shoe to achieve a certain "look." The shoe must work for the foot that's wearing it, not for an idealized image. How the shoe looks is of little consequence compared to how it fits and functions

A shorter shoe may create a better line and make the instep look higher, but it can also cause tendinitis or a bone spur on the back of the foot. Wearing shoes too short prevents the arch from expanding. Once the elasticity of the arch is lost, the ability to jump is lost. Short shoes can also lessen a dancer's plié.

Shoes that are too big lessen control over movements. A shoe that fits correctly allows full flexion and full ability to spread the arch as well as control the foot and ankle. Stuffing a large shoe with lamb's wool to "make it fit" will not allow adequate control. A large shoe can cause sprained ankles, overstretched tenons, and overdevelopment of muscles that are straining to hang on to the shoe. Rigidity may also be created in the back, shoulders, and neck when the body tries to compensate for the loss of range of motion experienced when control of the foot is lost.

Think in terms of strengthening joints to accomplish the maximum possible at the end of *your* range of motion. Don't risk injury by imitating someone else. Each body has its own range of motion; each body cand do some things better than others.

Stretching and working on the instep and forefoot will lessen the chances of ankle problems.

John Gossett at the Houston Body Conditioning Studio suggests thinking of the feet and toes as hands and fingers as they are exercised. Open the toes to stengthen all the small muscles. Work to articulate the foot.

Gossett also recommends icing the feet at the end of the day. Muscles swell as the dancer works and although applying heat to them may feel good, ice is a better idea. After a heat application, the muscles tighten up. After an ice "treatment," the blood vessels are constricted and the body temperature is lowered. Swelling and aching are lessened after icing. Use ice water or ice water with ice cubes.

Keep the skin on the feet dry and pliant at all times. Don't let it dry out so that it cracks or becomes moist and tender, allowing it to rub off and form blisters or soft corns between the toes. Do this by massaging vaseline into the skin of the toes each night; push vaseline into the space around the toenails and rub it on the heels. Massage each toe and knead the metatarsal arch with the thumbs.

Be particulary careful when fatigue sets in. Medical specialists have noted that the majority of ballet injuries happen between four and six in the afternoon, when physical and mental fatigue appear after a long day of class and/or rehearsal.

NOTES

1. Howse, Justin. *Dance Technique and Injury Prevention.* (New York: Theatre Arts Books, 1988), p. 59.
2. Wright, Stuart. *Dancer's Guide to Injuries of the Lower Extremities: Diagnosis, Treatment, and Care.* (Cranbury, NJ: Cornwall Books, 1985), p. 14.
3. Much of the information included in this chapter was gathered through interviews with medical professionals who specialize in the treatment of dancers. These professionals include the following:

Orthopedists

Dr. James G. Garrick currently heads the Center for Sports Medicine at St. Francis Hospital in San Francisco, a facility which includes a unique Dancemedicine Division. Dr. William G. Hamilton has been the orthopedic consultant for the New York City Ballet since 1973; he has also been affiliated with American Ballet Theatre since 1979 and School of American Ballet since 1975. He is an attending surgeon at St. Luke's—Roosevelt Hospital Center.

Podiatrists/Podiatric Surgeons

Dr. Steven Baff, Diplomat with the American Board of Podiatric Foot Surgery Ambulatory Division, the International Society of Podiatric Laser Surgery, the

National Board of Podiatry, and the Academy of Ambulatory Foot Surgery, has a practice that includes many professional dancers. Dr. Richard T. Braver, a podiatrist specializing in dance and sports medicine and foot and ankle surgery, is affiliated with the physical therapists for the New York City Ballet. Dr. Tom Novella, who works with many patients who are members of major dance companies in New York City, has been treating dancers since 1978, and often lectures on dancers' foot problems.

Physical Therapists

Marika Molnar is director of Westside Dance Physical Therapy and holds an M.A.P.T.

Shirley Hancock is principal physiotherapist to the Royal Ballet Schools, the Royal Academy of Dancing, and the Remedial Dance Clinic, London, England.

Chiropractors

Dr. Nathan Novick, a favorite of many professional dancers and teachers, retired after practicing for fifty-two years in New York. He is president emeritus of the American College of Chiropractors. Dr. Janiz A. Minshew is a chiropractor whose New York City practice includes many performing arts professionals.

4. Garrick, James G. "Ballet Injuries," *Medical Problems of Performing Artists.* (Philadelphia: Hanley and Belfus, Inc., 1986), pp. 123-127.

5. Benson, Joan. "Relationship of Nutrient Intake, Body Mass Index, Menstrual Function, and Ballet Injury," *Journal of the American Dietetic Association,* vol. 89 (January 1989), p. 58.

6. Garrick, James G. op. cit., p. 125.

7. For further guidance in identifying, understanding, and treating dance injuries, we recommend James G. Garrick and Peter Radetsky, *Peak Condition* (Crown, 1986); Celia Sparger, *Anatomy and Ballet* (Theatre Arts, 1970); Justin Howse and Shirley Hancock, *Dance Technique and Injury Prevention* (Theatre Arts, 1988); Daniel Arnheim, *Dance Injuries* (Princeton Books, 1991); and Stuart Wright, *Dancer's Guide to Injuries of the Lower Extremity* (Cornwall Books, 1985).

8. TAP, the Technical Assistance Project, has a publication on constructing, finishing, and surfacing dance floors. Write them c/o American Dance Festival, 1697 Broadway, New York, New York 10019. An introduction to resilient flooring can be found in G. James Sammarco, ed., *Clinics in Sports Medicine: Symposium on Injuries to Dancers* (W. B. Saunders Company, 1983). For information about permanent, semipermanent, and portable flooring designed for dance use, request information from Jay Seals, Robbins Inc., 4777 Eastern Avenue, Cincinnati, Ohio 45226, a leading floor manufacturer.

Stagestep, 2000 Hamilton Street, Suite C200, Philadelphia, PA 19103, Tel: 1-800-523-0960, has a full line of custom-tailored dance flooring and floorcare products. American Harlequin Corporation, 835 Industrial Highway, Suite 3, Riverton, NJ 08077-1929, Tel: 1-800-642-6440, has developed a full line of stage and studio flooring products.

11

Conversations on Pointe

After the various theories about dancing on pointe have been debated and the facts relating to pointe shoes have been clearly defined, the true nature of the experience of dancing on pointe remains elusive. A deeper understanding of the relationship between a ballerina and her blocked satin slippers can be gained only by listening to dancers speak about their shoes.

As we traveled around the country gathering information for this book, we spent many hours talking to dancers about pointe shoes. They shared their professional secrets about selecting shoes, preparing them, and working in them. Perhaps more importantly, they revealed how they feel about these unique instruments that are so much a part of their ability to create magic on stage. In closing, we would like to share conversations, reflections on pointe by great contemporary dancers, special to this revised edition of *The Pointe Book*.

LARISSA PONOMARENKO

Larissa Ponomarenko, principal dancer with the Boston Ballet since 1993, has been in the United States since 1991. Her parents still live in Odessa.

Ponomarenka was born in Ukraine and studied in St. Petersburg. She worked for one year in Ukraine after graduation and then came directly to the United States. Larissa joined the Boston Ballet after dancing in Jackson, Mississippi, and Tulsa, Oklahoma.

Even though dancing *en pointe* is not easy for anyone, Ponomarenka feels the school where she studied made it much easier because they had so many teachers who helped. In addition, she lived in a dormitory where the older girls used to come to the little girls' rooms and showed them how to sew the shoes and to make them more comfortable, and to share their own experiences.

Like most Russian dancers, Larissa sews above the vamp with cotton thread. When asked where she buys it, she laughed and said that she found it in the popular Boston supermarket, Stop n'Shop, next to the garlic and onions. When asked why she does it, she said that she had never analyzed it while in Russia—she just did it. Now that she can compare Russian shoes with American and English ones, she believes sewing helps to strengthen the softer Russian box. Also, when she goes onto demi-pointe, the shoe makes what she calls "ears" if she doesn't sew the front. When sewn, the shoe feels like a glove.

Ponomarenka explains that the elastic she wears around her ankle is not really to hold the shoe on her foot. For her, it is only mental and only for performance. When preparing her shoes, Larissa opens the binding which encloses the drawstring on the area that touches her heel. This makes the shoe higher on the back and the shoe stays on her feet perfectly. "I never wear elastic for rehearsals—it never comes down. Sometimes I put a little bit of resin on my heels. But when I go on stage, I don't want an accident to happen. Sometimes one heel can hit the other which would knock the shoe off." Larissa sews her ribbons and elastic with the same cotton thread used to sew up the vamp.

When Ponomarenka first came to the U.S., she wore Grishko pointe shoes, but now wears Russian Class. She does not wear custom shoes but is lucky to wear a stock shoe—size 32 in Russian Class pointe shoes (size 2 in Grishko). Larissa does bang them with a hammer to take the noise out and sews the back of the platform to make a rim where her shoe seems to take a lot of wear. When it starts to fray from use, she trims the satin—not before wearing, as some dancers do.

When asked if she wears different strength shoes for different performances, Ponomarenka described her experience in *Swan Lake*. She wears the newest shoes for the Black Swan. They are then ready for her next performance as the White Swan, which calls for softer shoes. Since Larissa does not have much time between performances, she does not really break in her shoes. She feels Russian shoes are softer than American ones, which allows her to wear them for only one rehearsal before performing in them.

Ponomarenka switched from Grishko shoes (which were also not custom made) because the dimensions of the shoe were suddenly changed. It then came up too high on the foot which made her do too much work. Larissa had to make darts to keep her shoes from bagging. Now, after changing to Russian Class, she still opens up the lining to give her foot a little extra room since she believes she needs a slightly wider shoe for a perfect fit.

Unlike most dancers, Larissa ties her ribbons on the outside of her ankle. She feels the indentation on the foot is the perfect place to tuck the ribbons. She doesn't ever sew them to hold them intact because sometimes she has to change shoes too quickly. Instead, Ponomarenka puts a little bit of resin on her tights and on the end of the ribbons, and keeps checking them after each variation.

PALOMA HERRERA

Paloma Herrera, principal dancer with American Ballet Theatre, grew up in Argentina, where it was hard to find pointe shoes. From the very beginning, she wore Argentinean shoes that were custom ordered. Paloma remembers, "When I was around ten, we [my class] all went with our teacher and found the right shoes [for us].

When asked whether she had encountered any specific problem she needed to overcome concerning pointe work, Paloma answered,

> ...I guess... it was easy for me. Pointe always was my dear—always. When I started ballet at 7, it was always my dream to be on pointe shoes. When I got them, I loved it. It was like a dream. I remember that day well. I know that some people hate their pointe shoes, but I never did. I love them even today.
>
> I think it was easy, but from the very beginning, I worked very strong in my ballet shoes when I was 7, 8, 9—so when I went into pointe shoes, the transition was easy.

Because of a beautifully high instep, "I need a stronger shank (3/4) and a longer vamp. I try to have really strong feet to control my shoes better." She also uses an elastic drawstring to better conform to the shape of her foot.

Herrera wears made-to-order Capezio pointe shoes now. On first arriving in New York, she attended the School of American Ballet and tried regular Capezios. When she joined American Ballet Theatre (ABT), Freeds were the company shoe. However, she ended up back with Capezio. "One day I went to Capezio and they said, 'Ask for whatever you want and we'll do it.' And so I said OK! They really did a great job.... They did pretty much everything I asked. Since then I have always worn Capezios and I feel very, very comfortable [in them]."

While we spoke, Paloma was recycling her ribbons: unstitching them from an old pair of pointe shoes and putting them on a new one. She does this to "try and save ABT money." She uses Capezio wide, pink ribbons in one long piece sewn into the shoe under the heel and from side to side. Herrera does this so she can't lose a ribbon. When she ties her ribbons for a performance, she sews them, so the ends don't come out. Paloma wears elastic only for performances—not class or rehearsals.

When preparing her pointe shoes, Paloma does not use a hammer. Instead, she bangs them on the floor to take the noise out. She smashes the box in a door at the Metropolitan Opera House, where the doors are big and heavy. "I used to break a lot of doors at home, so that's why I never do it there." Herrera scuffs the sole with a shoe-scuffer for a better grip on the floor. Nothing comes between Paloma's toes and her shoes: "I never wear anything on my foot...nothing in the shoe. No paper towels, lambs wool, no bandaids. Nothing."

MARISA SOLTIS

Marisa Soltis studied in New York City at Harkness House under the tutelage of Nanci Clement. More recently, she has danced as principal dancer with Ballet Theatre of Boston and Fort Wayne Ballet.

Soltis has not had much difficulty with pointe shoes because her toes are all very even. She began her career wearing Bloch Serenades, but ran out of them in the middle of a long *Nutcracker* season and had to make an emergency switch. The day before doing Sugar Plum Fairy, she was faced with wearing a completely different shoe because her back-order had not yet arrived.

Marisa now wears Gambas, size 4-1/2 XX and feels completely at home in them. She finds that style 93 is better for performance, but wears 92 for rehearsal. The lighter weight 93 needs very little breaking in. Soltis simply sews on the ribbons and elastic, and goes right out onstage. She feels they have the quality that everyone likes in Freeds, but last longer. Freeds seem to wear out for her in about one half hour. Unlike many dancers who change shoes for each act of a full-length ballet, Soltis can wear the 93's for an entire *Coppelia*, plus one more act the next day.

When preparing her shoes, Marisa likes a wider elastic and criss-crosses it over her ankle. For rehearsal, she doesn't go to the trouble of sewing on ribbons because she feels somewhat freer in the shoe without them. When Soltis does put the ribbons on, she sews them directly on top of the elastic on the outside of the shoe. Her high arch feels more comfortable and not as confined as when the ribbon is sewn on the inside. She never cuts the satin off the tip because she does not find it slippery.

While dyeing her shoes and ribbons black for a role, Soltis discovered that Krylon works better than dyes she had used. It dries in about fifteen minutes and the dye never comes off on her foot—even when rehearsing without tights. Nor did it change the texture of the shoe. In the past, dyes occasionally both shrank her shoes and made them harder. Krylon did neither.

Bibliography

Adshead-Landsdale, Janet, and Layson, June, Editors. *Dance History: An Introduction, 2nd ed.* London/New York: Routledge, 1994.

Arnheim, Daniel D. *Dance Injuries: Their Prevention and Care, 3rd ed.* Pennington, NJ: Princeton Book Company, 1991.

Arnot, Michelle. *Foot Notes.* New York: Doubleday/Dolphin, 1980.

Barnes, Clive. "Barnes On …," *Ballet News* (February 1986) vol. 7.

Ben Sommers. Taped interview in files of the Dance Collection, Performing Arts Library, New York Public Library.

Benson, Joan. "Relationship of Nutrient Intake, Body Mass Index, Menstrual Function, and Ballet Injury," *Journal of the American Dietetic Association* (January 1989) vol. 89.

Bentley, Toni. "The Heart and Sole of a Ballerina's Art: Her Toe Shoes," *Smithsonian* (June 1984) vol. 15.

Berardi, Gigi. *Finding Balance: Fitness and Training for a Lifetime in Dance.* Princeton, NJ: Princeton Book Company, 1991.

Braver, Richard T. "Tendonitis Rond de Ankle," *Kinesiology for Dance* (September 1988) vol. 11.

Brinson, Peter, Editor. *The Healthier Dancer: Injuries to Dancers, a Worldwide Problem.* London: Laban Centre for Movement and Dance, 1991.

Brody, Jane. "Personal Health: Ankle Injury," *New York Times* (September 14, 1989) II:15:1.

Chmelar, Robin D., and Sally S. Fitt. *Diet: A Complete Guide to Nutrition and Weight Control.* Pennington, NJ: Princeton Book Company, 1990.

Chujoy, Anatole, and Manchester, P.W., Editors. *The Dance Encyclopedia.* New York: Simon & Schuster, 1967.

Cohen, Selma Jeanne. *Dance as a Theatre Art: Source Readings in Dance History from 1581 to the Present.* Pennington, NJ: Princeton Book Company, 1992.

Coussins, Craig. *A Fitting Manual for Ballet and Pointe Shoes.* London: England: Gamba Timestep Ltd., 1988.

Cox, Meg. "If She's on Her Toes, a Ballerina Devotes Hours to Her Shoes," *Wall Street Journal* (March 11, 1989) 1:1:2.

Cunningham, James P. *Dancing in the Inns of Court.* New York: Jordon, 1965.

Dozzi, Paula A. "Biomechanical Analysis of the Foot During Rises to Full Pointe: Implications for Injuries to the Metatarsal-Phalangeal Joints and Shoe Redesign," *Kinesiology and Medicine for Dance*. Pennington, NJ (fall/winter 1993/94) vol. 16, no. 1.

Farrell, Suzanne. *Holding on to the Air: An Autobiography*. New York: Summit Books, 1990.

Fitt, Sally Sevey. *Dance Kinesiology, 2nd ed*. New York: Schirmer Books; London: Prentice Hall International, 1996.

Frederick Freed. Folder of clippings in Dance Collection of Performing Arts Library, New York Public Library.

Featherstone, Donald F. *Dancing Without Danger*. New York: A. S. Barnes, 1977.

Gelabert, Raoul. *Anatomy for the Dancer*. New York: *Dance Magazine*, 1964.

Garrick, James G., M.D. "Ballet Injuries," *Medical Problems of Performing Artists*. Philadelphia, PA: Hanley and Belfus, Inc., 1986.

Garrick, James G., M.D. and Peter Radetsky. *Peak Condition*. New York: Crown, 1986.

Glasstone, Richard. "Some Thoughts on Pointe Work," *Dancing Times* [London] (August 1997).

Gow, Gordon. "Freed at 80," *The Dancing Times* [London], (October 1979).

Golovkina, Sophia. *Lessons in Classical Dance*. London: Dance Books, 1991.

Grant, Gail. *Technical Manual and Dictionary of Classical Ballet*. New York: Dover, 1967.

Grieg, Valerie. *Inside Ballet Technique*. Pennington, NJ: Princeton Book Company, 1994.

Guest, Ivor. *The Romantic Ballet in England*. Middletown, CT: Wesleyan University Press, 1966.

———. *The Romantic Ballet in Paris*. Middletown, CT: Wesleyan University Press, 1972.

Hamilton, William G., M.D. "Ballet and Your Body: An Orthopedist's View," *Dance Magazine* (January 1979).

Haskell, Arnold. *The Russian Genius in Ballet*. New York: Pergamon, 1963.

Hill, Lorna. *La Sylphide: The Life of Marie Taglioni*. New York: Evans, 1967.

Howard, Sharma L., "Taking the Pain Out of Pointe," *Dance Teacher Now* (January 1997).

Howse, Justin and Shirley Hancock. Dance *Technique and Injury Prevention, Rev. Ed*. London: A.C. Black; New York: Theatre Arts Books/Routledge, 1992.

Hughes, Rebecca. "Ouch! Rx For Beat Feet," *Family Circle* (August 1988).

Jacob, Ellen. *Dancing: A Guide for the Dancer You Can Be.* New York: Addison Wesley, 1981.

Jonas, Gerald. *Dancing: The Pleasure, Power, and Art of Movement.* New York: Abrams, 1992.

Kent, Allegra. *Once a Dancer.* New York: St. Martin's Press, 1997.

Kistler, Darci. *Ballerina: My Story.* New York: Pocket Books, 1993.

Kostrovitskaya, Vera S. *100 Lessons in Classical Ballet,* translated by Oleg Briansky. New York: Doubleday and Company, 1981.

Kostrovitskaya, Vera S., and Pisarev, Alexei. *School of Classical Dance.* London: Dance Books, 1995.

Kraus, Hans, M.D. *The Causes, Prevention and Treatment of Sports Injuries.* New York: Putnam, 1981.

Laws, Kenneth, and Cynthia Harvey. *Physics, Dance, and the Pas de Deux.* New York: Schirmer Books; Toronto: Maxwell Macmillan Canada; New York: Maxwell Macmillan International, 1994.

Lawson, Joan. "Seventy Years of Gamba," *The Dancing Times* (December 1973).

_____. "Shoes and Injuries," *The Dancing Times* (September 1983).

_____. "Shoe Problems," *The Dance Gazette* (July 1982) no. 180.

Lee, Carol. *An Introduction to Classical Ballet.* Hillsdale, NJ: Lawrence Erlbaum Associates, 1983.

Leonard, Maurice. *Markova: The Legend.* London: Hodder & Stoughton, 1995.

Levine, Ellen. *Anna Pavlova: Genius of the Dance.* New York: Scholastic, 1995.

Mara, Thalia. *On Your Toes.* New York: Dance Horizons, 1972.

Martin, John. *The Dance in Theory.* Princeton, NJ: Princeton Book Company, 1989.

_____. *John Martin's Book of the Dance.* New York: Doubleday, 1975.

Miller, E., H. Schneider, J. Bronson, and D. McLain. "A New Consideration in Athletic Injuries: The Classical Ballet Dancer," *Clinical Orthopedics* (1975) vol. 111, 181-91.

Moore, Lillian. *Artists of the Dance.* New York: Blom, 1969.

_____. *Images of the Dance: Historical Treasures of the Dance Collection, 1581–1861.* New York: New York Public Library, 1965.

Neale, Wendy. *On Your Toes.* New York: Crown, 1980.

Nicholoff, Michael and Ray Williams. *The Child in Ballet.* Baltimore: Colonial Press, 1951.

Novella, Thomas M. "Foot Care for Pointe Shoes," *Dance Magazine* (April 1994).

Page, Ruth. *Class Notes on Dance Classes Around the World: 1915–1980.* Princeton, NJ: Princeton Book Company, 1984.

Paskevska, Anna. Ballet: *From the First Plié to Mastery, An Eight-Year Course.* London: Dance Books, 1990.

_____. *Both Sides of the Mirror: The Science and Art of Ballet, Second*

Edition. Pennington, NJ: Princeton Book Company, 1992.

Quirk, R. "Ballet Injuries: The Australian Experience, *Clinical Sports Medicine* (1983) vol. 2, 507-14.

Reid, D. C. "Prevention of Hip and Knee Injuries in Ballet Dancers," *Sports Medicine* (November 1988) vol. 6, 295-307.

Reyna, Ferdinanda. *A Concise History of Ballet*. New York: Grosset and Dunlap, 1964.

Roberts, Elizabeth. *On Your Feet*. Emmaus, PA: Rodale, 1975.

Roses, Cynthia Ann, "Preparing for Pointe," *Dance Teacher Now* (Nov./Dec. 1991).

Sachs, Curt. *World History of the Dance*. New York: Norton, 1963.

Schorer, Suki. *Balanchine Pointework*. Society of Dance History Scholars, 1995.

Selva and Son. Folder of clippings in file of the Dance Collection, Performing Arts Library, New York Public Library.

Solomon, Ruth, Minton, Sandra C., and Solomon, John, Editors. *Preventing Dance Injuries: An Interdisciplinary Perspective*. Reston, VA: American Alliance for Health, Physical Education, Recreation and Dance, 1990.

Sorell, Walter. *The Dance Has Many Faces*. Chicago: A Cappella Books, 1992.

_____. *The Dance Through the Ages*. New York: Grosset, 1967.

Sorine, Daniel and Stephanie. *Dancershoes*. New York: Alfred Knopf, 1979.

Sparger, Celia. *Anatomy and Ballet,* New York: Theatre Arts Books, 1970.

Spilken, Terry L. *The Dancer's Foot Book: A Complete Guide to Footcare and Health for People Who Dance*. Princeton, NJ: Princeton Book Company, 1990.

Taffy's of Cleveland Ohio. Folder of clippings in file of the Dance Collection, Performing Arts Library, New York Public Library.

Tallchief, Maria. *America's Prima Ballerina*. New York: Henry Holt, 1997.

Terry, Walter. *On Pointe*. New York: Dodd Mead, 1962.

Thomasen, Eivind, and Rachel-Anne Rist. *Anatomy and Kinesiology for Ballet Teachers*. London: Dance Books, 1996.

Tobias, Toby. "Toe Shoes: Satin Thorns under Every Ballerina's Feet," *New York Times* (September 21, 1975) III, 26:1.

Trucco, Terry. "To the Pointe," *Ballet News* (March 1982) vol. 3.

Vaganova, Agrippina. *Basic Principles of Classical Ballet: Russian Ballet Techniques*. New York: Dover, 1969.

Vincent, L. M. *Competing with the Sylph: Dancers and the Pursuit of the Ideal Body*. New York: Berkeley, 1979.

_____. *The Dancer's Book of Health*. Princeton, NJ: Princeton Book Company, 1988.

Warren, Gretchen Ward. *The Art of Teaching Ballet: Ten Twentieth Century Masters.* Gainesville: University Press of Florida, 1996.

Watkins, Andrea. *Dancing Longer, Dancing Stronger: A Dancer's Guide to Improving Technique and Preventing Injury.* Princeton, NJ: Princeton Book Company, 1990.

White, Thelma. "The Toe Shoe Dilemma," *Dance Teacher Now* (September–October 1980).

Woodle, Alan S. *Digital Length Discrepancies in Ballet Pointe Position: Conservative Treatment with Moldable Podiatric Compound.* Seattle, WA: Self-published, 1989.

Wright, Stuart. *Dancer's Guide to Injuries of the Lower Extremities: Diagnosis, Treatment, and Care.* Cranbury, NJ: Cornwall Books, 1988.

Index

Italicized numbers indicate illustrations.